1400503354

Fortran Codes for Mathematical Programming: Linear, Quadratic and Discrete

Fortran Codes for Mathematical Programming:

Linear, Quadratic and Discrete

A. H. Land

Reader in Operational Research,
London School of Economics

S. Powell

Research Fellow of St. Hilda's College, Oxford
and
the Atlas Computer Laboratory, Didcot

A Wiley—Interscience Publication

John Wiley & Sons

LONDON NEW YORK SYDNEY TORONTO

Library of Congress Catalog Card Number 73-2789

ISBN 0 471 51270 2

Printed in Great Britain by
William Clowes & Sons Limited, London, Colchester and Beccles

Preface

At the 1970 Symposium on Mathematical Programming at The Hague, there was a frequently expressed demand for the development of a Mathematical Programming computer language, or for the sophisticated commercial codes to be made accessible to the research user. There is no lack of published Fortran or Algol programs to perform Simplex calculations, some of them being quite highly developed. There are also, of course, efficient programs to solve large linear programming problems, although such refinements as Branch and Bound procedures are at the present time available only to users who can pay. There is the curious situation that a great deal of ingenuity is being displayed to develop, say, integer programming algorithms, at numerous Universities, which are published in an almost untested form. The commercial package producers are the only ones with the necessary programs which can be modified to test these algorithms, and no doubt they do pick out from the literature those which appear to them to be the most promising. There is little doubt that the person most likely to have the enthusiasm to develop programs to test a new idea is the author of the idea himself, but in many cases, this requires a basic, reliable, Simplex system, which he can 'get into' to adapt to his requirements.

The following programs have been developed for just this purpose. They do not claim to be either elegant or efficient, but they do claim to be reliable. The experience of running a problem on two different codes and obtaining two conflicting 'optimum' solutions will be familiar to some readers. We are confident that we have provided sufficient accuracy checks, re-inversion procedures and stopping rules to prevent this sort of thing happening, although we do not guarantee that a solution will always be reached.

These programs were not developed for publication, but to test certain ideas about cutting plane methods for integer programming. However, as the programs have developed it has proved possible to use them in a variety of ways not envisaged originally. For instance, a version of a Branch and Bound algorithm was quite easily grafted on, as was an inverse basis version of Beale's quadratic programming algorithm. Both of these programs, as well as one of the numerous versions of cutting plane algorithm, are included here. But it should be emphasized that this is not intended as a complete Mathematical Programming 'package' but rather as a research tool for use until the Mathematical Programming language appears. It should enable research students to test their own ideas about, say, alternative branching rules, or to experiment with the numerous versions of the so-called 'intersection cuts'. Time comparisons with commercial codes would be quite impossible, but such counts as the number of Simplex iterations may be good enough to assess comparative efficiency. The commercial users can have the job of developing efficiency once an algorithm has proved itself in these terms for moderate sized problems.

The bounds of these programs are set by the unit of calculation in all of them being the 'basis change' of the Simplex algorithm—the transformation of the inverse of a matrix, P, of rational numbers to the inverse of $\bar{P}$ which differs from P in one column only. Thus we have excluded the special 'unimodular' methods for the transportation model of linear programming, and so-called 'additive algorithms' for integer programming, without intending by these exclusions any judgement of relative importance.

We expect that different readers will approach this book with different purposes in mind. There will be those who simply wish to get the programs on to a computer because they want to solve a linear program with discrete variables, as well as those who want to develop their own algorithms. The 'Directions for Use' below attempt to guide the reader to the parts of the book which concern him. Note that these programs are not suitable for computers without a Fortran IV compiler, nor are they likely to be useful, except for teaching purposes, on a small computer (see Chapter 7 for storage requirements and tolerances).

DIRECTIONS FOR USE

The purpose and method of each algorithm are described briefly in Chapter 1. Each of the following chapters, up to Chapter 6, presents a Fortran program and subroutines designed to solve one class of problem—the longest being Chapter 2 which introduces many of the subroutines used in all of the algorithms. No comment statements are included in the programs, but each subroutine is preceded by a verbal description and by a list of the subroutines called and the COMMON variables used or altered by the subroutines.

Chapter 7 describes the modifications needed to adapt the programs for different computers; the tricky question of the setting of tolerance levels; how to change the programs to solve problems with different dimensions; how to use the programs for adding and deleting constraints other than those discussed here; and, finally, a brief record of the performance of the two different integer programming algorithms on some published problems.

Finally, the Appendices serve to index the subroutines and COMMON variables as thoroughly as possible. Appendix 1 lists the subroutines required by each program and the programs in which each subroutine occurs.

Appendix 2 gives first an alphabetical list of all COMMON variables, referring each to its appropriate labelled COMMON; secondly, all the COMMON variables in order of their labelled COMMON, with a full description of their function and where they are used and where they are altered.

Appendix 3 summarizes the data input, and Appendix 4 contains some small test problems.

There must be bugs in these programs, despite the care we have exercised in editing them, and we hope you will tell us about them. We should be pleased to hear about any corrections that you make.

Also we should be interested to hear of your uses and developments of these programs.

Arrangements have been made for distribution on magnetic tape of the programs in the text. Details of these arrangements may be obtained by writing to Dr. A. Land, MATHPROG, London School of Economics, Houghton Street, London WC2A 2AE, England.

London and Oxford,
October, 1972

A. H. LAND
S. POWELL

Acknowledgements

We recognize an enormous debt to those who have taught us and inspired our interest in this field, both personally like Martin Beale, Alison Doig (now Harcourt), Harold Kuhn, Helen Makower, George Morton, John Murchland, Alex Orden, and Steven Vajda; and those whose work we have known principally through the printed page such as G. B. Dantzig, and R. Gomory, to mention only those whose writings are the most obviously relevant.

We have to thank Dr. M. Wigan and N. Paulley of the Transport and Road Research Laboratory for their help on the section in Chapter 7 on an overlay structure for the programs.

We are grateful to the secretaries who have patiently typed and retyped our manuscript, Mrs. Pierrette Paquin and Miss Hazel Rice at LSE, and in particular Mrs. Trude Trewin at the Atlas Computer Laboratory. We thank Heather Booth for preparing the data and running the problems to test the algorithms.

Finally we must thank the Science Research Council for their financial support over a considerable period.

Contents

CHAPTER 1

An Introduction to the Algorithms

1. NOTATION

The following conventions will be observed.

Matrices are denoted by capital letters and vectors by lower case letters with no distinction between row and column vectors. Where there appears to be any ambiguity the vector is defined as a row or column, but where conformability calls for a row or a column, no explicit definition will be stated. For instance, in

Maximize cx subject to $Ax \geqslant b$

it should be obvious that c is a row, x and b are columns.

Capital letter superscripts are used to signify a partition of a vector (more rarely, of a matrix). Lower case superscripts to a lower case version of the matrix name indicate a column or a row of a matrix. Lower case subscripts to a vector indicate a single element of a vector.

For example,

$x = [x^R \, x^S]$ where x^R and x^S are partitions of x.
a^k is the kth column (or row, as specified) of A.
x_k is the kth element of x.
x_j^R is the jth element of x^R.
0 may be a scalar, vector or matrix according to context.

For brevity LP is used to signify linear programming and QP is used for quadratic programming.

We shall be concerned with the maximization or minimization of a linear or a quadratic function subject to inequality and equality constraints. Since a minimization problem can always be converted to a maximization problem (or vice versa) by a simple multiplication of the coefficients of the function by -1, the programs are designed only to maximize a function.

The particular LP problem

$$\begin{aligned} &\text{maximize } cx \\ &\text{subject to } Ax \leqslant b \\ &\qquad\qquad\quad x \geqslant 0 \end{aligned}$$

is referred to as the *standard problem*.

The constraints dealt with will be of the following kinds:

1. Upper and lower bounds on single variables.
2. Interrelationships between variables expressed as linear equalities or inequalities.
3. Individual variables restricted to taking one of a set of discrete values.

Initially we shall consider constraints of types (1) and (2) only. Constraints of type (3) are considered in Section 11 Discrete (integer) programming below.

2. THE FEASIBLE REGION

Constraints of types (1) and (2) can be regarded as defining a *feasible region* in R^n, the n-dimensional Euclidean space of which the coordinates are the variables, x. The mathematical programming problem is to find the point within the feasible region–i.e. the values of the coordinates–which maximizes the function.

A linear equality $a_1x_1 + \ldots + a_nx_n = b$ can be regarded as an $(n-1)$-dimensional hyperplane, which partitions R^n into two sets:

$$(x \mid a_1x_1 + \ldots + a_nx_n > b) \text{ an open half-space}$$

and

$$(x \mid a_1x_1 + \ldots + a_nx_n \leqslant b) \text{ a closed half-space.}$$

[Alternatively we might consider the two half-spaces: $(x \mid a_1x_1 + \ldots + a_nx_n < b)$ and $(x \mid a_1x_1 + \ldots + a_nx_n \geqslant b)$.]

These are all convex sets, S, by which we mean that if there are two points in S, $x^{(1)}$ and $x^{(2)}$, then every point on the one-dimensional line from $x^{(1)}$ to $x^{(2)}$ is also in S. More formally:

$$x^{(1)} \in S,\ x^{(2)} \in S \rightarrow (\lambda x^{(1)} + (1-\lambda)x^{(2)}) \in S, \quad \text{for } 0 \leqslant \lambda \leqslant 1.$$

The intersection of two or more convex sets is itself a convex set (although it may be an empty set). In particular, the intersection of two or more closed half-spaces is a convex set, called a closed convex polytope, or, in the mathematical programming context, the feasible region defined by a set of linear inequalities. For example, see Figure 1.1. The shading indicates the infeasible side of each constraint. The feasible region may not be bounded in all directions, as for example in Figure 1.2. An equality *may* be regarded for some purposes as a *pair* of opposed inequalities, as in Figure 1.3.

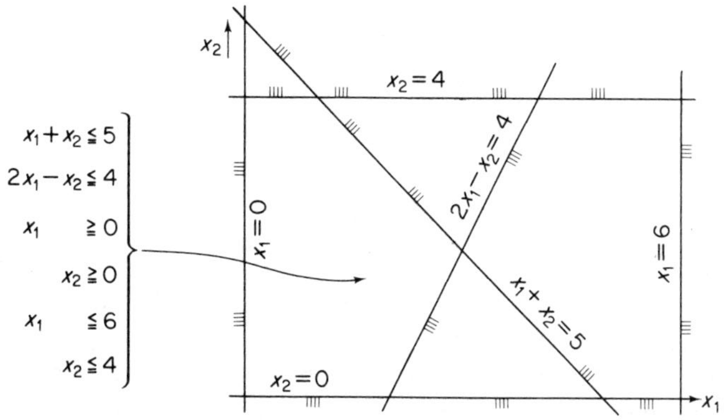

Figure 1.1

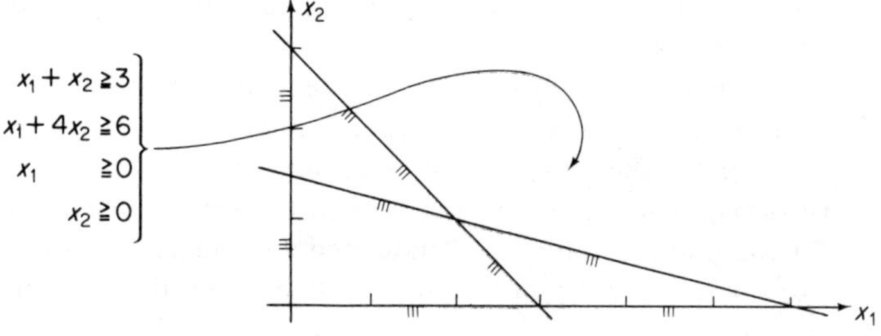

Figure 1.2

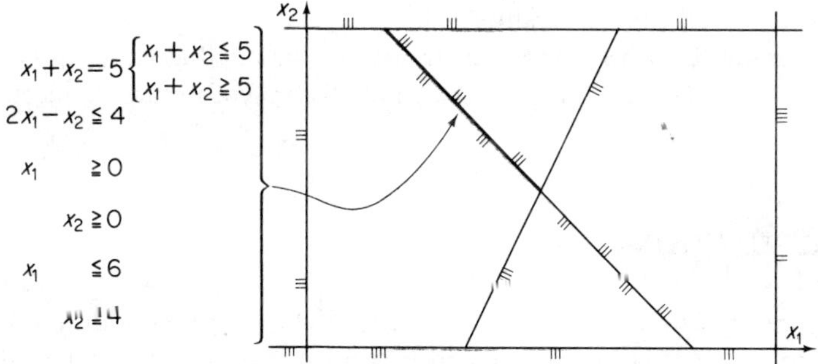

Figure 1.3

The numerical coefficients of a constraint can be multiplied by any positive number without affecting its domain of feasibility, e.g.:

$$129x_1 + 301x_2 + 473x_3 \leqslant 3053$$

is identically the same constraint as:

$$3x_1 + 7x_2 + 11x_3 \leqslant 71 \text{ (dividing by 43).}$$

A constraint may be multiplied by a negative number so long as the sign of the inequality is reversed:

$$-2x_1 + x_2 \geqslant -4$$

is the same constraint as

$$2x_1 - x_2 \leqslant 4.$$

Hence all equality, inequality, non-negativity, and upper bounding constraints can be written (in matrix terms) either $Ax \leqslant b$, or as $Ax \geqslant b$.

Just as all the elements of a row in $Ax \leqslant b$ (including the element in b) may be multiplied by a positive number without affecting the domain of the corresponding constraint, so may all the elements in a column (including the element in c), since this merely alters the unit level, changing the scale on the coordinate axis.

For computational purposes we find it convenient to treat $x_j \geqslant 0$ and $x_j \leqslant b_j$ as special cases of inequalities.

Basic points are those which satisfy n independent constraints as equalities, which lie on n independent bounding hyperplanes of the half-spaces.

Extreme points (of the feasible region) are basic points which also satisfy all the constraints, including those which do not enter their definition.

An *edge* is the intersection of $n-1$ independent constraints as equalities.

An *edge of the feasible region* is that part of an edge (if any) which satisfies all the constraints.

A *k-dimensional face* is the intersection of $n-k$ independent constraints as equalities.

A *k-dimensional face of the feasible region* is that part of the face (if any) which satisfies all the constraints.

Degeneracy. If more than n constraints are satisfied as equalities at a basic point we call this a degenerate point. We may also have a degenerate edge, face, etc.

3. THE FUNCTION

We shall restrict ourselves to problems in which $f(x)$ takes a unique value at each point of the feasible region and is continuous, and in fact algorithms will be presented only for linear and quadratic functions. We can represent the function in n-space by contours of equal value, as in Figure 1.4. Note that the quadratic contours might have been derived either from a convex function or from a concave function, as illustrated in Figure 1.5

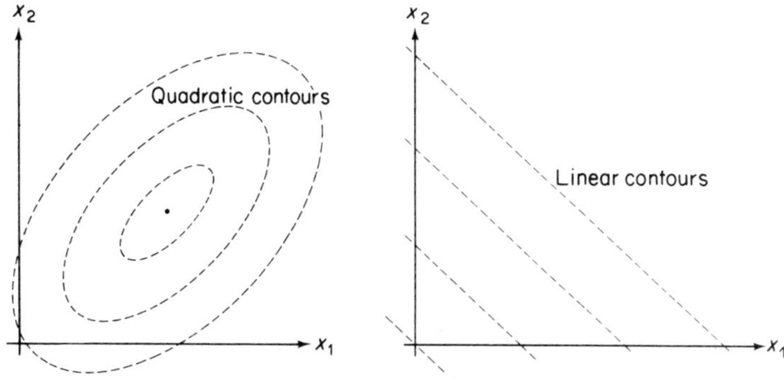

Figure 1.4

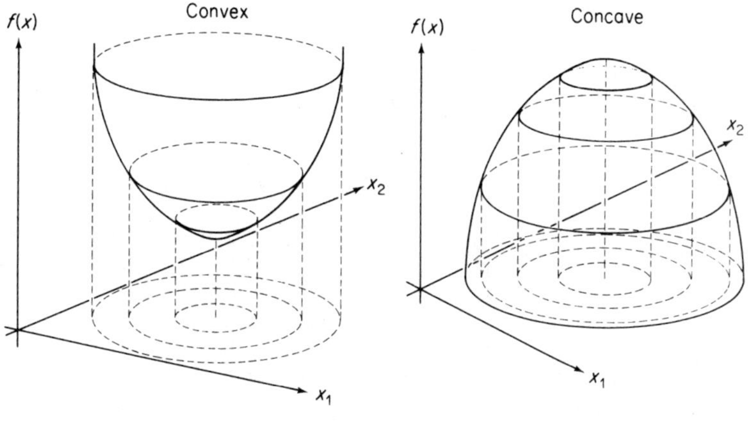

Figure 1.5

4. LINEAR AND QUADRATIC FUNCTIONS ON A CONVEX POLYTOPE

A linear function always reaches its optimum at an extreme point of the feasible region, as illustrated in Figure 1.6. In some cases a linear function may also reach its optimum value on an entire $(n - k)$-dimensional face of the feasible region, as illustrated in Figure 1.7.

If the feasible region is unbounded, the function may or may not also be unbounded, as illustrated in Figure 1.8.

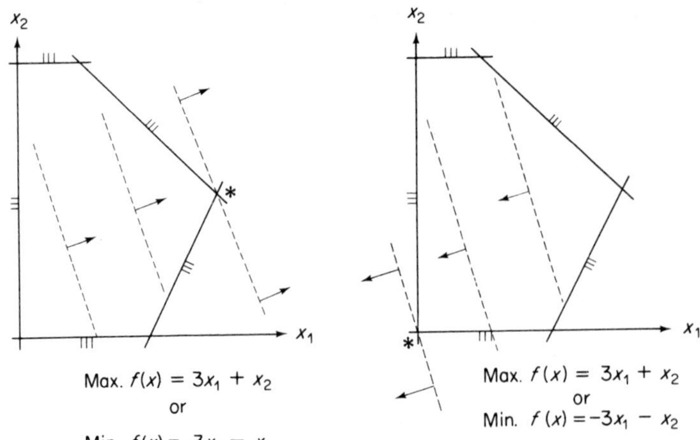

Figure 1.6

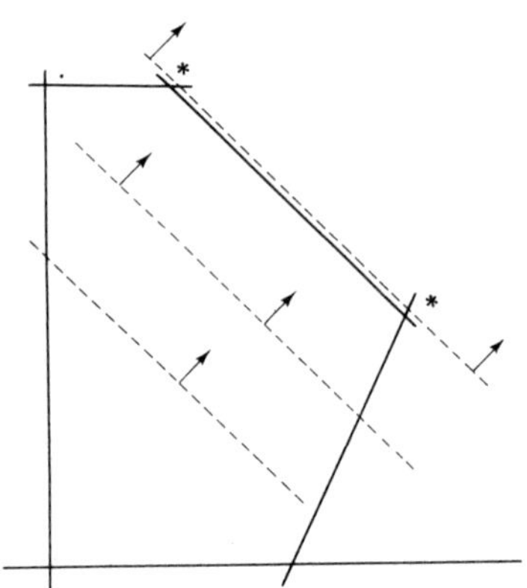

Figure 1.7

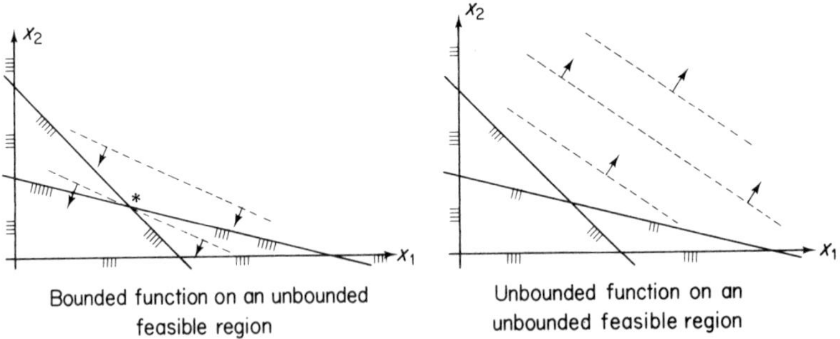

Figure 1.8

A quadratic function, if it has a bounded optimum, may reach its optimum value on any type of face of the feasible region, from zero-dimensional (an extreme point) to n-dimensional (the case where the ordinary calculus maximum or minimum point lies in the interior of the feasible region). Some simple cases are illustrated in Figure 1.9.

Note that in cases like Figure 1.9(a) a locally optimal point is also globally optimal, but that in Figure 1.9(b) there are two (or more) locally optimal points marked with an asterisk.

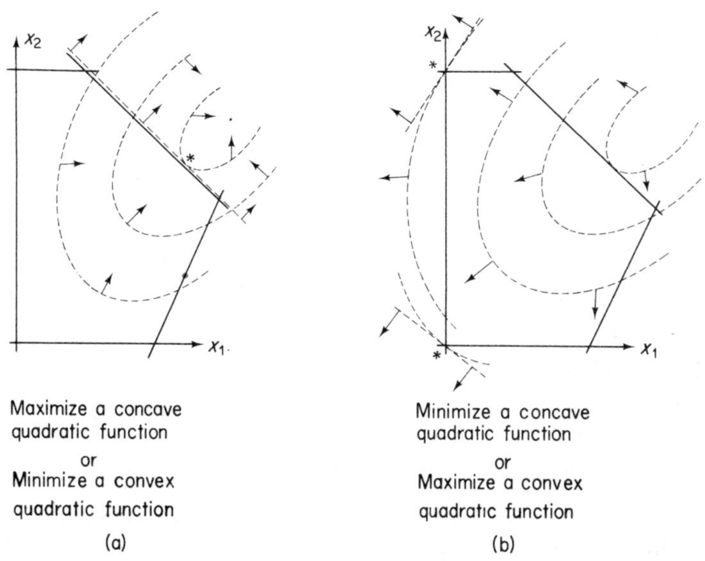

Figure 1.9

5. SUFFICIENT CONDITIONS FOR MAXIMIZATION OF A LINEAR FUNCTION

Maximize cx, subject to $Ax \leqslant b$.

If there is a vector of non-negative elements $\bar{y}$ such that $\bar{y}A = c$, then

$$\bar{y}Ax \leqslant \bar{y}b$$

for all feasible points, x, i.e.

$$cx \leqslant \bar{y}b.$$

If, in addition,

$$\bar{y}(b - Ax) = 0\dagger$$

† i.e. if the vectors $\bar{y}$ and $b - A\bar{x}$ are *orthogonal.*

for a particular feasible $\bar{x}$, then

$$\bar{y}b = \bar{y}A\bar{x} = c\bar{x},$$

and therefore

$$cx \leqslant c\bar{x},$$

i.e. $c\bar{x}$ is the maximum value of cx for feasible x.

5.1. Example

$$\begin{array}{ll} \text{Max} & 2x_1 + 3x_2 \\ \text{s.t.} & 2x_1 + x_2 \leqslant 4 \\ & 2x_1 + 5x_2 \leqslant 10 \\ & -x_1 \leqslant 0 \\ & -x_2 \leqslant 0. \end{array}$$

Any non-negative multiple of the four constraints is also a valid constraint. For example, taking $\bar{y}_1 = 0, \bar{y}_2 = 1, \bar{y}_3 = 0, \bar{y}_4 = 2$:

$$\begin{array}{l} 0.(2x_1 + x_2 \leqslant 4) \\ +1.(2x_1 + 5x_2 \leqslant 10) \\ +0.(-x_1 \leqslant 0) \\ +2.(-x_2 \leqslant 0) \\ \hline 2x_1 + 3x_2 \leqslant 10 \quad \text{i.e. } cx \leqslant 10. \end{array}$$

That is to say, the entire feasible region certainly lies in the feasible half-space of the constraint

$$\begin{array}{l} cx \leqslant \bar{y}b, \\ 2x_1 + 3x_2 \leqslant 10. \end{array}$$

But if we take $\bar{y}_1 = \frac{1}{2}, \bar{y}_2 = \frac{1}{2}, \bar{y}_3 = 0, \bar{y}_4 = 0$:

$$\begin{array}{l} \frac{1}{2}.(2x_1 + x_2 \leqslant 4) \\ +\frac{1}{2}.(2x_1 + 5x_2 \leqslant 10) \\ +0.(-x_1 \leqslant 0) \\ +0.(-x_2 \leqslant 0) \\ \hline 2x_1 + 3x_2 \leqslant 7 \end{array}$$

This is a tighter constraint on cx than the previous one. If we take the point $\bar{x}$ defined by the first two constraints as equalities (because the first two $\bar{y}$ values are positive),

$$\begin{array}{ll} & 2\bar{x}_1 + \bar{x}_2 = 4 \\ & 2\bar{x}_1 + 5\bar{x}_2 = 10 \\ \therefore & \bar{x}_1 = \frac{5}{4}, \bar{x}_2 = \frac{3}{2}. \end{array}$$

Since $\bar{x}$ also satisfies the constraints which do not enter its definition, it is an extreme point of the feasible region. The condition $\bar{y}(b - A\bar{x}) = 0$, together with $\bar{y} \geqslant 0$ and $(b - A\bar{x}) \geqslant 0$, means that the elements of the vector $\bar{y}$ must be non-zero only on constraints which are satisfied as exact equalities at $\bar{x}$—constraints for which the elements of the vector $(b - A\bar{x})$ are zero. These two derived constraints on the value of the function are illustrated in Figure 1.10.

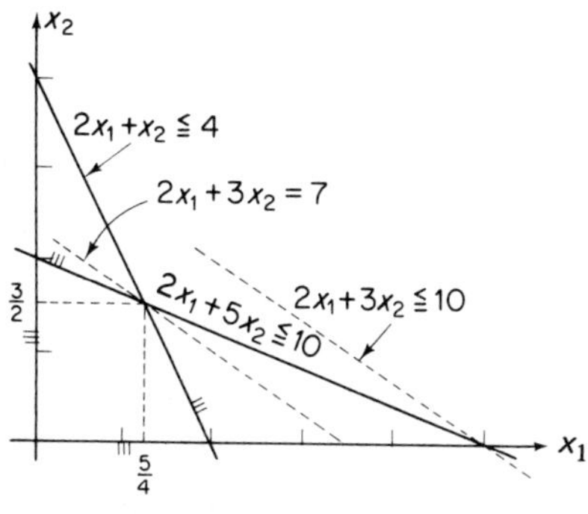

Figure 1.10

5.2. Non-negativity constraints

If the constraints of the problem include non-negativity constraints on all the variables, x, we can write the problem as:

$$\text{Maximize } cx, \text{ s.t. } Ax \leqslant b$$
$$-Ix \leqslant 0.$$

Then the sufficient conditions for optimality at the point $\bar{x}$ are:

$$\bar{y}A + \bar{v}(-I) = c$$
$$\bar{y} \geqslant 0, \bar{v} \geqslant 0$$
$$\bar{y}(b - A\bar{x}) = 0$$

and

$$\bar{v}(0 - (-I)\bar{x}) = 0$$

$$\therefore \quad \bar{v}\bar{x} = 0.$$

We can eliminate $\bar{v}$ since $\bar{v} = \bar{y}A - c$. Then the conditions are

$$\bar{y}A \geqslant c \text{ (since } \bar{v} \geqslant 0)$$
$$\bar{y} \geqslant 0$$
$$\bar{y}(b - A\bar{x}) = 0$$
$$(\bar{y}A - c)\bar{x} = 0.$$

6. DUALITY

We can state a pair of *dual* problems as follows:

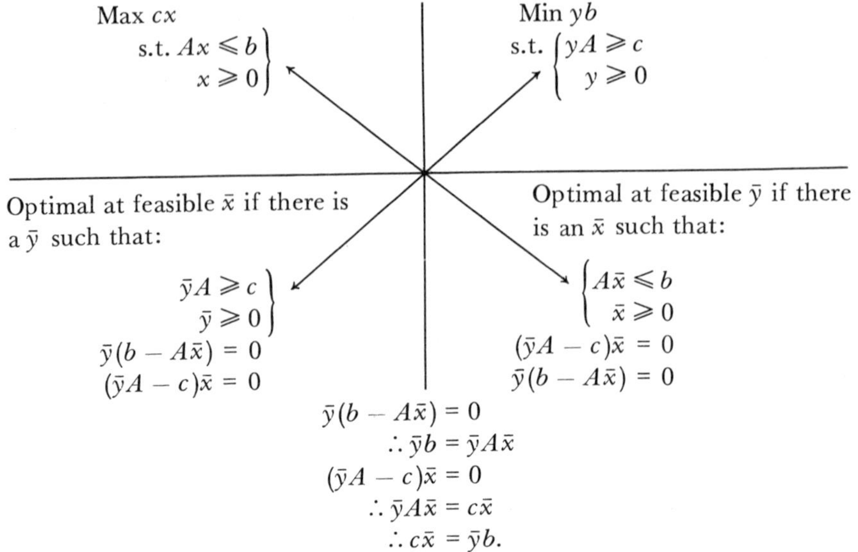

7. NECESSARY CONDITIONS FOR OPTIMALITY

It is also the case that *if* $\bar{x}$ maximizes cx s.t. $Ax \leqslant b$, *then there exists* $\bar{y} \geqslant 0$, such that $\bar{y}A = c$ and $\bar{y}(b - A\bar{x}) = 0$. But the proof of this is beyond the scope of this book, for example, see reference [7].

8. SIMPLEX ALGORITHM

All the routines in this book use the 'basis change' routine of the Simplex algorithm to move from one basic point to another until the conditions for feasibility and optimality of an LP are satisfied.

Briefly, this can be described as follows. Take a basic point, examine it for the conditions on x and y being satisfied. If they are not satisfied, relax one equality condition (so defining an edge) and move to an adjacent basic point. This unit of calculation is called a *basis change.* There are many different rules for choosing the sequence of basic points. These programs satisfy the 'primal' (x) conditions first by the 'sequential procedure', i.e., take one infeasibility at a time and perform basis change iterations until it is satisfied (or until it is established that it is impossible to satisfy it), never violating any primal constraint which is already satisfied. Having achieved feasibility of the primal, perform further basis changes until the dual conditions are also satisfied (or until it is discovered that they cannot be satisfied, i.e., that the problem has an unbounded value of the function). The program is designed to start from any basis, feasible or infeasible in the primal, feasible or infeasible in the dual, so that it can be used as a subroutine in the more complex algorithms.

8.1. Slack variables

The operation of basis change is most easily described in terms of a problem formulated in equality constraints with all the inequalities of the problem expressed as non-negativities on individual variables. Any set of inequalities can be converted into equalities by the addition of non-negative *slack variables*, x_{n+i}, which are defined as $x_{n+i} = b_i - a^i x$ (where a^i is the ith row of A) in the case of a constraint $a^i x \leqslant b_i$, and $x_{n+i} = a^i x - b_i$, where $a^i x \geqslant b_i$.

For example:

$$
\begin{matrix} [x_1 & x_2] \end{matrix}
\begin{bmatrix} 3 & -2 \\ 4 & 1 \\ -2 & 3 \\ 6 & 4 \end{bmatrix}
\begin{matrix} \leqslant \\ = \\ \leqslant \\ \geqslant \end{matrix}
\begin{bmatrix} 10 \\ 8 \\ 15 \\ 9 \end{bmatrix}
\Longrightarrow
\begin{matrix} [x_1 & x_2 & x_3 & x_5 & x_6] \end{matrix}
\begin{bmatrix} 3 & -2 & 1 & 0 & 0 \\ 4 & 1 & 0 & 0 & 0 \\ -2 & 3 & 0 & 1 & 0 \\ 6 & 4 & 0 & 0 & -1 \end{bmatrix}
=
\begin{bmatrix} 10 \\ 8 \\ 15 \\ 9 \end{bmatrix}
$$

$$(x_1, x_2 \geqslant 0) \qquad\qquad (x_1, x_2, x_3, x_5, x_6 \geqslant 0)$$

The function to be optimized remains unchanged as a function of the *original variables* x_1 and x_2 only, i.e., $c_{n+i} = 0$.

An equivalent but less conventional approach is actually followed in these programs of regarding all slack variables as present in the formulation and all being of the form $x_{n+i} = b_i - a^i x$. Feasibility is attained only when those x_{n+i} which are associated with a constraint $a^i x \leqslant b_i$ are *non-negative*, those associated with $a^i x \geqslant b_i$ are *non-positive*, and those associated with $a^i x = b_i$ are *zero*. For example:

$$
\begin{matrix} [x_1 & x_2] \end{matrix}
\begin{bmatrix} 3 & -2 \\ 4 & 1 \\ -2 & 3 \\ 6 & 4 \end{bmatrix}
\begin{matrix} \leqslant \\ = \\ \leqslant \\ \geqslant \end{matrix}
\begin{bmatrix} 10 \\ 8 \\ 15 \\ 9 \end{bmatrix}
\Longrightarrow
\begin{matrix} [x_1 & x_2 & x_3 & x_4 & x_5 & x_6] \end{matrix}
\begin{bmatrix} 3 & -2 & 1 & 0 & 0 & 0 \\ 4 & 1 & 0 & 1 & 0 & 0 \\ -2 & 3 & 0 & 0 & 1 & 0 \\ 6 & 4 & 0 & 0 & 0 & 1 \end{bmatrix}
=
\begin{bmatrix} 10 \\ 8 \\ 15 \\ 9 \end{bmatrix}
$$

$$(x_1, x_2 \geqslant 0) \qquad\qquad (x_1, x_2, x_3, x_5 \geqslant 0, x_4 = 0, x_6 \leqslant 0)$$

In this formulation, with m equality constraints on $m + n$ variables, a basic point is represented by a selection of n variables to be set equal to zero, in such a way that the remaining $m \times m$ matrix is non-singular. We speak of partitioning the set x of $m + n$ variables into x^Q of n *non-basic variables* set equal to zero, and x^P, the remaining m *basic variables.* Then the equations

$$Ax = b$$

become

$$Px^P + Qx^Q = b,$$
$$Px^P = b - Qx^Q,$$

and, so long as $|P| \neq 0$,

$$x^P = P^{-1}(b - Qx^Q).$$

If $x^Q = 0$, $x^P = P^{-1}b$.

Then the basic point is feasible (and hence an extreme point) if the non-negativity, non-positivity and zero conditions on the elements of x^P are satisfied at the point $x^P = P^{-1}b$, $x^Q = 0$.

If any element of x^P does *not* satisfy the required conditions, an element of x^Q is sought such that increasing that element from zero (or decreasing it if it is an element which must be non-positive) will drive the element of x^P in the desired direction. (In the algorithm, this search is conducted in the subroutine SEEKX.) If x_r is the infeasible element of x^P, we can pick out the corresponding row of the equations

$$x^P = P^{-1}(b - Qx^Q),$$

i.e.,

$$x_r = p^r b - p^r Q x^Q \quad \text{where } p^r \text{ is the } r^{\text{th}} \text{ row of } P^{-1}$$
$$= p^r b - h x^Q \quad \text{where } h = p^r Q.$$

Then $p^r b$ is the (infeasible) value of x_r at the basic point, and each element of the row h represents the potential impact on x_r of a unit increase in the corresponding element in x^Q. In geometrical terms the n elements of h represent the rates of change in x_r along each of the n edges which intersect at the basic point (each defined by $n - 1$ of the n hyperplanes of $x^Q = 0$).

If there is no variable in x^Q which can be moved in a feasible direction and simultaneously drive x_r towards feasibility, then there is no feasible solution to the whole problem.

Otherwise some rule of choice is employed to select one element, x_k, in x^Q to *introduce to the basis,* i.e., to select one of the n edges along which to move. Having made this selection of x_k, the impact of x_k on the other basic variables must be considered, since x_k must not be so increased (decreased) as to drive some other element of x^P into infeasibility. Since all other elements of x^Q apart from x_k are to remain at zero,

$$x^P = P^{-1}b - P^{-1}Qx^Q$$

can be reduced to

$$x^P = P^{-1}b - P^{-1}q^k x_k \quad \text{where } q^k \text{ is the column of } Q \text{ associated with } x_k$$

or

$$x^P = P^{-1}b - gx_k \quad \text{where } g = P^{-1}q^k.$$

Points where all m elements of x^P are non-zero and so also is x_k are not basic—only $n - 1$ independent inequalities are satisfied as exact equalities. Since we are moving in a direction in which x_k is increasing (decreasing), we must find some element in x^P which first reaches zero in order to identify a new basic point. One variable will certainly approach zero—x_r itself, since otherwise x_k would not have been selected. It may be, however, that some other element of x^P, feasible at the original basic point, may become infeasible if the edge is followed until x_r becomes feasible. The particular algorithm followed here will (in SEEKY) select x_s as (one of) the first variable(s) to reach zero as x_k increases (decreases). If this is not, in fact, x_r, one or more further basis changes will be required to make x_r feasible.

8.2. Optimality

Once feasibility has been attained, the algorithm tests the current basic solution for optimality, it checks to see if the dual variables $y = c^P P^{-1}$ take their allowed signs, non-negative for $a^i x \leqslant b_i$, non-positive for $a^i x \geqslant b_i$, and unconstrained for $a^i x = b_i$. It also checks to see if

$$yQ \geqslant c^Q$$

on all variables in x^Q. If these conditions are not fulfilled, the algorithm follows the usual Simplex rule of selecting that variable x_k to move from zero which is associated with the *greatest* violation of the optimality conditions, where x_k may be an original variable or a slack variable. This choice is carried out in the subroutine ISOPT. Once the choice of entering variable is made the algorithm follows the same path as when it is pursuing the goal of feasibility. Thus once it has become feasible it can never become infeasible (except in the more complex algorithms where additional constraints are added). Proofs of convergence will be found in the standard texts on linear programming, e.g. [3].

8.3. Basis change

We had a basis associated with a partition of x into x^P, x^Q, and correspondingly of A into $[P\ Q]$. We have now identified an element x_k of the non-basic set, x^Q, to become basic, and an element x_s of the basic set, x^P, to become non-basic. To proceed further we need the inverse of the new matrix $\bar{P}$ which differs from the previous matrix P in one column only, q^k instead of p^s.

Let us make the assumption that $\bar{P}$ is non-singular, and that the transformation from P^{-1} to $\bar{P}^{-1}$ can be achieved by the pre-multiplication of P^{-1} by a non-singular transformation matrix, T.

$$\begin{aligned} \bar{P}^{-1} &= TP^{-1}. \\ \therefore \bar{P} &= PT^{-1} \\ P^{-1}\bar{P} &= P^{-1}PT^{-1} \\ &= T^{-1}. \end{aligned}$$

But $\bar{P}$ differs from P in only one column, therefore

$$P^{-1}\bar{P} = \begin{bmatrix} I & & 0 \\ 0 & g & 0 \\ 0 & & I \end{bmatrix} \quad \text{where } g = P^{-1}q^k.$$

The sth element of g is known as the *pivot*, Δ, of the basis change.

$$T^{-1} = \begin{bmatrix} I & g^{(1)} & 0 \\ 0 & \Delta & 0 \\ 0 & g^{(2)} & I \end{bmatrix}$$

hence

$$T = \begin{bmatrix} I & \dfrac{-1}{\Delta}g^{(1)} & 0 \\ 0 & \dfrac{1}{\Delta} & 0 \\ 0 & \dfrac{-1}{\Delta}g^{(2)} & I \end{bmatrix}$$

Note that the non-singularity of T and hence of $\bar{P}$ depends only on Δ being non-zero. But Δ is precisely that element of $g = P^{-1}q^k$ which indicates the impact of the newly-basic variable x_k on the departing basic variable, x_s. The variable x_s would not have been chosen as the one to become zero if Δ had been zero. Thus the rules of the Simplex algorithm ensure that if one starts with a non-singular matrix P, all transformations will be to further non-singular matrices. (In practice, Δ must be not merely non-zero, but also not 'too small' if problems due to ill-conditioned matrices are to be avoided. The problem of the proper setting of tolerances is discussed in Chapter 7, Section 2.)

If no other basis and its inverse is available, the algorithm starts with the simplest basis—the unit matrix of the m slack variable columns. This has the advantage of having an inverse which is also the unit matrix.

8.4. The reduced basis

For the purpose of exposition we regard every row i of the A matrix as having an associated slack variable x_{n+i} with a unit vector column in the expanded A matrix, and zero function element. In practice these slack vectors are not explicitly recorded. Associated with every basic point there is a partitioning of $[A\ I]$ into $[P\ Q]$, where P is the $m \times m$ basis matrix. P may, in general, contain $m - k$ of the slack variable columns, where $0 \leqslant m - k \leqslant m$. With suitable re-ordering, we can partition P into $\begin{bmatrix} R & 0 \\ S & I \end{bmatrix}$.

Since $P^{-1} = \begin{bmatrix} R^{-1} & 0 \\ -SR^{-1} & I \end{bmatrix}$, it is only necessary to keep in the computer the matrix R^{-1}, not the whole of P^{-1}. We can if we wish express the conditions for feasibility and optimality in terms of this *reduced basis, R*. Consider the standard problem:

$$\begin{aligned} \text{Maximize } & cx \\ \text{s.t. } & Ax \leqslant b \\ & x \geqslant 0 \end{aligned}$$

where A is of order $m \times n$, and b, c and x are conformable. Associated with this problem there is a dual problem:

$$\begin{aligned} \text{Minimize } & yb \\ \text{s.t. } & yA \geqslant c \\ & y \geqslant 0. \end{aligned}$$

For x and y such that $cx = yb$, the conditions for the optimality of the first (primal) problem are the feasibility conditions of the dual problem and vice versa.

A *basic* solution of both problems is associated with a (re-ordering and) partitioning of A, and of the associated vectors, such that the square sub-matrix R is non-singular:

$$A = \begin{bmatrix} R & U \\ S & V \end{bmatrix}, \quad \begin{array}{l} R \text{ is of order } k \times k,\ k \leqslant m,\ k \leqslant n. \\ S \text{ is of order } (m-k) \times k \\ U \text{ is of order } k \times (n-k) \\ V \text{ is of order } (m-k) \times (n-k). \end{array}$$

Re-ordering and partitioning x, y, b, and c in conformity with A:

$$\begin{array}{ccc} & [x^R \quad x^U] & \\ \begin{bmatrix} y^R \\ y^S \end{bmatrix} & \begin{bmatrix} R & U \\ S & V \end{bmatrix} & \begin{bmatrix} b^R \\ b^S \end{bmatrix} \\ & [c^R \quad c^U] & \end{array}$$

Primal $\left\{\begin{array}{r} Ax \leqslant b \\ x \geqslant 0 \end{array}\right\}$ becomes

$$\left.\left\{\begin{array}{rll} Rx^R + Ux^U \leqslant b^R & (k \text{ inequalities}) \\ Sx^R + Vx^U \leqslant b^S & (m - k \text{ inequalities}) \\ x^R \geqslant 0 & (k \text{ inequalities}) \\ x^U \geqslant 0 & (n - k \text{ inequalities}) \end{array}\right.\right\} m + n \text{ inequalities}$$

Dual $\left\{\begin{array}{r} yA \geqslant c \\ y \geqslant 0 \end{array}\right\}$ becomes

$$\left.\left\{\begin{array}{rll} y^R R + y^S S \geqslant c^R & (k \text{ inequalities}) \\ y^R U + y^S V \geqslant c^U & (n - k \text{ inequalities}) \\ y^R \geqslant 0 & (k \text{ inequalities}) \\ y^S \geqslant 0 & (m - k \text{ inequalities}) \end{array}\right.\right\} m + n \text{ inequalities.}$$

So long as $|R| \neq 0$ we can define a *basic* solution of the primal problem by taking as equalities n of the $m + n$ primal inequalities, and a basic solution of the dual problem by taking as equalities m of the $m + n$ dual inequalities, as follows:

$$\left.\left\{\begin{array}{rll} Rx^R + Ux^U = b^R & (k \text{ equalities}) \\ x^U = 0 & (n - k \text{ equalities}) \end{array}\right.\right\} n \text{ equalities}$$

$$\therefore Rx^R = b^R$$

$$x^R = R^{-1}b^R,$$

and

$$\left.\left\{\begin{array}{rll} y^R R + y^S S = c^R & (k \text{ equalities}) \\ y^S = 0 & (m - k \text{ equalities}) \end{array}\right.\right\} m \text{ equalities}$$

$$\therefore y^R R = c^R$$

$$y^R = c^R R^{-1}.$$

For any basic solution, $cx = c^R x^R = c^R R^{-1} b^R = y^R b^R = yb$.

We shall say that a given basic solution is *feasible* if the remaining m inequalities of the primal are satisfied, namely:

$$Sx^R + Vx^U \leqslant b^S$$

i.e.,

$$Sx^R \leqslant b^S$$

and

$$x^R \geqslant 0.$$

We shall say that a given basic solution is *optimal* (whether or not it is feasible) if the dual problem is feasible, i.e., if the remaining n inequalities of the dual are satisfied, namely:

$$y^R U + y^S V \geqslant c^U$$

i.e.,

$$y^R U \geqslant c^U$$

and

$$y^R \geqslant 0.$$

A basic solution, therefore, is associated with a $k \times k$ submatrix of A, where k may be of any size from zero to the lesser of m and n.

In the usual form of Simplex, a vector w of slack variables (with elements x_{n+i}), are added to convert the original inequalities to equalities:

$$\begin{array}{lcl} \text{Max } cx & & \text{Max } \bar{c}\bar{x} & & \bar{x} = [x \quad w] \\ \text{s.t. } Ax \leqslant b & \text{becomes} & \text{s.t. } \bar{A}\bar{x} = b & \text{where} & \bar{A} = [A \quad I\,] \\ \quad x \geqslant 0 & & \quad \bar{x} \geqslant 0 & & \bar{c} = [c \quad 0\,] \end{array}$$

Then a basis in $\bar{A}$ is associated with a partitioning $\bar{A} = [P\; Q]$, $|P| \neq 0$, $x^Q = 0$, $x^P = P^{-1}b$, the basis being feasible if $x^P \geqslant 0$. P can be partitioned,

$$P = \begin{bmatrix} R & 0 \\ S & I \end{bmatrix}, \quad \text{and} \quad P^{-1} = \begin{bmatrix} R^{-1} & 0 \\ -SR^{-1} & I \end{bmatrix}.$$

$$x^P = P^{-1}b = \begin{bmatrix} R^{-1} & 0 \\ -SR^{-1} & I \end{bmatrix} \begin{bmatrix} b^R \\ b^S \end{bmatrix}$$

$$= \begin{bmatrix} R^{-1}b^R \\ -SR^{-1}b^R + b^S \end{bmatrix} = \begin{bmatrix} x^R \\ b^S - Sx^R \end{bmatrix}.$$

Thus the non-negativity of x^P expresses the same feasibility conditions which we specified in terms of the reduced basis. Similarly, the equivalence of the optimality conditions can be established.

One further equivalence should be noted, and that is to the Simplex tableau, the 'updated' coefficients of the non-basic variables,

$$P^{-1}Q = \begin{bmatrix} R^{-1} & 0 \\ -SR^{-1} & I \end{bmatrix} \begin{bmatrix} U & I \\ V & 0 \end{bmatrix} = \begin{bmatrix} R^{-1}U & R^{-1} \\ -SR^{-1}U + V & -SR^{-1} \end{bmatrix}.$$

We have occasion to refer at times to an updated row, h, or column, g, of coefficients, in which case we mean a row or a column of the above matrix.

The vector $yA - c$, the 'function row', the 'z row', the 'reduced costs', or whatever jargon is fancied, is, like x and $b - Ax$, kept updated at each basis change.

In the algorithms to be described here, the inverse matrix is principally R^{-1}, although under certain circumstances there may be one or more unit vectors and associated rows of S in the basis. The terms *basic variable* will refer principally to the original x variables currently in the basis, but may include one or more unit vector variables, x_{n+i} (where the unit element is in the ith row). The term *effective constraint* refers principally to the constraints $Ax \leqslant b$ which are currently satisfied as exact equalities, but also to those for which a unit vector is explicitly present in the basis.

At each basis change the inverse is *reduced* by the removal of the row and column associated with a basic unit vector on any feasible constraint (one satisfying the appropriate non-negativity, non-positivity, or zero conditions), so long as this does not reduce the size of the inverse to zero.

8.5. Upper bounded variables

For simplicity, the foregoing discussion of the reduced basis was conducted in terms of the simplest form of linear programming constraint set. In fact, a basic solution is here defined not by setting $x^U = 0$, but by setting some elements of x^U at zero and some at their upper bounds. Thus we can consider A and the associated vectors partitioned as follows:

$$\begin{matrix} [x^R & x^U & x^W] \\ \begin{bmatrix} R & U & W \\ S & V & Z \end{bmatrix} & & \begin{bmatrix} b^R \\ b^S \end{bmatrix} \\ [c^R & c^U & c^W] \end{matrix}$$

where x^U are the variables set equal to zero, and x^W those set equal to their upper bounds, $\bar{x}^W$. Thus $x^R = R^{-1}(b^R - W\bar{x}^W) \geqslant 0$ for feasibility, and $y^R U \geqslant c^U$ but $y^R W \leqslant c^W$ for optimality.

8.6. Mixed equality and inequality constraints

The foregoing exposition was in terms of the constraints being all of the form $Ax \leqslant b$. It is familiar LP theory that (in a maximization problem) the dual (y) variable associated with a greater-than-or-equal constraint must be non-positive for optimality, and that the dual variable associated with an equality constraint is not sign constrained, that it is a 'free variable'. Thus in this algorithm, feasibility and optimality are dependent on the signs of the constraints.

9. NON-LINEAR PROGRAMMING

Consider a general non-linear programming problem:

$$\begin{aligned}&\text{Min } f(x)\\ &\text{s.t. } g(x) \geqslant 0.\end{aligned}$$

Without proof we can state necessary conditions for a (local) minimum:

If $\bar{x}$ minimizes $f(x)$ (and the so-called 'constraint qualification' holds) then there exists $\bar{y} \geqslant 0$ such that

$$\begin{cases}\bar{y}\nabla g(\bar{x}) = \nabla f(\bar{x})\\ \bar{y}g(\bar{x}) = 0\end{cases}$$
(where $\nabla g(\bar{x})$ is the gradient vector of $g(x)$ evaluated at the point $\bar{x}$).

(This is the most succinct statement of the Kuhn-Tucker conditions, see [7].) We shall be concerned only with cases in which $g(x) \geqslant 0$ is a convex polytope, i.e., $(Ax - b) \geqslant 0$. In this case the constraint qualification always holds.

Note that LP is a special case of this general statement:

$$\nabla f(\bar{x}) = c; \quad \nabla g(\bar{x}) = A$$

so

$$\bar{y}\nabla g(\bar{x}) = \nabla f(\bar{x}) \text{ becomes } \bar{y}A = c,$$

and

$$\bar{y}g(\bar{x}) = 0 \text{ becomes } \bar{y}(A\bar{x} - b) = 0.$$

9.1. Non-negative *x*'s

$$\begin{aligned}&\text{Min } f(x)\\ &\text{s.t. } g(x) \geqslant 0\\ &\qquad\; x \geqslant 0\end{aligned}$$

If $\bar{x}$ is a local minimum there exists

$$\begin{aligned}&\bar{y} \geqslant 0, \bar{v} \geqslant 0\\ &\bar{y}\nabla g(\bar{x}) + \bar{v}I = \nabla f(\bar{x})\\ &\underbrace{\bar{y}g(\bar{x})}_{\geqslant 0} + \underbrace{\bar{v}\bar{x}}_{\geqslant 0} = 0\end{aligned}$$

i.e.

$$\bar{y}g(\bar{x}) = 0, \bar{v}\bar{x} = 0.$$

As in the LP case, we can eliminate $\bar{v} = \nabla f(\bar{x}) - \bar{y}\nabla g(\bar{x})$:

$$\begin{aligned}
&\bar{y} \geqslant 0 \\
&\bar{y}g(\bar{x}) \leqslant \nabla f(\bar{x}) \\
&\bar{y}g(\bar{x}) = 0 \\
&(\nabla f(\bar{x}) - \bar{y}\nabla g(\bar{x}))\bar{x} = 0
\end{aligned}$$

We present here an algorithm only for the special case of a quadratic function to be maximized on a convex polytope. (Obviously a quadratic function can be minimized if it is multiplied by -1.)

10. QUADRATIC PROGRAMMING

Quadratic programming has been used to fit a function to observations by least squares when the coefficients of the function are subject to linear inequalities; to maximize profit in a situation where price is a function of quantity; and in the context of minimizing variance where uncertainty is an important aspect of a problem.

$$\begin{aligned}
&\text{Min } f(x) = px + \tfrac{1}{2}xDx \\
&\text{s.t. } Ax - b \geqslant 0 \\
&\qquad\qquad x \geqslant 0.
\end{aligned}$$

If $\bar{x}$ is a local minimum,

since $\nabla g(\bar{x}) = A,\ \ \nabla f(\bar{x}) = p + D\bar{x}$

there exists

$$\begin{aligned}
&\bar{y} \geqslant 0 \\
&\bar{y}A \geqslant p + \bar{x}D \\
&\bar{y}(A\bar{x} - b) = 0 \\
&\bar{x}(p + D\bar{x} - \bar{y}A) = 0
\end{aligned}$$

Note: If the row vector is defined as $\bar{c} = \nabla f(\bar{x}) = p + \bar{x}D$, i.e. the vector of derivatives of the function evaluated at the point $\bar{x}$, then $\bar{x}$ minimizes the *linear* function $\bar{c}x$,

$$\begin{aligned}
&\text{s.t. } Ax \geqslant b \\
&\qquad\quad x \geqslant 0.
\end{aligned}$$

i.e. $\bar{c}\bar{x} \leqslant \bar{c}x$ for any x satisfying the constraints.

10.1. Sufficient conditions for a global minimum of a convex quadratic function

If $f(x)$ is *convex* within the region defined by the constraints,

$$\nabla f(\bar{x})(x^0 - \bar{x}) \leqslant f(x^0) - f(\bar{x}) \text{ (see lemma below)}$$

i.e.

$$\bar{c}(x^0 - \bar{x}) \leqslant f(x^0) - f(\bar{x})$$

$$\underbrace{\bar{c}x^0 - c\bar{x}}_{\geqslant 0} \leqslant \underbrace{f(x^0) - f(\bar{x})}_{\therefore \quad \geqslant 0}$$

i.e. $f(\bar{x}) \leqslant f(x^0)$ for any x^0 satisfying the constraints. That is to say, a local minimum is also the global minimum when the quadratic function is convex.

Lemma: $\nabla f(\bar{x})(x^0 - \bar{x}) \leqslant f(x^0) - f(\bar{x})$

Definition of a convex function:

$$f[(1-\lambda)\bar{x} + \lambda x^0] \leqslant (1-\lambda)f(\bar{x}) + \lambda f(x^0) \quad \text{for} \quad 0 \leqslant \lambda \leqslant 1$$

i.e.

$$f[\bar{x} + \lambda(x^0 - \bar{x})] \leqslant f(\bar{x}) + \lambda[f(x^0) - f(\bar{x})]$$

$$f(x^0) - f(\bar{x}) \geqslant \frac{f[\bar{x} + \lambda(x^0 - \bar{x})] - f(\bar{x})}{\lambda}$$

And by Taylor's theorem:

$$f[\bar{x} + \lambda(x^0 - \bar{x})] = f(\bar{x}) + \lambda \nabla f[\bar{x} + \lambda\theta(x^0 - \bar{x})]\,(x^0 - \bar{x}) \quad \text{for } 0 \leqslant \theta \leqslant 1$$

Hence

$$f(x^0) - f(\bar{x}) \geqslant \nabla f[\bar{x} + \lambda\theta(x^0 - \bar{x})]\,(x^0 - \bar{x}).$$

Let $\lambda \to 0$, then

$$\nabla f(\bar{x})(x^0 - \bar{x}) \leqslant f(x^0) - f(\bar{x}).$$

10.2. Beale's quadratic programming algorithm

This algorithm is designed to solve problems of the form

$$\text{Max } px + \tfrac{1}{2}x'Dx$$

$$\text{s.t. } Ax \lesseqgtr b \text{ (mixed inequality and equality constraints)}$$

$$x \geqslant 0.$$

Such a problem is (at least locally) optimized if the *linear* programming problem:

$$\begin{aligned}&\text{Max } \bar{c}x\\ &\text{s.t. } Ax \leqslant b\\ &\qquad x \geqslant 0\end{aligned}$$

is maximized at the point $\bar{x}$, where $\bar{c} = p + \bar{x}D$.

If in addition the function is concave (because the function is to be maximized) within the convex polytope, the local optimum is also the global optimum.

As illustrated in Figure 1.9, the optimum point $\bar{x}$ of a *QP* need not be an extreme point of the feasible region, i.e., it need not be a basic point. In order to use a Simplex algorithm on this type of problem, we can resort to the device of auxiliary constraints. Thus if the solution lies on a k-dimensional

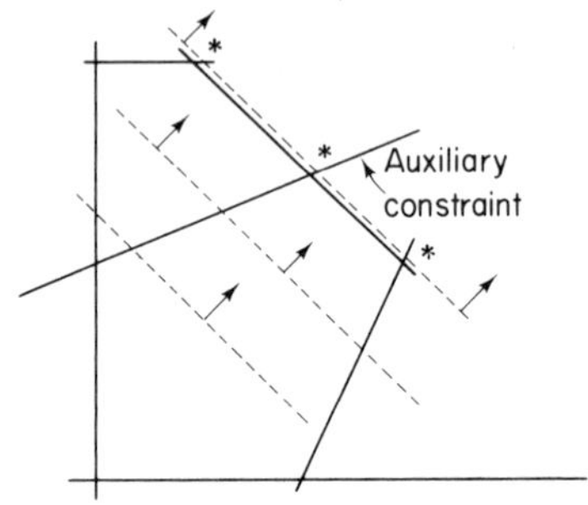

Figure 1.11

face of the feasible region, k auxiliary constraints can be found which intersect with the other $n - k$ to form a basic point. These constraints do not actually constrain the feasible region, because they are of the form

$$a^i x \lesseqgtr b$$

meaning that $a^i x$ is free to be either $\leqslant b_i$ or $\geqslant b_i$. The slack variable $x_{n+i} = b_i - a^i x$ is a free variable, and the corresponding dual variable y_i must be equal to zero. Alternatively we could think of such a constraint as having two non-negative slack variables, one with a positive unit vector of coefficients and the other with a negative unit vector of coefficients. Note that such a constraint could also be added to an LP without affecting the optimum value of the function although it might yield a different basic point for the solution if it were a problem with multiple solutions†. For example, we could add such a 'constraint' to Figure 1.7 and produce a third basic optimal solution as in Figure 1.11.

† An obvious additional use for this device is in the sub-problems of a decomposition algorithm to resolve the indeterminacy of their multiple solutions.

It might be helpful to summarize at this point the types of constraints used in these algorithms, bearing in mind in each case that the coefficients of the slack variable are in every case the positive unit vector:

i^{th} *constraint*	*slack,* x_{n+i}	*dual variable,* y_i
$a^i x \leqslant b_i$	$x_{n+i} \geqslant 0$	$y_i \geqslant 0$
$a^i x \geqslant b_i$	$x_{n+i} \leqslant 0$	$y_i \leqslant 0$
$a^i x = b_i$	$x_{n+i} = 0$	$y_i \gtreqless 0$ (free variable)
$a^i x \lesseqgtr b_i$	$x_{n+i} \lesseqgtr 0$ (free variable)	$y_i = 0$

The constraints suggested by Beale, [2], are (when expressed in terms of the original variables, see [9]):

$$(g^R D^R - d^k)x \leqslant -g^R p^R + p_k$$

where g^R is the vector $R^{-1}a^k$, the updated column of the entering variable, x_k; D^R† is the rows of D associated with the current basic variables, and d^k with the entering variable, x_k; p^R is the elements of p associated with the current basic variables, and p_k the p element of the entering variable, x_k.

Such a constraint has zero dual value when it is first imposed, and it remains at zero so long as only additional auxiliary constraints determine the extent of successive basis change moves. Its dual value departs from zero only if an original constraint, which was not effective when the constraint was first added, becomes effective.

Once a feasible point has been obtained, by the usual Simplex procedure, the algorithm presented in Chapter 3 proceeds by computing the linear function $c^0 = \nabla f(x^0) = p + Dx^0$ at each basic point x^0. It then checks the optimality of the linear function $c^0 x$. If the check fails, it follows the usual Simplex rule of moving in the direction indicated by the greatest violation of the linear optimality conditions, i.e., to increase x_k where

$$y^0 a^k \leqslant c_k^0 \quad (y^0 = c^{0R} R^{-1}).$$

In some circumstances, when the function first increases and then decreases along that edge of the feasible region, the movement is limited not by the next naturally occurring constraint to become effective, but by the auxilliary constraint

$$ya^k \leqslant c_k \quad \text{(taking } y \text{ and } c \text{ now as functions of } x\text{)}$$

† N.B. Although the matrix D is symmetrical so that both rows and columns refer to the basic and non-basic variables, x^R and x^U, the submatrix D^R refers only to the rows associated with x^R, but to *all* of the columns, both x^R and x^U. If we think of D as partitioned:

$$D = \begin{matrix} & x^R & x^U \\ x^R & \\ x^U & \end{matrix}\!\!\begin{bmatrix} D^{RR} & D^{RU} \\ D^{UR} & D^{UU} \end{bmatrix}; \quad D^R \text{ is } [D^{RR} \quad D^{RU}].$$

which is equivalent to

$$(g^R D^R - d^k)x \leqslant -g^R p^R + p_k \quad \text{as above.}$$

The new constraint may be effective in limiting the immediate movement, but thereafter it is treated as:

$$(g^R D^R - d^k)x \lesseqgtr -g^R p^R + p_k,$$

i.e., as having two slack variables.

Any auxiliary constraints which do not become effective when first imposed are immediately eliminated (in the subroutine PURGE). During the course of the calculation the dual value of an auxiliary constraint may depart from zero, and the slack variable may therefore enter the basis (either positively or negatively). The constraint would be eliminated in this case also.

The algorithm terminates when an LP solution is reached for the linear function which is the gradient vector at the current point, with the dual value of any still-present auxiliary constraint equal to zero.

11. DISCRETE (INTEGER) PROGRAMMING

Maximization and minimization of linear and quadratic functions over convex polytopes as defined by constraints of types (1) and (2) can be used to solve very many real problems. However, many other problems demand constraints of type (3)—discrete values of single variables. These may arise because of the 'lumpy' or non-continuous nature of economic variables—there may be two blast furnaces or three, but not 2·75. Or the variables may be logically 0 or 1, with no meaning for any other value. With greater or less degree of approximation *any* non-convex feasible region may be represented with the use of discrete (customarily integer) variables. And many of the awkward non-linearities in the function can be similarly converted into non-convexities of the feasible region. It is not, however, necessarily a help to finding a solution to make such a formulation of a real problem.

In two dimensions, we can represent the integer programming feasible region as the set of lattice points lying within the convex polytope defined by the ordinary equality and inequality conditions, as in Figure 1.12.

None of the nice mathematical properties which depend on the convexity of the feasible region carry over to this class of problem. It is not possible to examine a proposed solution in isolation to see if it satisfies conditions for optimality—a locally optimal point has no guarantee of being globally optimal. In many problems, the LP solution ignoring the discrete constraints is quite meaningless.

There is by now no difficulty in solving *small* problems with some or all variables integer or discrete. It is, on the other hand, not difficult to define problems which are essentially combinatorial in character and which are beyond the capability of any existing computer. The line between soluble and insoluble problems depends on the nature of the problem, the pay-off from obtaining the optimum, the size of computer available, (and perhaps the charging policy of the computing service). It should always be borne in mind that discrete programming problems are at least an order of magnitude more difficult to solve than LP problems of comparable size.

Of the many different algorithms available or being developed for solving discrete programming problems, a sample of two is included here. But we

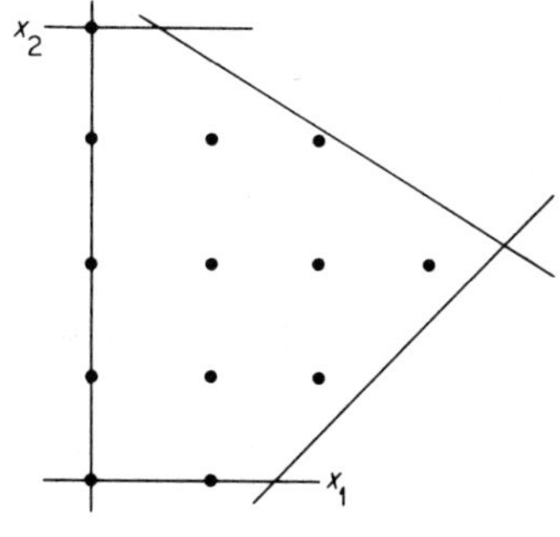

Figure 1.12

should like to stress that the programs could be easily adapted to alternative approaches. Chapter 7, Section 5 is devoted to explaining how to make this type of adaptation.

11.1. The method of integer forms

One continuing theme in the development of solution methods has been that of trying to cut down the feasible region defined by constraints of type (1) and (2) to the *convex hull* of the points which also satisfy constraints (3). If constraints, or *cutting planes,* can be found which do so restrict the feasible region at least in the neighbourhood of the solution, the resulting LP can be solved and the extreme point solution will be an integer point. The first automatic procedure for generating such constraints for an all-integer problem was Gomory's Method of Integer Forms [5].

The constraints of the Method of Integer Forms are normally applied in the updated tableau form. This may be familiar to the reader, but we shall give an alternative explanation of these constraints, which conforms to our practice of imposing the constraints in terms of the original variables of the problem.

Consider a maximization problem expressed entirely in less-than-or-equal constraints, with the non-negativity constraints also explicitly expressed as less-than-or-equal constraints. Note that this formulation is always valid, since a greater-than-or-equal constraint can be converted to a less-than-or-equal by multiplication by -1, and an equality constraint can be replaced by two inequalities.

$$\text{Max } cx$$
$$\left.\begin{aligned} \text{s.t. } Ax &\leqslant b \\ -Ix &\leqslant 0 \end{aligned}\right\} \text{ where } A \text{ is of order } m \times n.$$

A basis in this formulation corresponds to a selection of n of these $m + n$ inequalities to be solved as equalities:

$$\begin{array}{r} \\ k \\ n-k \\ m-k \\ k \end{array} \begin{array}{c} [x^R \quad x^U\,] \\ \begin{bmatrix} R & U \\ 0 & -I \end{bmatrix} \\ \begin{bmatrix} S & V \\ -I & 0 \end{bmatrix} \end{array} \begin{array}{c} \\ = \\ = \\ \leqslant \\ \leqslant \end{array} \begin{array}{l} \\ \left.\begin{bmatrix} b^R \\ 0 \end{bmatrix}\right\} n \text{ equalities} \\ \left.\begin{bmatrix} b^S \\ 0 \end{bmatrix}\right\} m \text{ inequalities} \end{array}$$

The basis yields a feasible solution if the remaining m inequalities are satisfied. The basis

$$P = \begin{bmatrix} R & U \\ 0 & -I \end{bmatrix}$$

is associated with an optimal solution if $y = cP^{-1} \geqslant 0$. Or, to put it another way, if $yP = c$, for some vector y of non-negative elements.

The LP problem is to select a basis which maximizes the function cx. The problem facing us when trying to determine a cutting plane which will cut off the current LP optimum point is the converse: to find a linear function which is maximized at the point associated with a given basis. Of course, it is extremely easy to find such a function. We can add any non-negative multiples, λ_i, of the rows of the basis and they will give us a row, p, which is a function maximized at this point:

$$\lambda P = p$$

i.e.,

$$pP^{-1} = \lambda \geqslant 0.$$

But we are only interested in functions p of *integer* coefficients which reach a *non-integer* maximum at this point. For if the maximum is:

$$px = d_0 + f_0,$$

where d_0 is an integer and f_0 is a positive fraction, and if p and x are integers, then we have a valid new constraint:

$$px \leqslant d_0$$

which cuts off the current basic point. These are not quite so easy to find. But one way of finding them is the Method of Integer Forms, which is to take as weights, λ_i, the non-negative fractional parts, f, of a row of the current tableau. This method assumes that the problem is expressed entirely in integer coefficients. If necessary this can be achieved by multiplying each row of the problem by its lowest common denominator.

Consider the matrix of all integer elements,

$$P = \begin{bmatrix} R & U \\ 0 & -I \end{bmatrix},$$

and the all-integer vector, $\begin{bmatrix} b^R \\ 0 \end{bmatrix}$, and the inverse of P,

$$P^{-1} = \begin{bmatrix} R^{-1} & R^{-1}U \\ 0 & -I \end{bmatrix}.$$

$\bar{x}$, the extreme point $= P^{-1} \begin{bmatrix} b^R \\ 0 \end{bmatrix}$. Take the kth row, w, of P^{-1} such that

$$\bar{x}_k = W \begin{bmatrix} b^R \\ 0 \end{bmatrix} \text{ is not integer, i.e.,}$$

$$\bar{x}_k = d_0 + f_0, \text{ where } 0 < f_0 < 1, \text{ and } d_0 \text{ integer.}$$

(If there is not such a row, the extreme point, $\bar{x}$, is an integer solution.)

Let

$$w = d + f$$

where d is a row vector of integers, d_i, and f is a row vector of elements, f_i,

$$0 \leqslant f_i < 1.$$

Then the row t:

$$t = fP$$

is integer, and $t\bar{x}$ is not integer, for:

$$wP = e_k,$$

the kth unit row vector (since w is the kth row of P^{-1}), i.e.

$$(d + f)P = e_k = \text{an integer vector.}$$

But dP is integer, since d is integer and so is P,

$$\therefore t = fP$$
$$= (w - d)P \quad \text{is integer.}$$

Also

$$t\bar{x} = fP\bar{x}$$
$$= f\begin{bmatrix} b^R \\ 0 \end{bmatrix}$$
$$= (w - d)\begin{bmatrix} b^R \\ 0 \end{bmatrix}$$
$$= w\begin{bmatrix} b^R \\ 0 \end{bmatrix} - d\begin{bmatrix} b^R \\ 0 \end{bmatrix}$$
$$= \bar{x}_k \text{ minus an integer, } \therefore \text{ not integer.}$$

Actually it is not necessary to have the whole inverse, P^{-1}. In the first place, we are not interested in the rows $[0\ -I]$, nor in the rows corresponding to effective upper bounds on single variables, since we cannot obtain a row, w, with non-integer right-hand-side from these rows.

But, further, we do not need to know $R^{-1}U$. For consider the multiplication to obtain

$$t = fP$$
$$= [f^R \quad f^U]\begin{bmatrix} R & U \\ 0 & -I \end{bmatrix}$$
$$= [t^R \quad t^U]$$

i.e., $t^U = f^R U - f^U$.

In other words, the elements of t^U are the elements of $f^R U$ rounded down to an integer.

The algorithm proceeds by solving the LP, checking whether it has integer solution values, if not adding a constraint derived from each non-integer variable, re-entering and solving the LP from the now infeasible basis, and repeating until either it finds an integer solution to one of the sequence of LPs, or exceeds the maximum allowed number of iterations, or until the 'cuts' become too small to give any hope of reaching a solution.

11.2. A Branch and Bound Method

Whereas the Method of Integer Forms is applicable only if *all* the variables must take integer values, Branch and Bound can be applied also to problems in which only some of the variables are so constrained—the so-called 'mixed integer' problems. As a matter of convenience, the version here can be used directly on problems with the discrete steps other than one, e.g., a step size of 1000, which means that the variable may take values 0, 1000, 2000, 3000, . . . etc. Of course, any such problem could always be reformulated with simple integer variables, but it is preferable to use a large step size for a variable if the alternative would be a unit step size and a very large coefficient within the A matrix. For simplicity of exposition, the following discussion is in terms of the variables taking simple integer values only.

The principle of this type of algorithm is that the convex feasible region of the LP is partitioned into convex subsets and an upper bound on the function is obtained for each subset in the partition. If a solution satisfying the integer constraints can be found which has a function value no less than the upper bound on all the subsets, then it is the optimum solution. In practice the partitioning is carried out sequentially (the branching operation), and a record of the subsets for which a bound has been obtained can be represented by a tree graph. There are many alternative possibilities both for the method of branching and for the determination of bounds. The particular algorithm presented here has not been tested against alternative versions. It is based principally on the original Land and Doig method [8], for no better reason than that it has apparently not previously been programmed.

The partitioning, or branching, proceeds as follows. The LP solution is obtained and the values of the variables which have to take discrete values are examined. If they are all at genuinely feasible integer values, there is, of course, no need to proceed further: the LP solution is also the integer solution. Otherwise, one variable, say, x_k, which is not at an integer value is selected, according to the same 'penalty' criteria used by Little *et al.* [10], as described in the description of the subroutine BRANCH. A consequence of the convexity of the LP feasible region is that the value of the function will decrease not merely monotonically but at an increasing rate as x_k is fixed at values further (either higher or lower) from its value at the LP optimum point. The solution tableau of the LP provides information which can be used to obtain upper bounds on the function for all values of x_k, both higher and lower than its value at the LP optimum point. Obviously the integer values immediately above and below the optimum value will have the highest bounds on the function. Of the two, let us suppose $x_k = \gamma$ gives the higher bound. Then the feasible region can be considered to be partitioned into the following mutally exclusive and exhaustive convex sets:

Set A in which $x_k \leqslant \gamma - 1$;
Set B in which $\gamma - 1 < x_k < \gamma$;
Set C in which $x_k = \gamma$;
Set D in which $\gamma < x_k < \gamma + 1$;
Set E in which $x_k \geqslant \gamma + 1$.

There can be no integer feasible solution in set B or set D, since x_k cannot there take an integer value. There are therefore three sets to be considered: A, in which $x_k \leqslant \gamma - 1$, will be referred to as the *left hand branch*; C, in which $x_k = \gamma$, is the *main branch*; and E, in which $x_k \geqslant \gamma + 1$, is the *right hand branch*.

The main branch (or partition) is the one in which a solution will be sought first. A record is kept that at *level 1* of the tree the left hand value of x_k is $\gamma - 1$, with its upper bound on the function, and the right hand value of x_k is $\gamma + 1$, with its upper bound.

Then a new LP is defined with, in effect, the additional constraint $x_k = \gamma$. In practice, the variable x_k is removed from the problem by giving it an upper bound of zero and the right hand side, or b vector, is modified by subtracting from it γ times the column of coefficients belonging to x_k in the A matrix. This makes the existing LP solution infeasible, so the LP routine is called to restore feasibility and optimality. At this point it may turn out that the function is lower than the bound obtained initially, in which case the bound on either the left hand or the right hand branch can also be tightened as explained in the description of the subroutine ISTAIL.

The situation is now again as at the original LP solution, except that one variable is definitely fixed at an integer value. If the solution is still not integer feasible, another variable is selected for branching, the level of the tree is increased by one and again a record kept of the left hand and right hand values of the new variable and their upper bounds.

Note that the algorithm does not branch from the vertex of the tree with the greatest bound on the function (as in the original Land-Doig algorithm), but proceeds down the main branch until a *tail* is reached. There are three types of tail:

1. An integer solution.
2. An LP solution with function value at least as low as the best solution discovered so far.
3. An infeasible LP.

Obviously, only cases 1 or 3 can occur on the first tail reached.

When a tail is reached the subsets of the feasible region which have been neglected on the 'left' and the 'right' of the main branch must be investigated. Starting with the level at which the tail was found, the bounds on the sets to the left and the right are looked at. Any which are no better than an integer solution already obtained (if any) or are infeasible (indicated by an upper bound on the function of a very large negative value) can be deleted and the level of the tree reduced. But if a level is reached for which either the left or the right bound still offers the possibility of there being a better integer solution within its set, this becomes the main branch and a further-out value of the appropriate variable has to be defined as the left or right value. The level may then increase again until another tail is reached.

Eventually, if the algorithm is allowed to run long enough, the backing-up investigation will get all the way back to level zero, indicating that no subset has an upper bound better than the best integer solution found (or that there is no integer solution).

If a limit on the number of iterations is set, the algorithm will terminate with a record of the final state of the tree, which can be punched out on cards (or dumped on tape, etc) and used to restart the algorithm if it is judged worth while.

A word of warning: it is important to scale the input coefficients as close to unity as possible to avoid the risk of spurious infeasibility, which may result in large parts of the tree being omitted from due consideration.

Note that although the total exploration performed by the algorithm could be described by a tree graph, the actual order in which it is carried out means that only a chain need be stored in the computer. The chain at any one time consists of a list of variables which have been fixed at each level, together with a record of the upper bounds on the function for the next values of the fixed variables to the 'left' and the 'right' which have not yet been explored. The maximum length of the chain is the number of variables constrained to take discrete values.

12. PARAMETRIC PROGRAMMING

When an LP problem is formulated for solution by a numerical process, such as the Simplex method, the values of the coefficients of A, b and c have to be exactly specified. This condition that the coefficients can only take one value often misrepresents the situation of which the LP is a model. Most LP models are concerned with the level of activities in the future, yet often the exact quantity of resources that will be available is not known. All the fuel that has been ordered may not arrive by next week. The extension to the warehouse may not be complete in six months. The threatened dock strike will probably disrupt our supplies of certain raw materials. It is usually the case that the amount of resource that will be available is known to be within a range of values. Similarly the expected profit from a new product may be anywhere within a range of values.

The values of such elements of b or c that are customarily used to specify the LP are the 'expected' or 'most probable' values. Clearly it is possible to find how the solution is affected by different values of the elements of b or c by solving a series of LPs. However, it is possible with parametric programming to evaluate the effect of changes in the values of elements of b or c. Parametric programming is concerned with the changes in the solution values and in the value of the objective function of an LP as the value of a parameter, an element of b or c, varies. This may involve a series of basis changes as the value of the parameter is increased or decreased.

Parametric programming is often presented in terms of varying a whole b vector or c vector over a range, rather than single elements. If this is the required investigation it can be carried out with these programs by adding an extra variable and an extra constraint, as illustrated by the table below:

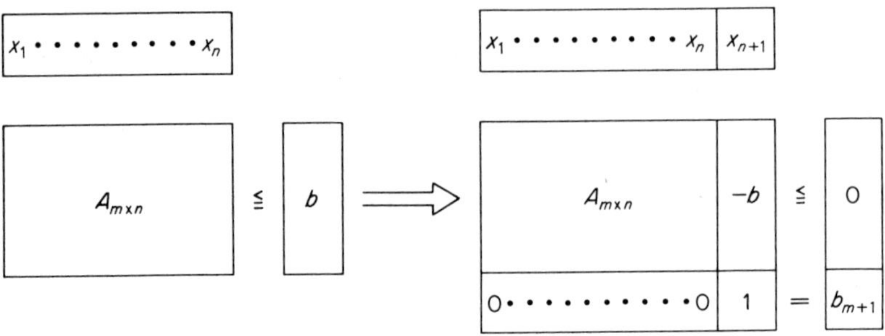

The PLP program can then be used to vary b_{m+1} over any desired range. Obviously, if only a subset of the b elements are to be varied, only they need be moved into the coefficient matrix and the rest may be left as constants on the right-hand side.

If there are two alternative b vectors, $b^{(1)}$ and $b^{(2)}$ and it is desired to explore the response of the LP over the range from $b = b^{(1)}$ to $b = b^{(2)}$, the following table suggests how this program can be used by adding two variables and two constraints.

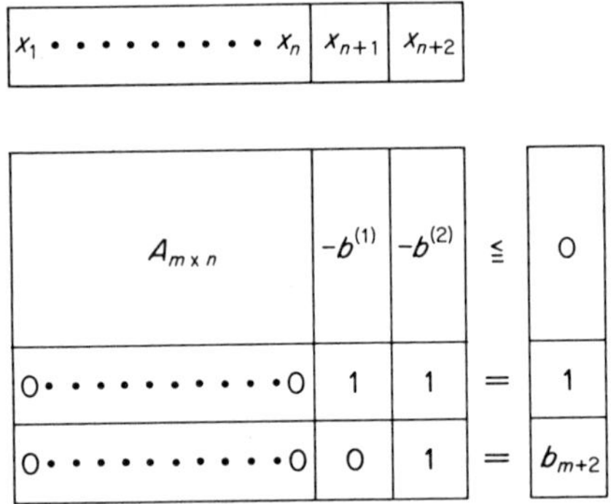

b_{m+2} can then be varied over the range 0 to 1.

Exactly analogous formulations can be used for variations in the c vector.

The remainder of this section is concerned with the mathematical details of parametric programming. The first discussion considers varying an element of b. This is followed by a discussion of varying an element of c and finally there is a short note on sensitivity and range analysis. The analysis is in terms of the standard problem.

12.1. Variation of the value of b_i

A basis is *feasible* if

$$\begin{aligned} Rx^R &= b^R \\ Sx^R &\leqslant b^S \\ x^R &\geqslant 0. \end{aligned}$$

x^S, the slack variables, are defined by $Sx^R + x^S = b^S$. Thus for feasibility $x^S \geqslant 0$.

The parameter is the ith element of b, b_i. The value of the parameter is initially b_i^* and it is to be varied between $b_i min$ and $b_i max$ ($b_i min \leqslant b_i^* \leqslant b_i max$). If the element b_i^* is contained in b^S at the (feasible) LP optimum then:

$$s^i x^R + x_i^S = b_i^*$$

where s^i is the ith row of S and x_i^S is the slack variable on the ith constraint. As the ith constraint is a less-than-or-equal constraint x_i^S is constrained to be non-negative, $x_i^S \geqslant 0$. Thus the value of the parameter, b_i, can vary from $s^i x^R$ to plus infinity without causing any infeasibility or a change in the value of the objective function; only the value of the slack variable, x_i^S, will change. If $s^i x^R$ is less than $b_i min$ then the value of b_i can vary over the complete range $b_i min$ to $b_i max$ without affecting the feasibility of the initial LP optimum basis. However if $s^i x^R$ is greater than $b_i min$ then decreasing b_i below the value of $b_i^* - x_i^S$ will cause the basis to become infeasible.

As the first step to preserve feasibility the ith constraint must be made effective, that is added to the constraints in R, with a value of b_i of $b_i^* - x_i^S$. The analysis of the variation of the value of b_i is now the same as if the ith constraint had been effective at the initial LP optimum. The following discussion considers varying b_i when the ith constraint is effective.

As the value of b_i *decreases* the values of the basic original and slack variables, x^R and x^S, will change until one of the variables, x_s, reaches zero; x_s must be made non-basic to preserve feasibility.

At a feasible basis:

$$\begin{bmatrix} x^R \\ x^S \end{bmatrix} = \begin{bmatrix} R^{-1}b^R \\ b^S - Sx^R \end{bmatrix} = \begin{bmatrix} R^{-1}b^R \\ b^S - SR^{-1}b^R \end{bmatrix} \geqslant 0$$

Let $\alpha(\alpha \geqslant 0)$ be the change in b_i and let e_i be the ith unit vector; $\bar{x}^R$ and $\bar{x}^S$ are the changed values of x^R and x^S. The new value of b^R is $b^R - \alpha e_i$

$$\begin{bmatrix} \bar{x}^R \\ \bar{x}^S \end{bmatrix} = \begin{bmatrix} R^{-1}(b^R - \alpha e_i) \\ b^S - SR^{-1}(b^R - \alpha e_i) \end{bmatrix}$$

$$= \begin{bmatrix} x^R - \alpha R^{-1} e_i \\ x^S - \alpha(-SR^{-1} e_i) \end{bmatrix}$$

$$= \begin{bmatrix} x^R \\ x^S \end{bmatrix} - \alpha \begin{bmatrix} R^{-1} e_i \\ -SR^{-1} e_i \end{bmatrix}$$

$$= \begin{bmatrix} x^R \\ x^S \end{bmatrix} - \alpha \begin{bmatrix} g^R \\ g^S \end{bmatrix} \tag{1}$$

that is

$$\bar{x}^P = x^P - \alpha g$$

where $\begin{bmatrix} g^R \\ g^S \end{bmatrix} = g$ is the 'updated' vector associated with bringing the slack on the ith constraint into the basis.

For feasibility,

$$\bar{x}^P = x^P - \alpha g \geqslant 0$$

Hence

$$\alpha = \min_{i, g_i > 0} \frac{x_i^P}{g_i}$$

Let the variable that defines α be x_s. The evaluation of α is the same as the search conducted (in SEEKY) in a basis change, to determine which variable is to leave the basis when the value of the variable entering is increasing. x_s is the variable that if it remained in the implicit basis (i.e., an element of x^P) would become infeasible (i.e., negative). Corresponding to the decrease in value of b_i by α the values of x^R and x^S are changed to $\bar{x}^R$ and $\bar{x}^S$ as in expression†. Clearly this changes the value of x_s to zero. In order to continue decreasing the value of b_i, x_s is made non-basic by a zero basis change.† As x^R and x^S are altered so is the value of the objective function.

The process of evaluating α, changing the values of x^R and x^S and remov-

† By a zero basis change we mean one in which the coefficients of the inverse basis, the dual variables, and the function row variables are altered. The values of the real and slack variables and the objective are not altered because the value of the variable leaving the basis is zero. Note that as in any basis change a variable is made non-basic and a different variable is made basic.

ing x_s from the basis, is continued until b_i takes a value less than $b_i min$. However, if no value for α can be found or if the ith constraint becomes ineffective then the value of b_i can decrease to minus infinity without causing infeasibility. If it is not possible to perform a zero basis change to make x_s non-basic then any value of b_i below that at the current basis will cause infeasibility; at this stage, in the computer program no further decrease in the value of b_i is analysed.

Similarly as the value of b_i *increases* the value of a variable, x_s, will become zero and would become infeasible if it remained in the implicit basis and b_i continued to increase. A zero basis change is necessary to make x_s non-basic and thus preserve feasibility as b_i increases. The analogous expression to (1) is

$$\begin{bmatrix} \bar{x}^R \\ \bar{x}^S \end{bmatrix} = \begin{bmatrix} x^R \\ x^S \end{bmatrix} + \alpha \begin{bmatrix} g^R \\ g^S \end{bmatrix} \tag{2}$$

that is

$$\bar{x}^P = x^P + \alpha g$$

where $\alpha(\alpha \geqslant 0)$ is the change in b_i, so that the new value of b^R is $b^R + \alpha e_i$.

For feasibility,

$$\bar{x}^P = x^P + \alpha g \geqslant 0$$

Hence

$$\alpha = \min_{i, g_i < 0} \frac{x_i^P}{-g_i}$$

The variable which defines α is x_s. As before the evaluation of α is the same as the search conducted in SEEKY when the value of the variable entering the basis is decreasing. Corresponding to the increase in the value of b_i by α the values of the variables are changed as in expression (2). x_s now has a value of zero and is made a non-basic variable in order to continue increasing the value of b_i and maintain feasibility. The process of increasing the value of b_i is continued until b_i has a value greater than $b_i max$. If no value can be found for α or the ith constraint becomes ineffective the value of b_i can increase to plus infinity. If it is not possible to perform a zero basis change to make x_s non-basic, then any value of b_i greater than that at the current basis will cause infeasibility.

The changes in the value of the objective function are represented in Figure 1.13 below. We shall describe the changes in terms of increasing the value of b_i, decreasing the value of b_i is essentially the same.
The variation of the value of b_i starts at A with an initial value of the parameter of b_i^*. The algorithm used in the computer program explores on either

side of b_i^* and calculates the changes, α_0 and α_1 in the value of the parameter for which the initial basis remains feasible. The value of b_i is increased by α_1 and the resultant changes to the basic and slack variables are computed in the subroutine CHXSL, to reach the basis represented by B in the diagram. Then 'at a corner point', a zero basis change is made, B to C, so that for further increases in the value of b_i feasibility can be maintained. From C the next increment, α_2, in the value of b_i is evaluated, the variables changed, to reach D, and a zero basis change made, to E. This is repeated until an increment, α_3, would increase the value of b_i beyond the upper limit, $b_i max$. The value of the parameter is increased by α_4 to $b_i max$ and the values of the variables are altered to correspond. From F the subroutine

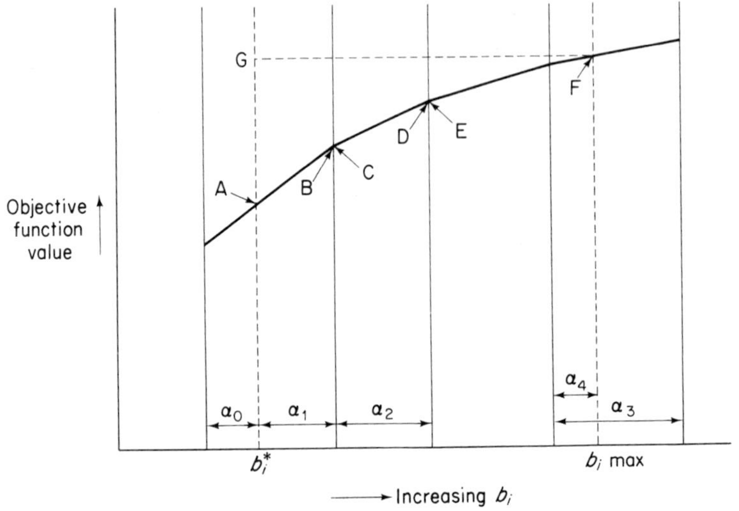

Figure 1.13

MIDBI returns to the initial value of the parameter, b_i^*, in one move. This basis, G, is attained by overshooting, if necessary, in CHXSL; feasibility and thus the basis represented by A is restored by the subroutine DOANLP.

In a similar fashion the changes that result from decreasing the value of the parameter are explored. In the computer program these explorations, both increasing and decreasing the value of b_i, are conducted by the subroutine PARAB.

12.2. Variation of the value of c_j

The analysis of the change to the value of the objective function that results from a change in the value of c_j, the parameter, is analogous to the change that results from a change in the value of b_i. In the case of varying an element of c_j we are concerned with the changes in the values of the dual variables of the effective constraints and the function row variables, and basis changes are necessary to preserve optimality (dual feasibility). In the case of varying an element of b_i we are concerned with changes in the values of the basic and slack variables, and basis changes are necessary to preserve feasibility (primal feasibility). A basis is *optimal* if

$$\begin{aligned} y^R R &= c^R \\ y^R U &\geqslant c^U \\ y^R &\geqslant 0. \end{aligned}$$

z^U, the function row variables, are defined as $y^R U + z^U = c^U$. Thus for optimality $z^U \geqslant 0$.

The parameter is the jth element of c, c_j. The jth variable is an original variable not a slack variable. The value of the parameter is initially c_j^* and it is to be varied between $c_j min$ and $c_j max$ ($c_j min \leqslant c_j^* \leqslant c_j max$). If the element c_j^* is contained in c^U at the LP optimum then:

$$y^R u^j - z_j^U = c_j^*$$

where u^j is the jth column of U and z_j^U is the function row variable of the jth variable. As the jth variable is non-basic at its lower bound of zero, z_j^U is constrained to be non-negative, $z_j^U \geqslant 0$. Thus the value of the parameter, c_j, can vary from minus infinity to $y^R u^j$ without causing the basis to become non-optimal and without changing the value of the objective function, only the value of the function row variable, z_j^U, will change. If $y^R u^j$ is more than $c_j max$ then the value of c_j can vary over the complete range $c_j min$ to $c_j max$ without affecting the optimality of the initial LP optimum basis. However if $y^R u^j$ is less than $c_j max$ then increasing c_j above the value of $y^R u^j$ will cause the basis to become non-optimal.

As the first step to preserve optimality the jth variable must be made basic, that is added to the variables in R, with a value of c_j of $y^R u^j$. The analysis of the variation of the value of c_j is now the same as if the jth variable had been basic at the initial LP optimum. The following discussion considers varying c_j when the jth variable is basic.

As the value of c_j *increases* the values of the dual variables of the effective constraints and the function row variables, y^R and z^U, will change until one of these reaches zero and the associated slack or original variable, x_k, must be introduced into the basis to preserve optimality.

At an optimal basis:

$$\begin{bmatrix} y^R \\ z^U \end{bmatrix} = \begin{bmatrix} c^R R^{-1} \\ y^R U - c^U \end{bmatrix} = \begin{bmatrix} c^R R^{-1} \\ c^R R^{-1} U - c^U \end{bmatrix} \geqslant 0$$

Let $\alpha (\alpha \geqslant 0)$ be the change in c_j; $\bar{y}^R$ and $\bar{z}^U$ are the changed values of y^R and z^U corresponding to the change in c^R to $c^R + \alpha e_j$.

$$\begin{bmatrix} \bar{y}^R \\ \bar{z}^U \end{bmatrix} = \begin{bmatrix} (c^R + \alpha e_j)R^{-1} \\ (c^R + \alpha e_j)R^{-1}U - c^U \end{bmatrix}$$

$$= \begin{bmatrix} c^R R^{-1} + \alpha e_j R^{-1} \\ c^R R^{-1} U - c^U + \alpha e_j R^{-1} U \end{bmatrix}$$

$$= \begin{bmatrix} y^R \\ z^U \end{bmatrix} + \alpha \begin{bmatrix} e_j R^{-1} \\ e_j R^{-1} U \end{bmatrix}$$

$$= \begin{bmatrix} y^R \\ z^U \end{bmatrix} + \alpha \begin{bmatrix} h^R \\ h^U \end{bmatrix} \qquad (3)$$

where $\begin{bmatrix} h^R \\ h^U \end{bmatrix} = h$ is the 'function' vector associated with removing the jth variable from the basis.

For optimality,

$$\begin{bmatrix} \bar{y}^R \\ \bar{z}^U \end{bmatrix} = \begin{bmatrix} y^R \\ z^U \end{bmatrix} + \alpha \begin{bmatrix} h^R \\ h^U \end{bmatrix} \geqslant 0$$

Hence

$$-\alpha = \max \left[\max_{i,\, h_i^R < 0} \frac{y_i^R}{h_i^R},\ \max_{j,\, h_j^U < 0} \frac{z_j^U}{h_j^U} \right]$$

Let the variable that defines α be x_k. The evaluation of α is the same as the search conducted (in SEEKX) to determine which variable is to enter the basis to remove an infeasible variable when the infeasible variable has to be increased to make it feasible. x_k is the variable that if it remained non-basic (i.e., an element of x^Q) would become non-optimal. Corresponding to the increase in value of c_j by α the values of y^R and z^U are changed to $\bar{y}^R$ and $\bar{z}^U$. This reduces either y_k^R, or z_k^U, depending whether x_k is slack or an original variable, to zero, and in order to continue increasing the value of c_j, x_k must be made a member of the implicit basis (i.e., an element of x^P). If x_k is an original variable then it is made basic (i.e., an element of R) while if x_k is a slack variable on the ith constraint then the ith constraint is made ineffective. Making x_k a member of the implicit basis involves a basis change in which the dual variables of the effective constraints and the function row variables do not change values, i.e., a dual zero basis change.

The process of evaluating α, changing the values of y^R and z^U and introducing x_k into the implicit basis is continued until c_j takes a value greater than $c_j max$. However, if no value for α can be found or if the jth variable becomes non-basic then the value of c_j can increase to plus infinity without causing non-optimality. Also if it is not possible to perform a dual zero basis change then any value of c_j above that at the current basis will cause non-optimality; at this stage, in the computer program no further increase in the value of c_j is analysed.

Similarly as the value of c_j *decreases* either a dual variable of an effective constraint, y^R, or the function row element of an original variable, z^U, will become non-optimal. The analogous expression to (3) is

$$\begin{bmatrix} \bar{y}^R \\ \bar{z}^U \end{bmatrix} = \begin{bmatrix} y^R \\ z^U \end{bmatrix} - \alpha \begin{bmatrix} h^R \\ h^U \end{bmatrix}$$

Hence

$$-\alpha = \max \left[\max_{i, h_i^R > 0} \frac{y_i^R}{-h_i^R}, \max_{j, h_j^U > 0} \frac{z_j^U}{-h_j^U} \right]$$

As in the case of varying the value of b_i, the analysis of the changes that result from increasing or decreasing the value of C_j is the same, *mutatis mutandi.*

The changes in the value of the objective function as c_j increases could be represented by a diagram analogous to Figure 1.13. The interpretation of the diagram is the same. When c_j increases the initial value of the parameter is c_j^* and its upper limit is $c_j max$. The changes to the dual variables of the effective constraints and the function row variables are performed by subroutine CHAGY and subroutine MIDCJ returns the value of the parameter to c_j^* in one move; optimality is restored by DOANLP. Subroutine PARAC organizes the computation to increase the value of the parameter to $c_j max$ and then decrease it to $c_j min$.

12.3. Sensitivity and range analysis

A *sensitivity analysis* of an element of b_i evaluates the range of values of b_i within which the optimal LP basis remains feasible. Thus, with reference to Figure 1.13, a sensitivity analysis would show that the same LP basis is feasible within the range of values of b_i, $b_i^* - \alpha_0$ to $b_i^* + \alpha_1$. One of the options in the computer program is to perform a sensitivity analysis upon specified elements of b. The program computes and prints the feasible range and also it prints (depending upon the printing option) the values of the solution variables when b_i has a value of $b_i^* - \alpha_0$ and when b_i has a value of $b_i^* + \alpha_1$.

A *range analysis* of b evaluates simply the range of values for *each* element of b within which the optimal LP basis remains feasible but it does not print the values of any solution variables at the limits of the range. The evaluation of the range is done independently of each other for all the elements of b. An option in the computer program is to perform a range analysis of b.

A sensitivity analysis of an element of c_j and a range analysis of c is analogous to those of b_i and b. In this case the range of values is the range of values of c_j within which the optimal LP basis remains optimal. As before both options are available in the computer program.

CHAPTER 2

A Program to Solve LP

1. PROGRAM LINP (linear programming)

The first program (LINP) and subroutine (LP) presented here simply set up the necessary conditions to enter the central routine of nearly all of these programs, DOANLP (do an LP). If the user's only purpose is to solve LP problems, he could easily combine these two routines. They have been separated only because those instructions which are included in the subroutine LP are required not only here but also in more complex algorithms where linear programming is only a subroutine.

The first card of the program is as required for the CDC 6600 in order to specify 5 as the input channel, and 6 as the output channel. This is not necessary on all computers. The COMMON and TYPE statements are omitted in the listing and are described separately immediately after the listing of the DOANLP subroutine.

DATA is the subroutine which reads in a problem for solution. If this routine fails and ISDONE (a COMMON variable) equals 1, the program stops. ISTATE = 0 indicates to the LP routine that it has no initial basis to operate upon. After LP, ISTATE will take values other than zero, according to the outcome of the LP calculation, and the subroutine IEXIT controls the output of the program.

MORE is a COMMON variable, read in DATA, which is zero only if there is no other LP problem to be solved.

Subroutines called in LINP

DATA
IEXIT
LP

COMMON variables altered in LINP

ISTATE

COMMON variables used in LINP

ISDONE
MORE

```
      PROGRAM LINP (INPUT,OUTPUT,TAPE5=INPUT,TAPE6=OUTPUT)
*********************** COMMON AND TYPE STATEMENTS ********************
   10 CALL DATA
      IF(ISDONE.EQ.1) GO TO 20
      ISTATE = 0
      CALL LP
      CALL IEXIT(ISTATE)
      IF(MORE.NE.0) GO TO 10
   20 STOP
      END
```

2. LP

This subroutine, which is also called in the discrete programming algorithms, sets the iteration count, ITR, and the re-inversion count, IR, to zero. ISTATE is a variable which indicates the starting situation for the LP. If the routine has been entered from the program LINP, ISTATE = 0. The significance of ISTATE = 10 will emerge in later programs (or can be discovered in Appendix 2).

ISTATE = 1 signifies that the outcome of DOANLP (do an LP) is optimality; ISTATE = 2 signifies infeasibility; ISTATE = 3 signifies an unbounded solution. Other values of ISTATE signify incomplete solutions of one kind or another. Only for completed solutions does the routine call CHACC (check accuracy). If the accuracy check fails, ISTATE = 7, and so long as the re-inversion count is less than IRMAX, a re-inversion is performed in REVERT, after which DOANLP is again called with ISTATE = 11, signifying that a basis is available.

Obviously, the heart of this program is DOANLP, and it is described in full detail immediately after the listing of LP.

If a version of LP without an accuracy check is required (because of limited storage, for instance) everything between '10 CALL DOANLP' and '20 RETURN' may be deleted and the two subroutines CHACC and REVERT removed from the program.

Conversely, if desired, an accuracy check can be made by calling CHACC at other points in this or the more complex programs, and similarly REVERT can be called at other points.

Subroutines called in LP

CHACC
DOANLP
REVERT

COMMON variables altered in LP

INREV
IR
ISTATE
ITR

COMMON variables used in LP

IRMAX

```
      SUBROUTINE LP
********************** COMMON AND TYPE STATEMENTS ********************
      ITR = 0
      IR = 0
      IF (ISTATE .EQ. 10) INREV = 1
   10 CALL DOANLP
      IF (ISTATE .GT. 3) GO TO 20
      CALL CHACC
      IF(ISTATE.NE.7) GO TO 20
      IF(IR.GE.IRMAX) GO TO 20
      CALL REVERT
      ISTATE = 11
      GO TO 10
   20 RETURN
      END
```

3. DOANLP (do an LP)

A flow chart for DOANLP precedes the actual listing.

The basic Simplex procedure presented here is designed to maximize a linear function of n non-negative variables, subject to m assorted equality and/or inequality constraints, with positive, negative, or zero right hand sides, and subject to simple upper bounds on some or all of the n variables.

DOANLP is the name of a Fortran subroutine which itself principally calls a series of other subroutines.

Communication between the main program and DOANLP, and between the latter and its subroutines, is entirely by means of blocks of COMMON storage to which all the routines have access. The details of that COMMON store are described immediately after the listing of DOANLP.

In some of the more complicated programs described in later chapters, DOANLP may be entered with a basic solution which may be feasible or infeasible, optimal or non-optimal, and the routine will then proceed to perform Simplex iterations to find a feasible, optimal solution, or to discover that one does not exist. Initially, however, the simplest version of DOANLP, without an initially given basis, will be presented in the flow chart, as indicated by ISTATE = 0.

The first step is to set up a 1 x 1 inverse matrix, consisting of a unit vector on the first constraint. This is done in FIRSTB (first basis).

In this and every case, the algorithm first performs iterations to satisfy the feasibility conditions, and only then satisfies the optimality conditions, preserving feasibility as it does so. Feasibility is attained as follows. The basic variables are checked for feasibility, that is to say, they are checked to see whether they lie within their upper and lower bounds. The variable with the greatest violation of its feasibility conditions determines the indicator variable, NEGINV, which signifies the row of the inverse associated with this greatest violation. The values of $b^S - Sx^R$ are computed (or inspected). These values are called the SLACK array (and are set equal to 0·0 on effective constraints). Elements of SLACK(I) may have to be non-negative or non-positive, or actually equal to zero for feasibility, according to the sign of the S(I) element, which signifies whether the Ith constraint is a $\leqslant$, a $\geqslant$, or an =. The row of A with the greatest violation of its feasibility condition is signified by the variable NEGROW.

If both NEGROW and NEGINV are zero, the current solution is feasible, and the algorithm proceeds to examine optimality.

If NEGINV is positive, the algorithm will make Simplex iterations until that variable reaches feasibility. This may involve driving the variable up to its lower bound (in which case the variable DRIVER = 1·0) or down to its upper bound (in which case DRIVER = −1·0). The iterations to achieve feasibility proceed as follows. First a variable to enter the basis is chosen in the subroutine SEEKX (seek x). If there is no non-basic variable (either an x variable or a slack variable) which can enter the basis and reduce the infeasibility of the NEGINV row, the problem is infeasible, and the program terminates with ISTATE = 2. If a candidate for entry to the basis, NEWX, is found, the variable to be removed from the basis must next be discovered, in the subroutine SEEKY (seek y). Using dual Simplex, the variable to leave the basis would, of course, be the one in the NEGINV position. This might then cause some other variable to depart from feasibility. SEEKY, however, chooses the variable to leave the basis according to normal primal basis change rules; any constraint, either an explicit equality or inequality constraint or a non-negativity or an upper bound, which is already satisfied, will not be violated. That one which most restricts the entry of the new variable will determine the variable leaving the basis. If this is an explicit constraint, the preliminary step of augmenting the inverse by the appropriate unit vector and row of S is carried out, in the subroutine ADDCON. (This is one of the numerous places where the algorithm is aiming less at efficiency than at being relatively easy for its authors to use!)

Then the solution is changed in the subroutine CHBSIS, any slack vectors in the basis (other than infeasible ones) are removed in REDUCE (but not to reduce the SIZE to zero); the SLACK array, etc., is updated in CHSLCK; and NEGROW and NEGINV are again inspected for feasibility. Note that once a basic variable has been designated NEGINV, it will so remain until feasibility is attained on that variable, or until infeasibility of the problem is recognized, even though it may no longer be the greatest violation of the feasibility conditions on basic variables.

If NEGINV is zero, but NEGROW is not, the inverse is augmented by a slack vector in ADDCON and the augmenting row designated as NEGINV. The succeeding steps are then as detailed above.

If NEGROW and NEGINV are both zero, the current solution is feasible and the new variable to enter the basis, NEWX, is determined in ISOPT rather than in SEEKX (although these are really very similar routines). If NEWX = 0, the LP is optimal, and ISTATE = 1.

Subroutines called in DOANLP

ADDCON	NEWVEC
CHBSIS	REDUCE
CHSLCK	SEEKX
FIRSTB	SEEKY
ISOPT	

COMMON variables altered in DOANLP

DRIVER	NEGINV
ISTATE	NEWY

COMMON variables used in DOANLP

ITR	SIZE
ITRMAX	SIZE1
NEGROW	SLACK(I)
NEWX	

4. FLOWCHART FOR DOANLP

The five points marked * are five possible endings of the subroutine. Three of them are obvious: ISOPT may discover that the LP is optimal; SEEKX, that it is infeasible; and SEEKY, that it is unbounded. The fourth and fifth

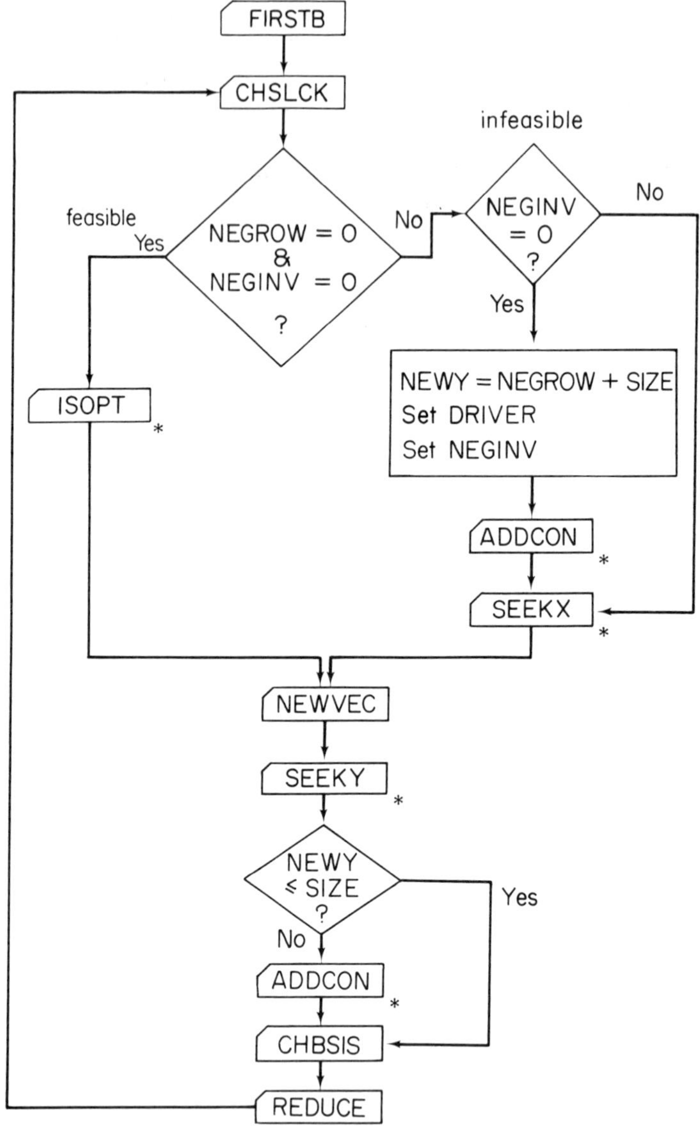

exits, both from ADDCON, are to deal with the case where MXSIZE, the maximum size of the inverse, is less than the number of constraints, M, and where this size limit is about to be exceeded.

```
      SUBROUTINE DOANLP
********************** COMMON AND TYPE STATEMENTS ********************
      IF (ISTATE .EQ. 0) CALL FIRSTB
      IF (ISTATE .EQ. 11) GO TO 20
      IF (ISTATE .EQ. 12) GO TO 50
   10 CALL CHSLCK
      IF (ITR .LE. ITRMAX) GO TO 20
      ISTATE = 5
      GO TO 80
   20 IF (NEGROW.EQ.0 .AND. NEGINV.EQ.0) GO TO 40
      IF (NEGINV.NE.0) GO TO 30
      NEWY = NEGROW + SIZE
      DRIVER = 1.0
      IF (SLACK(NEGROW).GT.0.0) DRIVER = -1.0
      NEGINV = SIZE1
      CALL ADDCON
      IF(ISTATE.EQ.4) GO TO 80
   30 CALL SEEKX
      IF (NEWX.NE.0) GO TO 50
      ISTATE = 2
      GO TO 80
   40 CALL ISOPT
      IF (NEWX.NE.0) GO TO 50
      ISTATE = 1
      GO TO 80
   50 CALL NEWVEC
      CALL SEEKY
      IF (NEWY.NE.0) GO TO 60
      ISTATE = 3
      GO TO 80
   60 IF (NEWY.LE.SIZE) GO TO 70
      CALL ADDCON
      IF(ISTATE.EQ.4) GO TO 80
   70 CALL CHBSIS
      CALL REDUCE
      GO TO 10
   80 RETURN
      END
```

5. ARRANGEMENT OF THE STORE FOR DOANLP

The communication between subroutines in this program is almost entirely by the use of COMMON storage. In effect, all routines have access to and can operate upon a common set of data. We have found it convenient to think of the data store as laid out in the following way:

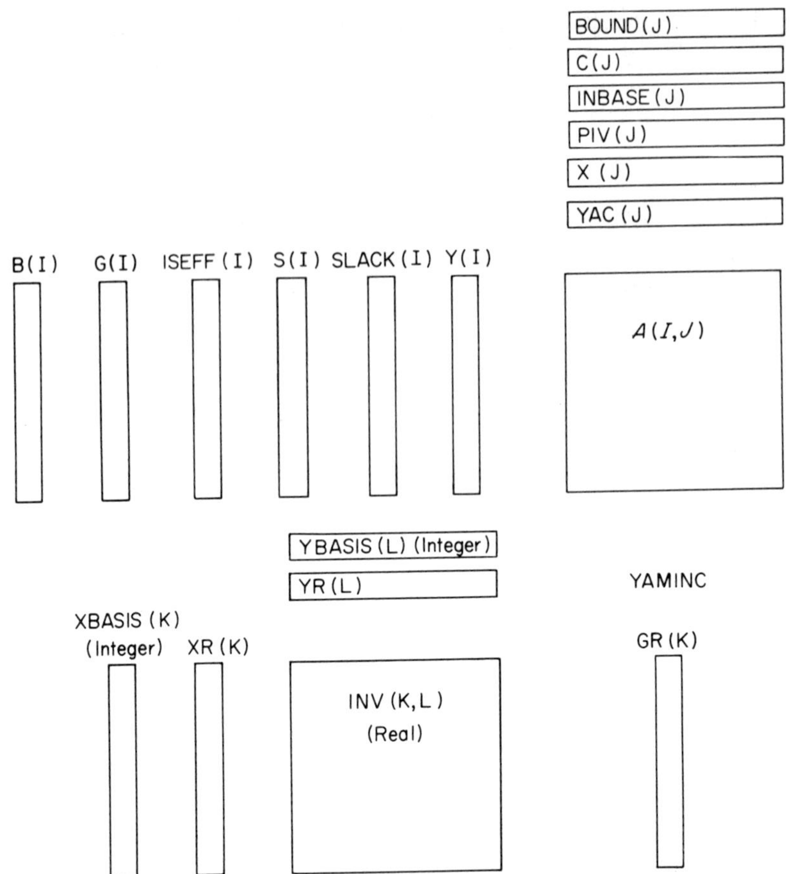

To solve small, 'student-type' problems of up to, say 25 x 50, the TYPE statements and COMMON statements to follow the subroutine name, *in every subroutine* where indicated by asterisks, might be as follows:

```
  REAL INV
  INTEGER SIZE, SIZE1, XBASIS, YBASIS
  COMMON BOUND(50),C(50),INBASE(50),PIV(50),X(50),YAC(50),
2            B(25),G(25),ISEFF(25),S(25),SLACK(25),Y(25),
3            INV(25,25),XBASIS(25),XR(25),YBASIS(25),YR(25),GR(25),
4  TOL(8),BIG,DRIVER,INREV,IR,IRMAX,ISBIG,ISBND,ISDONE,ISTATE,ITR,
5  ITRMAX,M,MARKI,MARKK,MAXM,MAXN,MNOW,MORE,MOREPR,MXSIZE,N
6  NEGINV,NEGROW,NEWX,NEWY,NUMSLK,OBJ,R,SIZE,SIZE1,SMALL,XKPOS
7  YAMINC
```

Note that for larger problems it may be worth specifying an inverse size (continuation card 3) much smaller than the number of rows in A (card 2), if there is reason to believe that the number of *effective* constraints throughout the calculation will be less than the total number of constraints. The procedure to be followed to alter the dimensions will be found in Chapter 7, Section 4.

Some of the variables in COMMON are either obvious or have already been referred to. Others will be identified as we come to them. A glossary of variables is contained in Appendix 2, with a key to the place where each is discussed, and a list of the routines in which it may change.

Note that the A matrix does not feature in COMMON. In fact, A(I,J) is a function subroutine, and the statement:

AIJ = A(I,J)

evaluates the element in the (notional) i^{th} row and j^{th} column of the A matrix, from the list of stored non-zero elements.

The cards in the COMMON statement are arranged so that the first card refers to the maximum dimension of N, the second card to the maximum dimension of M, and the third card to the maximum value of SIZE, the dimension of the INV matrix. This is simply to facilitate the labour of changing the dimensions. However, this is a machine-dependent facility, since some machines specify the order in which different types of variables may appear in COMMON.

Note that we use the subscript I for the rows of A and associated arrays; J for the columns of A and associated arrays; K for the rows of INV(K,L); and L for the columns. These are conventions which we use wherever possible. I, J, K, and L are local variables, not in COMMON.

There is a considerable degree of redundancy in the recording of information, which would never have occurred if we had had a proper respect for efficiency. The array XR(K) contains the values of the current basic variables, and the identity of these variables is held in the array XBASIS(K). But simultaneously, the values of all the real variables are recorded in the array X(J). The array INBASE(J) is zero when the Jth variable is non-basic at zero; it is set at -1 when the Jth variable is non-basic at its upper bound; and it is set at K when the Jth variable is basic and is recorded in the Kth element of XR(K).

Similarly, there is redundancy in that the Y array contains the same information as the YR array relating to the effective constraints. YBASIS(L) indicates which row I of the A matrix is represented by the Lth column of the inverse, and the Lth element of YR. ISEFF(I) = 0 if the Ith constraint is not effective, and = L if the Ith constraint is represented by the Lth column of the inverse.

The array YAC(J) contains the elements of $yA - c$, the 'functional row', the values which have to be non-negative (along with the appropriate conditions on the y^R elements) if the current basic solution is to be optimal (or non-positive on non-basic variables at their upper bounds).

S(I) is the sign of the Ith constraint, 1·0 for a less-than-or-equal constraint, 0·0 for an equality, and −1·0 for a greater-than-or-equal constraint.

BOUND(J) is the upper bound of the Jth variable. If there is no upper bound on the Jth variable, BOUND(J) = −1·0. ISBND is the number of variables subject to upper bounds.

The arrays PIV(J) and G(I) are simply to hold a currently relevant 'updated' row and column of the A matrix, when otherwise they might have to be picked out and computed twice in successive subroutines.

The array GR(K) contains the column $R^{-1}a^j$, which is required when the jth column of A is to be made basic: that part of the 'updated' column of A associated with the basic original variables, x^R. YAMINC is the associated element of the function row, the minimum (most negative) yA minus c.

5.1. The arrangement of the A matrix

The non-zero elements of the A matrix are stored row by row in the AA array. On some machines, an integer variable can be accommodated in less space than that required for a real variable, and it may therefore be worth scaling the problem so that all the elements are integers and declaring AA to be integer. In any case the elements of A should be kept as close to unity as possible if problems of inaccuracy are to be avoided.

A second array of the same order as AA called JCOL is used to signify for every element AA to which column of the matrix of coefficients it belongs. A third array, called IROW, indicates in which element of AA each row of the coefficient matrix starts. This need be only of sufficiently great dimension to accommodate the greatest value of M to be solved by the current version, plus one.

The print routine included here (IPRINT) prints the arrays AA, JCOL and IROW, and the actual A matrix can be deduced as in the following example:

AA VECTOR AND JCOL VECTOR

1	2	3	4	5	6	7	8	9	10	11	12	13	14	15
9	10	22	6	15	19	22	15	14	16	−20	−45	−45	18	260
8	1	3	4	5	6	2	4	5	7	1	3	4	5	6

IROW VECTOR

1	2	3	4
1	2	7	11

Since the first row of A starts at the first element of AA, the second row at the second element, the third row at the seventh element and the fourth row at the eleventh element of AA, we can go through the AA array, dividing it into sectors by lines preceding each of these row-start indicators:

AA VECTOR AND JCOL VECTOR

1	2	3	4	5	6	7	8	9	10	11	12	13	14	15
9	10	22	6	15	19	22	15	14	16	–20	–45	–45	18	260
8	1	3	4	5	6	2	4	5	7	1	3	4	5	6

The four rows and eight columns are, therefore, as follows:

$$
\begin{array}{cccccccc}
1 & 2 & 3 & 4 & 5 & 6 & 7 & 8
\end{array}
$$

$$
\begin{bmatrix}
. & . & . & . & . & . & . & 9 \\
10 & . & 22 & 6 & 15 & 19 & . & . \\
. & 22 & . & 15 & 14 & . & 16 & . \\
-20 & . & -45 & -45 & 18 & 260 & . & .
\end{bmatrix}
$$

An all-zero row would be represented in the AA and JCOL arrays by a single zero for the first element of the row.

Since it is convenient to organize some of the DO loops to go through a part of AA, rather than through a part of A, these vectors are recorded in a labelled COMMON, available to all those subroutines which require them.

COMMON/AREF/AA(1000),JCOL(1000),IROW(26),MAXA

These would be appropriate dimensions to handle the problems of up to 25 x 50 if the A matrix were not more than 80% dense. MAXA would then be 1000 (see DATA routine).

This card is also omitted from the Fortran listings, and is indicated by:

************ COMMON/AREF **

where it should be inserted.

6. FUNCTION A(I,J)

This routine merely looks up the value of the element a_{ij} of the A matrix in the array AA, or sets it equal to zero if there is no element recorded for row I and column J.

This function subroutine enables the programs to use A(I,J) like a subscripted variable *on the right hand side* of any Fortran expression. For the addition of rows to A, of course, another device has to be used (the subroutine COPY).

COMMON/AREF variables used in A(I,J)

AA(LOOK)
IROW(I)
JCOL(LOOK)

```
      FUNCTION A(I,J)
*********************** COMMON/AREF ************************************
      ISTART = IROW(I)
      LAST = IROW(I+1) - 1
      A = 0.0
      DO 1 LOOK = ISTART,LAST
      JHERE = JCOL(LOOK)
      IF(JHERE.LT.J) GO TO 1
      IF(JHERE.GT.J) RETURN
      A = AA(LOOK)
      RETURN
    1 CONTINUE
      RETURN
      END
```

7. ADDCON (add constraint)

This routine is used to augment the inverse matrix by a row and a column (the SIZE1 row and column), either because an infeasible constraint is now to become the NEGINV row until it becomes feasible, or because the routine SEEKY has identified an implicit slack variable as the one which is to leave the basis. In either case, the row concerned, I, is identified by subtracting SIZE from NEWY. If the inverse is already at its maximum size limit ISTATE is set to 4 and control is returned to the calling routine.

To augment the inverse of a matrix which is increased by a row s and a unit column vector, the following relationship requires only the computation of sR^{-1}:

$$\begin{bmatrix} R & 0 \\ s & 1 \end{bmatrix}^{-1} = \begin{bmatrix} R^{-1} & 0 \\ -sR^{-1} & 1 \end{bmatrix}$$

ADDCON first sets the new row and column (SIZE1) of the inverse equal to zero, in 'DO 10'. In 'DO 30' the non-zero elements of the Ith row of A in the columns associated with the basic variables (s) are used to accumulate the vector-matrix product, sR^{-1}.

The other vectors associated with the inverse are also augmented, and finally SIZE and SIZE1 are increased by 1. If SIZE is greater than ISBIG, the greatest value of SIZE so far encountered, ISBIG is set equal to SIZE. NUMSLK, the number of slack variables explicitly present in the basis matrix R, is also increased by 1.

COMMON variables altered in ADDCON

INV(K,L)	SIZE
ISBIG	SIZE1
ISEFF(I)	XBASIS(K)
ISTATE	XR(K)

NEWY YBASIS(L)
NUMSLK YR(L)

COMMON variables used in ADDCON

INBASE(J) N
MXSIZE SLACK(I)

COMMON/AREF variables used in ADDCON

AA(LOOK) JCOL(LOOK)
IROW(I)

```
      SUBROUTINE ADDCON
*********************** COMMON AND TYPE STATEMENTS ********************
********************** COMMON/AREF ***********************************
      IF(SIZE1.GT.MXSIZE) GO TO 40
      I = NEWY - SIZE
      DO 10 L = 1,SIZE
      INV(L,SIZE1) = 0.0
   10 INV(SIZE1,L) = 0.0
      ISTART = IROW(I)
      LAST = IROW(I+1) - 1
      DO 30 LOOK = ISTART,LAST
      J = JCOL(LOOK)
      IF(INBASE(J).LE.0) GO TO 30
      K = INBASE(J)
      AIJ = AA(LOOK)
      DO 20 L = 1,SIZE
   20 INV(SIZE1,L) = INV(SIZE1,L) - AIJ * INV(K,L)
   30 CONTINUE
      INV(SIZE1,SIZE1) = 1.0
      XR(SIZE1) = SLACK(I)
      ISEFF(I) = SIZE1
      XBASIS(SIZE1) = I + N
      YBASIS(SIZE1) = I
      YR(SIZE1) = 0.0
      SIZE = SIZE1
      SIZE1 = SIZE1 + 1
      IF(SIZE.GT.ISBIG) ISBIG = SIZE
      NUMSLK = NUMSLK + 1
      NEWY = SIZE
      GO TO 50
   40 ISTATE = 4
   50 RETURN
      END
```

8. CHACC (check accuracy)

This routine computes $yA - c$ on the basic variables and $b - Ax$ minus the slack vector on all the constraints. Both of these sets of elements should theoretically be zero. They are checked to determine whether they differ from zero by more than a tolerance, and if they do so differ ISTATE is set to 7 and control returns to the calling routine. When solving an LP the calling routine is subroutine LP.

The 'DO 5' loop ensures that the slack vector is correct on any constraint for which the slack vector is explicitly present in the basis. This loop is not computed if there are no slack vectors explicitly in the basis, NUMSLK = 0.

The 'DO 40' loop accumulates YAC(J) on the basic variables (first set at −C(J) in 'DO 20') and computes individual elements BAXSL ($b - Ax -$ slack). As each element BAXSL is computed it is checked for accuracy with a tolerance, TOL(2), for its absolute value, and with a tolerance, TOL(6), for its value relative to the value of B(I). As soon as an error exceeding the tolerance is discovered, the checking ceases, a statement of error is printed and control returns to the calling routine with ISTATE = 7.

If no significant error is discovered in $b - Ax -$ slack, the now completed YAC(J) array is checked for absolute accuracy with TOL(4) and for accuracy relative to C(J) with TOL(7) in the 'DO 50' loop. Again checking is abandoned if a significant error is found.

There is a fuller description of the tolerances in Chapter 7, Section 2.

COMMON variables altered in CHACC

ISTATE	YAC(J)
SLACK(I)	

COMMON variables used in CHACC

B(I)	SIZE
C(J)	TOL(JK)
INBASE(J)	X(J)
ISEFF(I)	XBASIS(K)
MNOW	XR(K)
N	Y(I)

COMMON/AREF variables used in CHACC

AA(LOOK)	JCOL(LOOK)
IROW(I)	

```
      SUBROUTINE CHACC
*********************** COMMON AND TYPE STATEMENTS ********************
*********************** COMMON/AREF *************************************
 9000 FORMAT (1H0,'UNACCEPTABLE ERROR OF ',F16.8,' FOUND IN B-SLACK-AX O
     1F CONSTRAINT',I6)
 9004 FORMAT (1H0,'UNACCEPTABLE RELATIVE ERROR OF ',F16.8,' FOUND IN B-S
     1LACK-AX OF CONSTRAINT',I6/1H ,'THE ABSOLUTE ERROR IS ',F16.8,' AND
     2 B(I) IS ',F16.8)
 9008 FORMAT (1H0,'UNACCEPTABLE ERROR OF ',F16.8,' FOUND IN YA-C OF BASI
     1C VARIABLE ',I6)
```

```
9012 FORMAT (1H0,'UNACCEPTABLE RELATIVE ERROR OF ',F16.8,' FOUND IN YA-
    1C OF BASIC VARIABLE, ',I6/1H ,'THE ABSOLUTE ERROR IS ',F16.8,' AND
    2 C(J) IS ',F16.8)
      IF(NUMSLK.EQ.0) GO TO 10
      DO 5 K = 1,SIZE
      IF (XBASIS(K).LE.N) GO TO 5
      I = XBASIS(K) - N
      SLACK(I) = XR(K)
    5 CONTINUE
   10 DO 20 J = 1,N
      IF(INBASE(J).LE.0) GO TO 20
      YAC(J) = -C(J)
   20 CONTINUE
      TOL2 = TOL(2)
      TOL6 = TOL(6)
      DO 40 I = 1,MNOW
      ISEFFI = ISEFF(I)
      YI = Y(I)
      BAXSL = B(I) - SLACK(I)
      ISTART = IROW(I)
      LAST = IROW(I+1) - 1
      DO 30 LOOK = ISTART,LAST
      J = JCOL(LOOK)
      INJ = INBASE(J)
      IF(INJ.EQ.0) GO TO 30
      AIJ = AA(LOOK)
      BAXSL = BAXSL - X(J) * AIJ
      IF(INJ.GT.0.AND.ISEFFI.NE.0) YAC(J) = YAC(J) + YI * AIJ
   30 CONTINUE
      ERR = ABS(BAXSL)
      IF (ERR.GT.TOL2) GO TO 60
      ABSB = ABS(B(I))
      IF (ABSB.LT.1.0) ABSB = 1.0
      IF (ERR / ABSB .GT. TOL6) GO TO 65
   40 CONTINUE
      TOL7 = TOL(7)
      TOL4 = TOL(4)
      DO 50 J = 1,N
      IF (INBASE(J) .LE. 0) GO TO 50
      ERR = ABS(YAC(J))
      IF (ERR .GT. TOL4) GO TO 70
      ABSC = ABS(C(J))
      IF (ABSC.LT.1.0) ABSC = 1.0
      IF (ERR / ABSC .GT. TOL7) GO TO 75
   50 CONTINUE
      GO TO 90
   60 WRITE (6,9000) ERR,I
      GO TO 80
   65 RELERR = ERR / ABSB
      WRITE (6,9004) RELERR,I,ERR,ABSB
      GO TO 80
   70 WRITE (6,9008) ERR,J
      GO TO 80
   75 RELERR = ERR / ABSC
      WRITE (6,9012) RELERR,J,ERR,ABSC
   80 ISTATE = 7
   90 RETURN
      END
```

9. CHBSIS (change basis)

This routine makes the basis change to INV and to those arrays associated with it. In 'DO 30' XR(K) is updated, and the most infeasible element identified (HOWNEG in row MOSNEG). The NEGINV label is only changed at the end of the routine, however, if the basis change has resulted in making the NEGINV variable feasible.

Immediately after the 'DO 30' loop, the case of the new variable going immediately to its upper bound (or an upper bounded variable going immediately to its lower bound) is dealt with, and the basis change of the inverse is omitted.

Between 40 and 70, the newly basic variable is dealt with, and the labels INBASE(J) and XBASIS(K) updated.

At 80 OBJ is updated, and from 90 to 110 the columns of the inverse and the YR array are updated.

COMMON variables altered in CHBSIS

DRIVER	NUMSLK
INBASE(J)	OBJ
INV(K,L)	XBASIS(K)
ITR	XR(K)
NEGINV	YR(L)

COMMON variables used in CHBSIS

BOUND(J)	S(I)
GR(K)	SIZE
INREV	SMALL
N	TOL(JK)
NEWX	XKPOS
NEWY	YAMINC
R	

```
      SUBROUTINE CHBSIS
*********************** COMMON AND TYPE STATEMENTS ********************
      ITR = ITR + 1
      MOSNEG = 0
      HOWNEG = 0.0
      XOFNEG = 0.0
      DRITEM = 0.0
      TOL1 = TOL(1)
      IF(INREV.EQ.1) GO TO 90
```

```
      IF(R.EQ.0.0) GO TO 40
      DO 30 K = 1,SIZE
      XR(K) = XR(K) - R * GR(K) * XKPOS
      XXX = XR(K)
      IF(ABS(XXX).LE.TOL1) XR(K) = 0.0
      J = XBASIS(K)
      IF(J.LE.N) GO TO 10
      XXX = XR(K)
      I = J -N
      SI = S(I)
      IF(SI .EQ. 0.0 .AND. XXX .GT. 0.0 .OR. SI .EQ. -1.0) XXX = -XXX
      GO TO 20
   10 BOUNDJ = BOUND(J)
      IF(ABS(BOUNDJ-XXX).LE.TOL1) XR(K) = BOUNDJ
      XXX = XR(K)
      IF(XXX .LE. BOUNDJ. OR. BOUNDJ .EQ. -1.0) GO TO 20
      XXX = BOUNDJ - XXX
   20 IF(K.EQ.NEGINV) XOFNEG = XXX
      IF(XXX.GE.HOWNEG.OR.K.EQ.NEGINV) GO TO 30
      MOSNEG = K
      DRITEM = 1.0
      IF(XR(K).GE.0.0) DRITEM =-1.0
      HOWNEG = XXX
   30 CONTINUE
      IF(NEWY.NE.-1) GO TO 40
      IT = INBASE(NEWX)
      INBASE(NEWX) = -1
      IF(IT.EQ.-1) INBASE(NEWX) = 0
      IXOUT = NEWX
      OBJ = OBJ - R * YAMINC
      GO TO 120
   40 IXOUT = XBASIS(NEWY)
      IF(IXOUT.GT.N) GO TO 50
      INBASE(IXOUT) = 0
      IF(GR(NEWY) * XKPOS.LT.0.0.AND.NEWY.NE.NEGINV) INBASE(IXOUT) = -1
      IF(NEWY.EQ.NEGINV.AND.XR(NEWY).GT.0.0) INBASE(IXOUT) = -1
   50 IF(NEWX.GT.N) GO TO 60
      IHOLD = INBASE(NEWX)
      INBASE(NEWX) = NEWY
   60 XBASIS(NEWY) = NEWX
      IF(NEWX.GT.N) NUMSLK = NUMSLK + 1
      IF(IXOUT.GT.N) NUMSLK = NUMSLK - 1
      XR(NEWY) = R
      IF(NEWX.LE.N) GO TO 70
      I = NEWX - N
      IF(S(I).EQ.-1.0) XR(NEWY) = -R
      GO TO 80
   70 IF(IHOLD.EQ.-1) XR(NEWY) = BOUND(NEWX) - R
   80 OBJ = OBJ - R * YAMINC
   90 RR = 1.0/ GR(NEWY)
      DO 110 L = 1,SIZE
      IF(ABS(INV(NEWY,L)).LT.SMALL) GO TO 110
      RL = INV(NEWY,L) * RR
      DO 100 K = 1,SIZE
      INV(K,L) = INV(K,L) - RL * GR(K)
  100 CONTINUE
      INV(NEWY,L) = RL
```

```
      IF(INREV.NE.1) YR(L) = YR(L) - RL * YAMINC * XKPOS
  110 CONTINUE
  120 IF (R.EQ.0.0 .OR. XOFNEG.LT.0.0 .AND. NEWY.NE.NEGINV) GO TO 130
      NEGINV = MOSNEG
      DRIVER = DRITEM
  130 RETURN
      END
```

10. CHSLCK (change slack)

The actual pivoting operation of Simplex is carried out in CHBSIS (change basis). But this operates only on the 'lower' part of the common store—that is to say, on the inverse and the vectors associated with it. CHSLCK completes the process by making the necessary changes to the vectors associated with the A matrix.

In the 'DO 10' loop of CHSLCK the elements of X(J) are set equal to zero or to their upper bounds if non-basic, or to the appropriate elements of XR(K) if basic, and the YAC(J) array is set equal to –C(J).

The 'DO 70' loop, running through the rows of A, updates the Y array and the SLACK array, and simultaneously accumulates the values of YAC(J) row by row. Note that the inner do loop, 'DO 20', which in principle runs through a row of A, in practice runs through the appropriate section of AA. The 'DO 40' loop has not been similarly treated simply because it is seldom used and the less efficient routine of using the A(I,J) function subroutine is good enough.

SLACK(I) is either set up initially or modified by the array G, according to whether INREV is 1 or 0. The array G (computed in SEEKY) contains the modifications to be made to the SLACK array *per unit increase* in the variable entering the basis. R is the absolute value of the level at which the new variable enters, and XKPOS (which is +1·0 or –1·0) indicates whether the variable is entering the basis positively or negatively. A variable may enter negatively either because it is a variable being brought down from its upper bound or because it is a slack variable on a greater-than-or-equal constraint.

If NEGINV is zero, the greatest infeasibility of a row of A is discovered and indicated by NEGROW.

Finally INREV is zeroed, and the atypical basic slack variable dealt with if necessary.

Subroutines called by CHSLCK

A(I,J)

COMMON variables altered in CHSLCK

INREV   X(J)

NEGROW	Y(I)
SLACK(I)	YAC(J)

COMMON variables used in CHSLCK

B(I)	N
BOUND(J)	NEGINV
C(J)	R
G(I)	S(I)
INBASE(J)	TOL(JK)
ISEFF(I)	XKPOS
MARKI	XR(K)
MARKK	YR(L)
MNOW	

COMMON/AREF variables used in CHSLCK

AA(LOOK)	JCOL(LOOK)
IROW(I)	

```
      SUBROUTINE CHSLCK
*********************** COMMON AND TYPE STATEMENTS ********************
*********************** COMMON/AREF ***********************************
      IF (R .NE. 0.0) NEGROW = 0
      HOWNEG = 0.0
      DO 10 J = 1,N
      YACJ = 0.0
      K = INBASE(J)
      IF(K.LE.0) YACJ = -C(J)
      YAC(J) = YACJ
      XJ = 0.0
      IF(K.EQ.-1) XJ = BOUND(J)
      IF(K.GT.0) XJ = XR(K)
   10 X(J) = XJ
      TOL2 = TOL(2)
      DO 70 I = 1,MNOW
      L = ISEFF(I)
      Y(I) = 0.0
      IF(L.EQ.0) GO TO 30
      YI = YR(L)
      Y(I) = YI
      SLACK(I) = 0.0
      LAST = IROW(I+1) -1
      ISTART = IROW(I)
      DO 20 LOOK = ISTART,LAST
      J = JCOL(LOOK)
      IF(INBASE(J).GT.0) GO TO 20
      AIJ = AA(LOOK)
      YAC(J) = YAC(J) + YI * AIJ
   20 CONTINUE
      GO TO 70
   30 IF(INREV.NE.1) GO TO 50
      SLKI = B(I)
```

```
      DO 40 J = 1,N
      IF(INBASE(J).EQ.0) GO TO 40
      SLKI = SLKI - A(I,J) * X(J)
   40 CONTINUE
      GO TO 60
   50 IF(R.EQ.0.0) GO TO 70
      SLKI = SLACK(I) - R * G(I) * XKPOS
   60 IF(ABS(SLKI).LE.TOL2) SLKI = 0.0
      SLACK(I) = SLKI
      IF(NEGINV.NE.0) GO TO 70
      SI = S(I)
      ABSLKI = ABS(SLKI)
      IF(SI .NE. 0.0 .AND. SI*SLKI .GE. HOWNEG .OR. SI .EQ. 0.0 .AND.
     1   -ABSLKI .GE. HOWNEG) GO TO 70
      HOWNEG = -ABSLKI
      NEGROW = I
   70 CONTINUE
      INREV = 0
      IF (MARKI .NE. 0) SLACK(MARKI) = XR(MARKK)
      RETURN
      END
```

11. COPY

Although COPY is used here merely as a subroutine to DATA, its function in the more complex programs is to extend the A matrix by a newly generated row of A, the MNOWth row. The row is initially stored in the PIV array in extended form (i.e., complete with zero elements), and is copied into an extension of the AA array without zero elements. COPY is complemented in the more complex programs by PURGE which eliminates rows which have become redundant.

Since the program makes frequent use of DO loops running from the first element of AA belonging to a particular row to the last element, It is important that every row be represented by at least one element. Thus the variable ISTRIV (is trivial) is set initially to one. If after 'DO 10' ISTRIV still equals one, showing that no non-zero element has been found, a zero element for the first column of the row is put into the AA array.

If the maximum size of AA or of M is about to be exceeded the subroutine calls IEXIT(6) and returns control to the calling subroutine (DATA, in the simple LP).

Subroutines called in COPY

IEXIT

COMMON variables used in COPY

ISDONE	N
MAXM	PIV(J)
MNOW	

COMMON/AREF variables altered in COPY

AA(LOOK)   JCOL(LOOK)
IROW(I)

COMMON/AREF variables used in COPY

MAXA

```
      SUBROUTINE COPY
********************** COMMON AND TYPE STATEMENTS ********************
********************** COMMON/AREF ***********************************
      IF (MNOW .LE. MAXM) GO TO 5
      CALL IEXIT(6)
      GO TO 30
    5 ISTRIV = 1
      IT = -1
      IRM = IROW(MNOW)
      DO 10 J = 1,N
      AIJ = PIV(J)
      IF(AIJ.EQ.0.0) GO TO 10
      ISTRIV = 0
      IT = IT + 1
      LOOK = IRM + IT
      IF(LOOK.GT.MAXA) CALL IEXIT(6)
      IF(ISDONE.EQ.1) GO TO 30
      AA(LOOK) = AIJ
      JCOL(LOOK) = J
   10 CONTINUE
      IF(ISTRIV.EQ.0) GO TO 20
      LOOK = IRM
      IF(LOOK.GT.MAXA) CALL IEXIT(6)
      IF(ISDONE.EQ.1) GO TO 30
      AA(LOOK) = 0
      JCOL(LOOK) = 1
   20 NEXTM = MNOW + 1
      IROW(NEXTM) = LOOK + 1
      NEXTM = MNOW + 2
      IROW(NEXTM) = LOOK + 1
   30 RETURN
      END
```

12. DATA

In Appendix 3 there is a summary of the input formats for all the programs.

The first two executable statements of this routine set BIG and SMALL. These are used as the greatest and least possible values of a real variable in the program, and are obviously machine dependent. The next four executable statements set upper limits on the size of problems which can be solved.

These four statements must be altered if dimensions are changed (see Chapter 7, Section 4). MXSIZE is the maximum dimension of the inverse matrix. In large problems it may be very much less than the total number of constraints, and need never exceed the lesser of M and N.

MAXA is the maximum number of non-zero elements in the A matrix.

MAXM is the maximum number of constraints in the problem. (For integer and quadratic programming this must allow for the constraints which will be added during the course of the calculation.)

MAXN is the maximum number of (original, not slack) variables which can be solved.

The first read statement reads a card with six 10-digit fields of integers to specify for a particular LP problem M, N, and ISBND, the number of variables with simple upper bounds. If *all* the variables have upper bounds of 1, ISBND can be set equal to −1, to avoid specifying all the individual bounds. The program checks that M and N are not greater than MAXM and MAXN respectively.

The remaining variables on the first card, MOREPR (more print), ITRMAX (maximum iterations), IRMAX (maximum number of re-inversions) can be left blank. If not specified by the user, ITRMAX will be set equal to three times the total number of variables plus constraints; MOREPR and IRMAX will be zero. MOREPR controls the amount of output, both in the DATA routine and in the subroutine IPRINT, as follows:

MOREPR = 0 data cards printed in DATA
inverse of the basis not printed in IPRINT
MOREPR = 1 data cards printed in DATA
inverse of the basis printed in IPRINT
MOREPR = 2 data cards not printed in DATA
inverse of the basis printed in IPRINT
MOREPR = 3 data cards not printed in DATA
inverse of the basis not printed in IPRINT

There then follows the reading of either three or four sets of cards, each in the same format. The sets are:

1. the C elements
2. the BOUND elements (which may be omitted if ISBND = 0 or −1).
3. the B elements
4. the non-zero elements of the A matrix

Each block is completed by a card with ten 9's in the first ten columns, to signify the end of the block. Each card is divided into eight fields of ten digits, and the eight fields further sub-divided into a 3-digit integer, a 1-digit integer, and a 6-digit real number.

C elements. Eight elements per card: the 3-digit integer specifies the identity, J, of each element, and the 6-digit real number contains the C(J) element, which may be punched with or without a decimal point. The 1-digit integer is not used. The elements may be entered in any order, and any not specified will be set at zero. A warning message will be printed if *all* the C elements are missing and hence set at zero but the program will proceed nevertheless, and any feasible solution will be an optimal solution.

BOUND elements. As C, but elements not specified are assumed to have no upper bound (which is signified by BOUND(J) = –1·0).

B elements. As C, except that the 3-digit integer specifies I, and the 1-digit integer specifies the sign of the constraint:

$$0 \text{ if } \sum_{j=1}^{n} a_{ij}x_j = b_i; \quad 1 \text{ if } \sum_{j=1}^{n} a_{ij}x_j \leqslant b_i; \quad \text{and } 2 \text{ if } \sum_{j=1}^{n} a_{ij}x_j \geqslant b_i.$$

Note that the 2 for the $\geqslant$ constraint is simply in order to signify the sign with a single digit on the input cards, and that S(I) will be –1·0 when the constraint is identified as a $\geqslant$. Any B elements which are not specified will be taken as $\leqslant$ BIG, and a warning message will be printed.

A matrix. The *A* matrix is read in row by row, in strict order, although any-all-zero row of coefficients may be omitted. A row cannot be entered after a row with a higher number, and if one is encountered it will cause a fatal error message to be printed and the program will not proceed.

The elements of *A* are punched only seven to a card, since the first 10-digit field is used to specify the row number. Only non-zero elements need be punched, in any order within a row, in the same format as for C, BOUND etc, i.e. the 3-digit integer to specify J and the 6-digit real number for the element itself.

Finally, after the 9's card signifying the end of the *A* elements, MORE is read. If MORE is zero the program will assume that no further problems are to be solved. Otherwise, if MORE is non-zero, the program will solve the current problem then return to the DATA routine to read the input for the next problem.

Apart from reading the cards, the DATA routine (from statement 600) sets up initial values for some of the COMMON variables and defines the values of certain tolerances, the details of which are described in Chapter 7, Section 2.

Obviously the user may substitute an alternative data-reading routine for this one, but if so he must take care to set all the COMMON variables at the beginning of this version, down to ISDONE = 0, and at the end of the routine, after statement number 600 from INREV = 0 to YAMINC = 0.0.

Note that for debugging purposes one may generally insert the statement 'CALL IPRINT' anywhere in the programs in order to print the present state of the calculation. However, IPRINT will fail if it is called before DATA has been completed.

Subroutines called in DATA

COPY

COMMON variables altered in DATA

B(I)	MORE
BIG	MOREPR
BOUND(J)	MXSIZE
C(J)	N
INREV	NEGINV
IR	NEGROW
IRMAX	NEWX
ISBIG	NEWY
ISBND	PIV(J)
ISDONE	R
ITR	S(I)
ITRMAX	SIZE
M	SMALL
MAXM	TOL(JK)
MAXN	YAMINC
MNOW	

COMMON/AREF variables altered in DATA

IROW(I)
MAXA

```
      SUBROUTINE DATA
********************** COMMON AND TYPE STATEMENTS ********************
********************** COMMON/AREF ***********************************
      REAL K3
      DIMENSION K1(8), K2(8), K3(8)
 9000 FORMAT (8I10)
 9004 FORMAT(1H0,'MOREPR = ',I5)
 9008 FORMAT(1H0,'IRMAX = ',I5)
 9012 FORMAT(1H0,'ITRMAX = ',I5)
 9016 FORMAT(1H1,'M (NO. OF CONSTRAINTS) = ',I5,', N (NO. OF VARIABLES--
     1REAL, NOT SLACK) = ',I5,','/1X,'NUMBER OF UPPER BOUNDED VARIABLES
     2= ',I5,'.')
 9020 FORMAT(1H0,'YOU ARE TRYING TO SOLVE A PROBLEM WHICH IS TOO BIG FOR
     1 THE PROGRAM.'/1X,'THE LARGEST PROBLEM HAS',I5,' CONSTRAINTS AND',
     1I5,' VARIABLES.')
 9024 FORMAT (1H0, 'IT IS NOT POSSIBLE TO HAVE A NEGATIVE NUMBER OF ROWS
     1 OR COLUMNS.')
```

```
9030 FORMAT (1H0,'INPUT CARDS FOR THE C ELEMENTS . . . .')
9034 FORMAT (1H0,'INPUT CARDS FOR THE UPPER BOUNDS ON SINGLE VARIABLES
    1. . . .')
9038 FORMAT (1H0,'INPUT CARDS FOR THE B VECTOR, THE RIGHT-HAND SIDES OF
    1 THE CONSTRAINTS . . . .')
9042 FORMAT (1H0,'INPUT CARDS FOR THE ROWS OF THE A MATRIX . . . .')
9050 FORMAT (8(I3,I1,F6.0))
9064 FORMAT (1H ,'CARD ',I4)
9068 FORMAT(1H ,4('(',I3,'/',I1,'/',F12.5,')')/1H ,4('(',I3,'/',I1,'/',
    1F12.5,')'))
9070 FORMAT(1H0,'YOU HAVE SPECIFIED AN ELEMENT FOR VARIABLE NO. ',I5,
    1' WHICH IS GREATER THAN N, ',I5,'.'/' IT HAS BEEN IGNORED.')
9074 FORMAT (1H0,'YOU HAVE SPECIFIED AN ELEMENT FOR ROW NO. ',I5,', WHI
    1CH IS GREATER THAN M, ',I5,'.'/' IT HAS BEEN IGNORED.')
9078 FORMAT (1H0,'THE ELEMENT IN THE 4TH COLUMN OF EACH FIELD OF 10 CAN
    1 ONLY BE 1 FOR A LESS-THAN-OR-EQUAL CONSTRAINT, OR 0 '/' FOR AN EQ
    2UALITY, OR 2 FOR GREATER-THAN-OR EQUAL.  YOU HAVE A ',I5,'.'/1X,
    3'IT HAS BEEN IGNORED')
9082 FORMAT (1H0,'YOU ARE TRYING TO READ ROW NO.',I5,' WHICH IS MORE TH
    1AN YOUR SPECIFIED NO. OF ROWS,',I5,'.')
9084 FORMAT (1H0,'YOUR PREVIOUS ROW WAS ',I5,', AND YOU ARE NOW TRYING
    1TO READ ROW NO.',I6,'.'/' IT IS ESSENTIAL THAT THE ROWS OF THE A M
    1ATRIX ARE ENTERED IN THE RIGHT ORDER.')
9088 FORMAT(1H0,'**** WARNING ****  ALL YOUR FUNCTION ELEMENTS ARE ZERO
    1')
9092 FORMAT(1H0,'**** WARNING ****  YOU HAVE NOT SPECIFIED A RIGHT HAND
    1 SIDE FOR ALL THE CONSTRAINTS.'/' ANY NOT SPECIFIED HAVE BEEN ASSU
    2MED TO BE A LARGE NUMBER')
9096 FORMAT(1H0,'****  YOU HAVE SPECIFIED THAT THERE ARE',I5,' ROWS AND
    1 YOU HAVE TRIED TO READ IN ELEMENTS OF A FOR',I5,' ROWS')
9098 FORMAT (1H0,'****** THERE IS A FATAL ERROR IN YOUR DATA INPUT ****
    1**')
     BIG = 1.0E11
     SMALL = 1.0E-9
     MXSIZE = 50
     MAXA = 1000
     MAXM = 70
     MAXN = 150
     ISDONE = 0
     ICARD = 1
     KC = 0
     KB = 0
     READ(5,9000) M,N,ISBND,MOREPR,ITRMAX,IRMAX
     IF(MOREPR.NE.0) WRITE(6,9004) MOREPR
     IF(IRMAX.NE.0) WRITE(6,9008) IRMAX
     IF(ITRMAX.LE.0) GO TO 10
     WRITE(6,9012) ITRMAX
     GO TO 30
  10 IJK = ISBND
     IF (IJK.EQ.-1) IJK = N
     ITRMAX = 3 * (M + N + IJK)
  30 WRITE (6,9016) M,N,ISBND
     IF(M.LE.MAXM.AND.N.LE.MAXN.AND.ISBND.LE.MAXN) GO TO 35
     WRITE(6,9020) MAXM,MAXN
     ISDONE = 1
     GO TO 610
  35 IF(M.GE.0.AND.N.GE.0 .AND. ISBND .GE. -1) GO TO 40
```

```
      WRITE(6,9024)
      ISDONE = 1
      GO TO 610
   40 MNOW = 1
      IROW(1) = 1
      ISTEP = 1
      BNDJ = -1.0
      IF(ISBND.EQ.-1) BNDJ = 1.0
      DO 50 J = 1,N
      C(J) = 0.0
      PIV(J) = 0.0
   50 BOUND(J) = BNDJ
      DO 60 I = 1,M
      B(I) = BIG
   60 S(I) = 1.0
      IF(MOREPR.LE.1) WRITE(6,9030)
  100 READ(5,9050)((K1(JK),K2(JK),K3(JK)),JK=1,8)
      ICARD = ICARD + 1
      IF(MOREPR.GE.2) GO TO 120
      WRITE(6,9064) ICARD
      WRITE(6,9068) ((K1(JK),K2(JK),K3(JK)),JK=1,8)
  120 IF(K1(1) .NE. 999) GO TO 130
      ISTEP = ISTEP + 1
      IF(ISTEP.EQ.2.AND.ISBND.LE.0) ISTEP = 3
      IF(ISTEP.EQ.5) GO TO 600
      IF(MOREPR.GE.2) GO TO 100
      IF (ISTEP .EQ. 2) WRITE(6,9034)
      IF(ISTEP .EQ. 3) WRITE(6,9038)
      IF (ISTEP .EQ. 4) WRITE (6,9042)
      GO TO 100
  130 IF(ISDONE.EQ.1) GO TO 100
      GO TO (200,300,400,500),ISTEP
  200 DO 210 JK = 1,8
      J = K1(JK)
      IF (J .LE. 0) GO TO 210
      IF (J .LE. N) GO TO 205
      WRITE (6,9070) J,N
      GO TO 210
  205 C(J) = K3(JK)
      KC = KC + 1
  210 CONTINUE
      GO TO 100
  300 DO 320 JK = 1,8
      J = K1(JK)
      IF (J .LE. 0) GO TO 320
      IF (J.LE. N) GO TO 315
      WRITE (6,9070) J,N
      GO TO 320
  315 BOUND(J) = K3(JK)
  320 CONTINUE
      GO TO 100
  400 DO 420 JK = 1,8
      I = K1(JK)
      IF(I .LE. 0) GO TO 420
      IF (I .LE. M) GO TO 405
      WRITE (6,9074) I,M
      GO TO 420
```

```
405 SI = K2(JK)
    IF (SI .EQ. 1.0 .OR. SI .EQ. 2.0 .OR. SI .EQ.  0.0) GO TO 410
    WRITE (6,9078) K2(JK)
    GO TO 420
410 IF (SI .EQ. 2.0) SI = -1.0
    S(I) = SI
    B(I) = K3(JK)
    KB = KB + 1
420 CONTINUE
    GO TO 100
500 I = K3(1)
510 IF(I.EQ.MNOW) GO TO 540
    IF (I .LE. M) GO TO 515
    WRITE (6,9082) I,M
    MOREPR = 0
    ISDONE = 1
    GO TO 100
515 IF (I .GT. MNOW) GO TO 520
    WRITE (6,9084) MNOW,I
    MOREPR = 0
    ISDONE = 1
    GO TO 100
520 CALL COPY
    IF(ISDONE.NE.1) GO TO 525
    MOREPR = 0
    GO TO 100
525 DO 530 J = 1,N
530 PIV(J) = 0.0
    MNOW = MNOW + 1
    GO TO 510
540 DO 550 JK = 2,8
    J = K1(JK)
    IF (J .LE. 0) GO TO 550
    IF (J .LE. N) GO TO 545
    WRITE (6,9070) J,N
    GO TO 550
545 PIV(J) = K3(JK)
550 CONTINUE
    GO TO 100
600 IF(ISDONE.EQ.0) CALL COPY
    IF(ISDONE.EQ.1) GO TO 610
    INREV = 0
    IR = 0
    ITR = 0
    NEGINV = 0
    NEGROW = 0
    NEWX = 0
    NEWY = 0
    R = 0.0
    SIZE = 0
    ISBIG = 1
    TOL(1) = 1.0E-6
    TOL(2) = 1.0E-5
    TOL(3) = 1.0E-6
    TOL(4) = 1.0E-5
    TOL(5) = 1.0E-5
    TOL(6) = 1.0E-5
```

```
      TOL(7) = 1.0E-5
      TOL(8) = TOL(5) * 10.0
      YAMINC = 0.0
      READ (5,9000) MORE
      IF(KC.EQ.0) WRITE(6,9088)
      IF(KB.LT.M) WRITE(6,9092)
      IF(MNOW.EQ.M) GO TO 610
      WRITE(6,9096) M,MNOW
      ISDONE = 1
  610 IF (ISDONE .EQ. 1) WRITE (6,9098)
      RETURN
      END
```

13. FIRSTB (first basis)

This routine, which is not called when DOANLP is entered with an existing basis, sets up a 1 x 1 inverse consisting of the slack variable on the first row of the A matrix. If the first constraint is satisfied by the origin point of x-space, NEGINV and DRIVER will be set at zero. If not, NEGINV is set at 1, indicating that the first row of the inverse is associated with an infeasibility at the current basis. If the slack variable in the basis is positive and infeasible, DRIVER is set equal to –1·0, indicating that feasibility requires it to be non-positive and that it must be driven *down,* otherwise DRIVER = 1·0.

MARKI and MARKK being equal to 1 indicate respectively that the first row of A and the first row of INV(K,L) are in the unusual situation of having a slack vector explicitly in the inverse, and NUMSLK = 1 indicates that one slack variable is explicitly in the basis.

Note that XBASIS(1) = N + 1. Throughout the program, a value for XBASIS(K) of N + I indicates that the Kth basic variable is the slack variable on the Ith row of A.

INREV is a variable used to indicate to the following routine, CHSLCK, that it has not been reached by the usual route through CHBSIS. It is also used in the re-inversion routine to be described later.

Note that 'DO 20' runs from 2 to MNOW rather than from 2 to M. In straight LP, MNOW = M. But MNOW (M now) may be greater than M if new constraints are added during the calculation.

COMMON variables altered in FIRSTB

DRIVER	NEWX
INBASE(J)	NUMSLK
INREV	OBJ
INV(K,L)	SIZE

ISEFF(I)	SIZE1
ITR	XBASIS(K)
MARKI	XR(K)
MARKK	YBASIS(L)
NEGINV	YR(L)

COMMON variables used in FIRSTB

B(I)	N
MNOW	S(I)

```
      SUBROUTINE FIRSTB
********************** COMMON AND TYPE STATEMENTS ********************
      DO 10 J = 1,N
   10 INBASE(J) = 0
      DO 20 I = 2,MNOW
   20 ISEFF(I) = 0
      DRIVER = 0.0
      NEGINV = 0
      SS = S(1)
      BB = B(1)
      IF(SS .EQ. 1.0 .AND. BB .GE. 0.0 .OR. SS .EQ. -1.0 .AND. BB .LE.
     10.0 .OR. SS .EQ. 0.0 .AND. BB .EQ. 0.0) GO TO 30
      NEGINV = 1
      DRIVER = 1.0
      IF(BB.GT.0.0) DRIVER = -1.0
   30 SIZE = 1
      SIZE1 = 2
      NEWX = N + 1
      XBASIS(1) = N + 1
      INV(1,1) = 1.0
      XR(1) = BB
      OBJ = 0.0
      YR(1) = 0.0
      YBASIS(1) = 1
      ISEFF(1) = 1
      NUMSLK = 1
      MARKI = 1
      MARKK = 1
      ITR = ITR + 1
      INREV = 1
      RETURN
      END
```

14. IEXIT

IEXIT is merely a collection of appropriate WRITE statements to conclude the program. The WRITE statements all assume that output is on to channel 6.

If the solution is optimal, the print routine (IPRINT) will print the inverse matrix or not, according to the setting of MOREPR (more print) by the user. But if the program terminates in any other way, MOREPR is set to 1, so that the inverse will be printed. If DATA has not been completed, IPRINT cannot be used.

If the LP solution is infeasible, the array PIV, generated in SEEKX, is printed, so that the user may discover whether an alteration of one of the tolerances, TOL(3), TOL(4), or TOL(5), would enable feasibility to be reached (see Chapter 7, Section 2).

For similar reasons, the arrays GR(K) and G(I) are printed if the solution is unbounded.

For completeness, we include here the statements which are only required for the more complex programs.

Subroutines called in IEXIT

IPRINT

COMMON variables altered in IEXIT

ISDONE
MOREPR

COMMON variables used in IEXIT

G(I)	MNOW
GR(K)	N
IR	PIV(J)
M	SIZE
MAXM	

COMMON/AREF variables used in IEXIT

MAXA

```
      SUBROUTINE IEXIT(JK)
*********************** COMMON AND TYPE STATEMENTS *********************
*********************** COMMON/AREF *************************************
 9001 FORMAT (1H0,'OPTIMUM')
 9002 FORMAT (1H0,'INFEASIBLE.')
 9003 FORMAT (1H0,'UNBOUNDED.')
 9004 FORMAT (1H0,'THE MAXIMUM SIZE OF THE INVERSE HAS BEEN EXCEEDED')
 9005 FORMAT (1H0,'THE MAXIMUM NUMBER OF ITERATIONS HAS BEEN REACHED')
 9006 FORMAT (1H0,'EITHER THE AA VECTOR IS FULL WITH',I6,' ELEMENTS, OR
     1THE NUMBER OF CONSTRAINTS IS ABOUT TO EXCEED',I6,'.'/1X,'THE PROGR
     2AM IS TRYING TO COPY ROW',I6,' WHICH IS AS FOLLOWS...')
 9007 FORMAT (1H0,'STILL INACCURATE AFTER ',I5,' REINVERSIONS.')
 9008 FORMAT (1H0,'INTEGER PROGRAM OPTIMUM.')
 9009 FORMAT (1H0,'QUADRATIC PROGRAM OPTIMUM.')
```

```
9011 FORMAT (1H0,'THE NEGINV ROW OF THE UPDATED A MATRIX IS AS FOLLOWS.
    1...')
9012 FORMAT (8(1X,F14.7))
9013 FORMAT (1H0,'THE VECTOR GR IS AS FOLLOWS...')
9014 FORMAT (1H0,'THE VECTOR G IS AS FOLLOWS...')
9015 FORMAT (/////)
     IF(JK.EQ.2.OR.JK.EQ.3) MOREPR = 1
     WRITE (6,9015)
     ISDONE = 1
     GO TO (1,2,3,4,5,6,7,8,9),JK
   1 WRITE(6,9001)
     GO TO 10
   2 WRITE (6,9002)
     WRITE (6,9011)
     WRITE (6,9012)(PIV(J),J=1,N)
     GO TO 10
   3 WRITE (6,9003)
     WRITE (6,9013)
     WRITE (6,9012)(GR(K),K=1,SIZE)
     WRITE (6,9014)
     WRITE (6,9012)(G(I),I=1,MNOW)
     GO TO 10
   4 WRITE (6,9004)
     GO TO 10
   5 WRITE (6,9005)
     GO TO 10
   6 WRITE (6,9006) MAXA,MAXM,MNOW
     WRITE (6,9012)(PIV(J),J=1,N)
     GO TO 10
   7 WRITE (6,9007) IR
     GO TO 10
   8 WRITE (6,9008)
     GO TO 10
   9 WRITE (6,9009)
  10 IF (MNOW.GE.M) CALL IPRINT
     RETURN
     END
```

15. IPRINT

This routine prints out on channel 6 almost the entire contents of COMMON and COMMON/AREF. The first three executable statements (after 9600 FORMAT) may be eliminated if SPRINT, the special print routine for teaching purposes, is not required.

All the format statements are collected at the beginning of the routine. To statement 200 the routine prints arrays AA, JCOL and IROW. This is followed by the objective function, OBJ, C(J), BOUND(J), X(J), and YAC(J), to statement 300. From 300 to 400 B(I), S(I), Y(I), and SLACK(I) are printed.

According to the value of MOREPR, the inverse is printed or not, from

400 to 500. And from 500 to the end, the single variables in COMMON are printed out (as an aid to diagnosis). Note that during the development of a new version of a program, it is frequently helpful to CALL IPRINT at intermediate stages of the program, but that it may not be called before the DATA routine is completed.

A sample of the printing for a small LP problem is displayed in Appendix 4, Section 3.

Subroutines called in IPRINT

SPRINT

COMMON variables used in IPRINT

B(I)	MOREPR
BIG	MXSIZE
BOUND(J)	N
C(J)	NEGINV
DRIVER	NEGROW
INBASE(J)	NEWX
INREV	NEWY
INV(K,L)	NUMSLK
IR	OBJ
IBMAX	R
ISBIG	S(I)
ISBND	SIZE
ISDONE	SLACK(I)
ISEFF(I)	SMALL
ISTATE	TOL(JK)
ITR	X(J)
ITRMAX	XBASIS(K)
M	XKPOS
MARKI	XR(K)
MARKK	Y(I)
MAXM	YAC(J)
MAXN	YAMINC
MNOW	YBASIS(L)
MORE	YR(L)

COMMON/AREF variables used in IPRINT

AA(LOOK)	JCOL(LOOK)
IROW(I)	MAXA

```
      SUBROUTINE IPRINT
*********************** COMMON AND TYPE STATEMENTS ********************
*********************** COMMON/AREF ***********************************
 8000 FORMAT (1H0,' THE SIGN(I) VECTOR INDICATES THE SIGN OF THE I-TH CO
     2NSTRAINT, 0 FOR EQ, 1 FOR LE, -1 FOR GE.')
```

```
9000 FORMAT (1H1,'NON-ZERO ELEMENTS OF THE A MATRIX, FOLLOWED BY THEIR
    1COLUMN LABELS....')
9001 FORMAT (1H0,12(4X,I6))
9002 FORMAT (1H ,12F10.3)
9003 FORMAT (1H ,12(4X,I6))
9004 FORMAT (1H0,'THE FOLLOWING VECTORS SHOW THE STARTING POINTS OF THE
    1 SUCCESSIVE ROWS OF A IN THE ABOVE LIST OF THE NON-ZERO ELEMENTS.'
    2'..')
9005 FORMAT (1H0,24(I5))
9006 FORMAT (1H ,24(I5))
9200 FORMAT (1H0,'OBJECTIVE ',F22.8)
9204 FORMAT(1H0,38X,'J ',8(3X,I3,4X))
9205 FORMAT(1H0,38X,'I ',8(3X,I3,4X))
9208 FORMAT (1H0,31X,'C VECTOR ',8(F9.1,1X))
9212 FORMAT (1H0,27X,'BOUND VECTOR ',8(F9.4,1X))
9220 FORMAT (1H0,31X,'X VECTOR ',8(F9.4,1X))
9228 FORMAT (1H0,34X,5HY'A-C,1X,8(F9.2,1X))
9232 FORMAT (////)
9234 FORMAT (1H0,12(6X,I3,1X))
9236 FORMAT (1H0,12(F9.1,1X))
9238 FORMAT (1H0,12(F9.0,1X))
9240 FORMAT (1H0,12(F9.4,1X))
9244 FORMAT (1H0,12(F9.2,1X))
9300 FORMAT (1H0,31X,'B VECTOR ',8(F9.1,1X))
9304 FORMAT (1H0,35X,'SIGN ',8(F9.0,1X))
9308 FORMAT (1H0,31X,'Y VECTOR ',8(F9.4,1X))
9312 FORMAT (1H0,34X,' B-AX ',8(F9.4,1X))
9404 FORMAT (1H1,12X,'COLUMN ',7(6X,I2,6X))
9408 FORMAT (1H0,12X,'YBASIS ',7(5X,I3,6X))
9412 FORMAT (1H0,16X,'YR ',2X,7(F12.4,2X))
9416 FORMAT (1H0,'ROW XBS ',4X,'XR',5X,'INVERSE MATRIX'/)
9420 FORMAT (2(I3,1X),8(F12.4,2X))
9424 FORMAT (1H1,5X,8(5X,I3,6X))
9428 FORMAT (1H0,5X,8(5X,I3,6X))
9432 FORMAT (1H0,5X,8(F12.4,2X))
9436 FORMAT (1H0,'ROW',5X,'INVERSE MATRIX CONTINUES'/)
9438 FORMAT (1H ,I3,2X,8(F12.4,2X))
9500 FORMAT (1H1)
9504 FORMAT(1H0,'   BIG',E12.4,', DRIVER',F12.1,',  INREV',I12,',      I
    1R',I12,',  IRMAX',I12,',  ISBND',I12/1H ,'ISDONE',I12,', ISTATE',I
    212,',    ITR',I12,', ITRMAX',I12,',       M',I12,',  MARKI',I12/1H
    3,' MARKK',I12,',   MAXA',I12,',   MAXM',I12,',   MAXN',I12,',    MO
    4RE',I12,', MXSIZE',I12/1H ,'      N',I12,', NEGINV',I12,', NEGROW',
    5I12,',   NEWX',I12,',   NEWY',I12,', NUMSLK',I12/1H ,'      R',
    6F12.5,',   SIZE',I12,',  SMALL',E12.4,', TOL(1)',E12.4,', TOL(2)',
    7E12.4,', TOL(3)',E12.4/1H ,'TOL(4)',E12.4,', TOL(5)',E12.4,
    8', TOL(6)',E12.4,', TOL(7)',E12.4,', TOL(8)',E12.4,',  XKPOS',
    9F12.1/1H ,'YAMINC',F12.5)
9516 FORMAT (1H0,'ISEFF'/1H ,40I3)
9520 FORMAT (1H0,'INBASE'/1H ,40I3)
9600 FORMAT (1H0,I5,' SIMPLEX ITERATIONS.')
9604 FORMAT (1H0,'(N.B., THE MAXIMUM SIZE OF THE INVERSE DURING THE CAL
    1CULATION WAS ',I4,')')
     IF (N .GE. 8) GO TO 90
     CALL SPRINT
     GO TO 400
  90 WRITE(6,9000)
```

```
      LAST = IROW(MNOW+1) - 1
      ISTART = 1
      IF(IEND.GT.LAST) IEND = LAST
      WRITE (6,9001) (IJ,IJ = ISTART,IEND)
      WRITE (6,9002) (AA(IJ),IJ = ISTART,IEND)
      WRITE (6,9003) (JCOL(IJ),IJ = ISTART,IEND)
      IF (IEND.EQ.LAST) GO TO 105
      ISTART = IEND + 1
      GO TO 100
  105 WRITE (6,9004)
      ISTART = 1
  110 IEND = ISTART + 23
      IF(IEND.GT.MNOW) IEND = MNOW
      WRITE (6,9005) (I,I = ISTART,IEND)
      WRITE (6,9006) (IROW(I),I = ISTART,IEND)
      IF(IEND.EQ.MNOW) GO TO 200
      ISTART = IEND + 1
      GO TO 110
  200 WRITE (6,9200) OBJ
      IEND = 8
      IF(N.LE.IEND) IEND = N
      WRITE (6,9204) (J,J = 1,IEND)
      WRITE (6,9208) (C(J),J = 1,IEND)
      IF(ISBND.EQ.0) GO TO 210
      WRITE (6,9212) (BOUND(J),J = 1,IEND)
  210 WRITE (6,9220) (X(J),J = 1,IEND)
      WRITE (6,9228) (YAC(J),J = 1,IEND)
  230 IF(N.LE.IEND) GO TO 300
      WRITE (6,9232)
      ISTART = IEND + 1
      IEND = IEND + 12
      IF(N.LE.IEND) IEND = N
      WRITE (6,9234) (J,J = ISTART,IEND)
      WRITE (6,9236) (C(J),J = ISTART,IEND)
      IF (ISBND.EQ.0) GO TO 235
      WRITE (6,9240) (BOUND(J), J = ISTART,IEND)
  235 WRITE (6,9240) (X(J), J = ISTART,IEND)
      WRITE (6,9244) (YAC(J), J = ISTART,IEND)
      GO TO 230
  300 IEND = 8
      IF(MNOW.LE.IEND) IEND = MNOW
      WRITE (6,9232)
      WRITE(6,8000)
      WRITE (6,9205)(I,I=1,IEND)
      WRITE (6,9300) (B(I), I = 1,IEND)
      WRITE (6,9304) (S(I), I = 1,IEND)
      WRITE (6,9308) (Y(I), I = 1,IEND)
      WRITE (6,9312) (SLACK(I), I = 1,IEND)
  310 IF(MNOW.LE.IEND) GO TO 400
      WRITE (6,9232)
      ISTART = IEND + 1
      IEND = IEND + 12
      IF(MNOW.LE.IEND) IEND = MNOW
      WRITE (6,9234) (I, I = ISTART,IEND)
      WRITE (6,9236) (B(I), I = ISTART,IEND)
      WRITE (6,9238) (S(I), I = ISTART,IEND)
      WRITE (6,9240) (Y(I), I = ISTART,IEND)
```

```
      WRITE (6,9240) (SLACK(I), I = ISTART,IEND)
      GO TO 310
  400 IF(MOREPR.LT.1.OR.MOREPR.GT.2) GO TO 600
      IEND = 7
      IF(SIZE.LE.IEND) IEND = SIZE
      WRITE (6,9404) (L, L = 1,IEND)
  410 WRITE (6,9408) (YBASIS(L), L = 1,IEND)
      WRITE (6,9412) (YR(L), L = 1,IEND)
      WRITE (6,9416)
      DO 430 K = 1,SIZE
  430 WRITE (6,9420) K,XBASIS(K),XR(K), (INV(K,L), L = 1,IEND)
  440 IF(SIZE.LE.IEND) GO TO 500
      ISTART = IEND + 1
      IEND = IEND + 8
      IF(SIZE.LE.IEND) IEND = SIZE
      WRITE (6,9424) (L, L = ISTART,IEND)
      WRITE (6,9428) (YBASIS(L), L = ISTART,IEND)
      WRITE (6,9432) (YR(L), L = ISTART, IEND)
      WRITE (6,9436)
      DO 445 K = 1,SIZE
  445 WRITE (6,9438) K, (INV(K,L), L = ISTART,IEND)
      GO TO 440
  500 IF(SIZE.LT.9) GO TO 510
      WRITE (6,9500)
  510 WRITE (6,9232)
      WRITE(6,9504)BIG,DRIVER,INREV,IR,IRMAX,ISBND,ISDONE,ISTATE,ITR,
     1   ITRMAX,M,MARKI,MARKK,MAXA,MAXM,MAXN,MORE,MXSIZE,N,NEGINV,
     2  NEGROW,NEWX,NEWY,NUMSLK,R,SIZE,SMALL,(TOL(K),K=1,8),XKPOS,YAMINC
  600 WRITE (6,9516) (ISEFF(I), I = 1,MNOW)
      WRITE (6,9520) (INBASE(J), J = 1,N)
      WRITE(6,9600) ITR
      WRITE(6,9604) ISBIG
      RETURN
      END
```

16. ISOPT (is optimal)

YAMINC (*yA* minus *c*) is the value of the element in the function row of the variable, NEWX, which is to enter the basis, according to the usual Simplex rule. If no variable is found for which YAMINC is less than zero (actually, less than a tolerance) NEWX remains zero, and the solution is considered to be optimal.

In 'DO 10' YAMINC is sought in the inverse, i.e., amongst the non-basic slack variables. The sign of the S array determines whether an element of YR(K) is associated with a positive slack, a negative slack, or zero slack. If a most negative value for YAMINC is found for the slack vector associated with the Ith row of A, NEWX is set equal to I + N.

'DO 20' continues the search for YAMINC through the YAC array, omitting those variables which are currently basic, and those which have zero upper bounds. Notice that setting BOUND(J) equal to zero can be used as a device to cause the program to ignore a subset of the variables and to solve the LP without them. It is used in this way in the Branch and Bound algorithm. If a variable is non-basic at its upper bound (INBASE(J) = −1) the function element considered is the negative of the YAC(J) element, since the variable could only enter the basis negatively.

COMMON variables altered in ISOPT

NEWX	YAMINC
YAC(J)	

COMMON variables used in ISOPT

BOUND(J)	SIZE
INBASE(J)	TOL(JK)
N	YBASIS(L)
S(I)	YR(L)

```
      SUBROUTINE ISOPT
********************** COMMON AND TYPE STATEMENTS ********************
      YAMINC = - TOL(3)
      NEWX = 0
      DO 10 L = 1,SIZE
      I = YBASIS(L)
      SI = S(I)
      IF(SI.EQ.0.0) GO TO 10
      YRL = YR(L) * SI
      IF(YRL.GE.YAMINC) GO TO 10
      YAMINC = YRL
      NEWX = I + N
   10 CONTINUE
      TOL4 = TOL(4)
      DO 20 J = 1,N
      INBJ = INBASE(J)
      IF(INBJ .GT. 0 .OR. BOUND(J) .EQ. 0.0) GO TO 20
      T = YAC(J)
      IF(ABS(T).LE.TOL4) T = 0.0
      YAC(J) = T
      IF(INBJ.EQ.-1) T = -T
      IF(T.GE.YAMINC) GO TO 20
      YAMINC = T
      NEWX = J
   20 CONTINUE
      RETURN
      END
```

17. NEWVEC (new vector)

This routine is concerned with computing GR, the 'updated' array of the variable NEWX which is to enter the basis—the vector of subtractions to be made to the current basic variables as NEWX increases by one unit. This vector, $g^R = R^{-1}a^k$, is computed by premultiplying by R^{-1} the column of those elements in A of the NEWX variable which belong to the effective constraints. If NEWX is a slack variable, a^k is a unit vector, and g^R is simply the appropriate column of the inverse. This case is dealt with separately in 'DO 50'.

In order to look up each element of the new vector only once in the A matrix the matrix-vector product is accumulated (in 'DO 30') in the GR array by multiplying each element of A(I,NEWX) in turn (in 'DO 20') by all the relevant elements of the inverse. This necessitates first setting all the elements of GR(K) to zero in 'DO 10'.

After 'DO 30' XKPOS is set to $-1{\cdot}0$ if in fact NEWX is to enter the basis negatively because it is a variable coming down from its upper bound. Similarly, after 'DO 50', XKPOS is set to $-1{\cdot}0$ if NEWX is a slack variable on a greater-than-or-equal constraint, which is to enter the basis at a negative level.

Subroutines called in NEWVEC

A(I, J)

COMMON variables altered in NEWVEC

GR(K)
XKPOS

COMMON variables used in NEWVEC

INBASE(J)	NEWX
INV(K,L)	S(I)
ISEFF(I)	SIZE
N	YBASIS(L)

```
      SUBROUTINE NEWVEC
********************** COMMON AND TYPE STATEMENTS *******************
      XKPOS = 1.0
      IF(NEWX.GT.N) GO TO 40
      DO 10 K = 1,SIZE
   10 GR(K) = 0.0
      DO 30 L = 1,SIZE
      I = YBASIS(L)
```

```
      AIJ = A(I,NEWX)
      IF(AIJ.EQ.0.0) GO TO 30
      DO 20 K = 1,SIZE
   20 GR(K) = GR(K) + AIJ * INV(K,L)
   30 CONTINUE
      IF(INBASE(NEWX).EQ.-1) XKPOS = -1.0
      GO TO 60
   40 I = NEWX - N
      L = ISEFF(I)
      DO 50 K = 1,SIZE
   50 GR(K) = INV(K,L)
      IF(S(I).EQ.-1.0) XKPOS = -1.0
   60 RETURN
      END
```

18. REDUCE

This routine is entered after each basis change to delete from the inverse any feasible slack variables, but not to reduce SIZE to zero. When a slack is deleted from the Kth row of the inverse, the last row of the inverse is moved into the Kth row (in 'DO 20'). L, the associated column of the inverse (which contains only a unit vector) is identified, and the last column of the inverse is moved into the Lth column (in 'DO 40'). The rest of the routine is simply the necessary associated alterations of the various labelling variables.

COMMON variables altered in REDUCE

INBASE(J)	SIZE
INV(K,L)	SIZE1
ISEFF(I)	SLACK(I)
MARKI	XBASIS(K)
MARKK	XR(K)
NEGINV	YBASIS(L)
NUMSLK	YR(L)

COMMON variables used in REDUCE

N
S(I)

```
      SUBROUTINE REDUCE
*********************** COMMON AND TYPE STATEMENTS ********************
      MARKI = 0
      MARKK = 0
      IF(NUMSLK.EQ.0) GO TO 80
      IT = SIZE
```

```
      DO 60 K = 1,IT
   10 IF(SIZE.LE.1) GO TO 70
      J = XBASIS(K)
      IF(J.LE.N) GO TO 60
      I = J - N
      SI = S(I)
      IF(SI * XR(K).LT.0.0.OR.SI.EQ.0.0.AND.XR(K).NE.0.0) GO TO 60
      IF(K.EQ.SIZE) GO TO 30
      DO 20 L = 1,SIZE
   20 INV(K,L) = INV(SIZE,L)
      J = XBASIS(SIZE)
      XBASIS(K) = J
      IF(J.LE.N) INBASE(J) = K
   30 SLACK(I) = XR(K)
      XR(K) = XR(SIZE)
      IF(NEGINV.EQ.SIZE) NEGINV = K
      L = ISEFF(I)
      ISEFF(I) = 0
      IF(L.EQ.SIZE) GO TO 50
      DO 40 KK = 1,SIZE
   40 INV(KK,L) = INV(KK,SIZE)
      YR(L) = YR(SIZE)
      YBASIS(L) = YBASIS(SIZE)
      I = YBASIS(SIZE)
      ISEFF(I) = L
   50 XBASIS(SIZE) = 0
      SIZE = SIZE - 1
      SIZE1 = SIZE1 - 1
      NUMSLK = NUMSLK - 1
      GO TO 10
   60 CONTINUE
   70 IF(SIZE.LT.2.AND.XBASIS(1).GT.N) MARKK = 1
      IF(NEGINV.EQ.0.AND.MARKK.EQ.0) GO TO 80
      J = 0
      IF(NEGINV.NE.0) J = XBASIS(NEGINV)
      IF(J.GT.N) MARKK = NEGINV
      IF(MARKK.EQ.0) GO TO 80
      MARKI = XBASIS(MARKK) - N
   80 RETURN
      END
```

19. REVERT (re-invert)

The re-inversion count, IR, is incremented.

The inverse matrix is replaced by a unit matrix (in 'DO 40'), one unit vector for each of the currently effective constraints. If any of the slack vectors was explicitly in the basis before the re-inversion, 'DO 20' ensures that its label (in XBASIS(K)) is re-positioned into the row which corresponds to its column (in YBASIS(L)).

In 'DO 40', all the elements of XBASIS(K) corresponding to original variables are multiplied by −1, which serves as an indicator of which variables have not yet been introduced.

In 'DO 50' all original variables are indicated as non-basic in INBASE(J).

'DO 90' is the heart of the routine, introducing each original variable, NEWX, to the basis in turn. The updated array, GR(K) is obtained in NEWVEC, then the row in which the pivot is to take place is chosen (in 'DO 80') amongst those in which there has not yet been a pivot, to yield the pivot with the least absolute difference from unity. If there is no possible pivot greater than TOL(8) (absolute) the variable is not introduced. In that case 'DO 80' is completed with NEWY still zero, and the next variable to enter the basis is chosen from XBASIS(K). If there is an acceptable pivot in row NEWY, the entry in XBASIS(NEWY) is held in IHOLD, since it will be introduced to the basis next, unless it happens that NEWY is in the same row as NEWX, in which case IHOLD = 0.

CHBSIS is called to introduce NEWX to the basis (but note that since INREV = 1 CHBSIS only operates on the inverse, not on XR(K) and YR(L)). If IHOLD = 0, 'DO 90' picks up the next available element of XBASIS(K) for NEWX. Otherwise NEWX = IHOLD and control returns to 60 to try to introduce another new variable.

In 'DO 110', INBASE(J) is corrected to show the original variables now in the basis, and those rows in which the unit vectors have not been pivoted out are renamed as their appropriate slack variables. NUMSLK is computed.

The remainder of the routine is concerned with computing XR(K) and YR(L) (in 'DO 140') and then checking for the presence of infeasibility, and if it is present for the row of the inverse associated with the greatest infeasibility, in 'DO 180'. REDUCE then removes any feasible slacks, CHSLK updates the arrays X, Y and SLACK, and identifies any infeasibility in the slacks; the iteration count is set back to its value on entering REVERT; and the objective function is recomputed. Finally a line of printing announces that there has been a re-inversion at iteration so and so.

Subroutines called in REVERT

A(I,J)	ISOPT
CHBSIS	NEWVEC
CHSLCK	REDUCE

COMMON variables altered in REVERT

DRIVER	NEWY
INBASE(J)	NUMSLK
INREV	OBJ
INV(K,L)	SMALL
IR	XBASIS(K)
ITR	XR(K)
NEGINV	YR(L)
NEWX	

COMMON variables used in REVERT

B(I)	N
BOUND(J)	S(I)
C(J)	SIZE
GR(K)	TOL(JK)
ISBND	X(J)
ISEFF(I)	YBASIS(L)

```
      SUBROUTINE REVERT
********************** COMMON AND TYPE STATEMENTS ********************
 9000 FORMAT (1H ,20X,'REINVERTED AT ITERATION ',I6)
      IR = IR + 1
      ITHOLD = ITR
      INREV = 1
      HOLD = SMALL
      SMALL = 0.0
      TOL8 = TOL(8)
      DO 20 K = 1,SIZE
   10 IF (XBASIS(K) .LE. N) GO TO 20
      I = XBASIS(K) - N
      L = ISEFF(I)
      IF (K .EQ. L) GO TO 20
      XBASIS(K) = XBASIS(L)
      XBASIS(L) = I + N
      J = XBASIS(K)
      IF (J .GT. N) GO TO 10
   20 CONTINUE
      DO 40 K = 1,SIZE
      IF (XBASIS(K) .LE. N) XBASIS(K) = -XBASIS(K)
      DO 30 L = 1,SIZE
   30 INV(K,L) = 0.0
   40 INV(K,K) = 1.0
      DO 50 J = 1,N
      IF (INBASE(J) .NE. -1) INBASE(J) = 0
   50 CONTINUE
      DO 90 K = 1,SIZE
      NEWX = -XBASIS(K)
      IF (NEWX .LT. 0 .OR. NEWX .GT. N) GO TO 90
   60 CALL NEWVEC
      NEWY = 0
      DO 80 KK = 1,SIZE
      IF (XBASIS(KK) .GT. 0) GO TO 80
      ABDIF = ABS(GR(KK))
      IF (ABDIF .LT. TOL8) GO TO 80
      IF (NEWY .NE. 0) GO TO 70
      BEST = ABS(1.0 - ABDIF)
      NEWY = KK
      GO TO 80
   70 ABDIF = ABS(1.0 - ABDIF)
      IF (ABDIF .GE. BEST) GO TO 80
      BEST = ABDIF
      NEWY = KK
   80 CONTINUE
```

```
      IF (NEWY .EQ. 0) GO TO 90
      IHOLD = -XBASIS(NEWY)
      IF (IHOLD .EQ. NEWX) IHOLD = 0
      CALL CHBSIS
      XBASIS(NEWY) = NEWX
      IF (IHOLD .EQ. 0) GO TO 90
      NEWX = IHOLD
      GO TO 60
   90 CONTINUE
      NUMSLK = 0
      DO 110 K = 1,SIZE
      J = XBASIS(K)
      IF (J .GT. 0) GO TO 100
      I = YBASIS(K)
      XBASIS(K) = N + I
      NUMSLK = NUMSLK + 1
      GO TO 110
  100 IF (J .LE. N) INBASE(J) = K
      IF(J.GT.N) NUMSLK = NUMSLK + 1
  110 CONTINUE
      SMALL = HOLD
      DO 120 K = 1,SIZE
      XR(K) = 0.0
  120 YR(K) = 0.0
      DO 140 K = 1,SIZE
      I = YBASIS(K)
      J = XBASIS(K)
      TC = 0.0
      IF (J .LE. N) TC = C(J)
      TB = B(I)
      DO 130 JJ = 1,N
      IF (INBASE(JJ) .NE. -1) GO TO 130
      TB = TB - BOUND(JJ) * A(I,JJ)
  130 CONTINUE
      DO 140 L = 1,SIZE
      XR(L) = XR(L) + TB * INV(L,K)
      YR(L) = YR(L) + TC * INV(K,L)
      IF (ABS(YR(L)).LE. SMALL) YR(L) = 0.0
      IF (ABS(XR(L)) .LE. SMALL) XR(L) = 0.0
  140 CONTINUE
      NEGINV = 0
      T = 0.0
      DO 180 K = 1,SIZE
      XRK = XR(K)
      J = XBASIS(K)
      IF (J .GT. N) GO TO 160
      IF (ISBND .EQ. 0) GO TO 150
      IF (BOUND(J) .EQ. -1.0) GO TO 150
      IF (XRK .GT. BOUND(J)) XRK = BOUND(J) - XR(K)
  150 IF (XRK .GE. T) GO TO 180
      GO TO 170
  160 I = J - N
      IF (S(I) .NE. 0.0 .AND. XRK * S(I) .GE. T .OR. S(I) .EQ. 0.0 .AND.
     1   ABS(XRK) * (-1.0) .GE. T) GO TO 180
  170 T = -1.0 * ABS(XRK)
      NEGINV = K
      DRIVER = 1.0
```

```
      IF (XR(K) .GT. 0.0) DRIVER = -1.0
  180 CONTINUE
      IF(NUMSLK.GE.1) CALL REDUCE
      CALL CHSLCK
      CALL ISOPT
      ITR = ITHOLD
      INREV = 0
      OBJ = 0.0
      DO 190 J = 1,N
      IF (INBASE(J) .EQ. 0) GO TO 190
      OBJ = OBJ + X(J) * C(J)
  190 CONTINUE
      WRITE (6,9000) ITR
      RETURN
      END
```

20. SEEKX (seek x)

This routine is basically similar to ISOPT, except that instead of seeking a new basic variable to increase the value of the function, the driving row is the one represented in NEGINV.

We could simply use that row analogously to the use of the function row in ISOPT, but we have chosen rather to make the dual Simplex type of choice of new variable. Strictly speaking, dual Simplex refers to the situation where all the function elements are already non-negative, whereas this is the case here only when DOANLP is being used to restore feasibility after a constraint has been added. However, the ratio test extends naturally to negative function elements, and preference is given to choosing variables which increase both the feasibility and the function. However, this can lead to very slow approaches to feasibility, by choosing variables which have very small contributions both to the function and to the driving row, but that have nevertheless a favourable ratio of the two. Therefore, if the variable being examined does not satisfy the dual (optimality) condition and if the element in the driving row exceeds −0·5, the ratio criterion is dropped in favour of choosing the largest negative element in the driving row. This element, PIVMAX, is recorded as occurring in variable JMAXP and is used to provide a new variable if NEWX is still zero after all non-basic variables have been examined (after 'DO 60').

Finally, it is useful to choose between ties on the ratio rule by the size of element in the driving row. In practice, only the ties in the case where the function element is zero are so distinguished by the value of DESPIV.

NEWX is sought first in the inverse (in 'DO 40') and secondly in the A matrix (in 'DO 60'). To enable advantage to be taken of the row-wise storage of A, the array PIV (the 'updated' driving row of the non-basic variables) is accumulated in 'DO 20' and used in 'DO 60'.

COMMON variables altered in SEEKX

NEWX	R
PIV(J)	YAMINC

COMMON variables used in SEEKX

BIG	S(I)
BOUND(J)	SIZE
DRIVER	TOL(JK)
INBASE(J)	YAC(J)
INV(K,L)	YBASIS(L)
N	YR(L)
NEGINV	

COMMON/AREF variables used in SEEKX

AA(LOOK)	JCOL(LOOK)
IROW(I)	

```
      SUBROUTINE SEEKX
*********************** COMMON AND TYPE STATEMENTS ********************
********************** COMMON/AREF ***********************************
      NEWX = 0
      R = -BIG
      PIVMAX = 0.0
      JMAXP = 0
      BESPIV = 0.0
      TOL3 = TOL(3)
      TOL4 = TOL(4)
      TOL5 = TOL(5)
      DO 10 J = 1,N
   10 PIV(J) = 0.0
      DO 40 L = 1,SIZE
      I = YBASIS(L)
      SI = S(I)
      YI = YR(L) * SI
      IF(ABS(YI).LT.TOL3) YI = 0.0
      RINVL = INV(NEGINV,L)
      ISTART = IROW(I)
      LAST = IROW(I+1) - 1
      DO 20 LOOK = ISTART,LAST
      J = JCOL(LOOK)
      IF (INBASE(J) .GE. 1 .OR. BOUND(J) .EQ. 0.0) GO TO 20
      AIJ = AA(LOOK)
      PIV(J) = PIV(J) + AIJ * RINVL
   20 CONTINUE
      IF (SI .EQ. 0.0) GO TO 40
      PIVOT = RINVL * SI * DRIVER
      IF (PIVOT .GE. -TOL5 .OR. PIVOT .GE. -0.5 .AND. NEWX .NE. 0
     1     .AND. YI .LT. 0.0) GO TO 40
      IF (PIVOT .GE. -0.5 .AND. YI .LT. 0.0) GO TO 30
      RATIO = YI / PIVOT
```

```
      IF (RATIO .LT. R .AND. NEWX .NE. 0) GO TO 40
      IF (RATIO .EQ. 0.0 .AND. PIVOT .GE. BESPIV) GO TO 40
      IF (RATIO .EQ. 0.0) BESPIV = PIVOT
      R = RATIO
      YAMINC = YI
      NEWX = N + I
      GO TO 40
   30 IF (PIVOT .GE. PIVMAX) GO TO 40
      YACP = YI
      JMAXP = N + I
      PIVMAX = PIVOT
   40 CONTINUE
      DO 60 J = 1,N
      INJ = INBASE(J)
      IF (INJ .GE. 1 .OR. BOUND(J) .EQ. 0.0) GO TO 60
      SJ = 1.0
      IF (INJ .EQ. -1) SJ = -1.0
      FUNC = YAC(J) * SJ
      IF (ABS(FUNC) .LT. TOL4) FUNC = 0.0
      PIVOT = PIV(J) * SJ * DRIVER
      IF (PIVOT .GE. -TOL5 .OR. PIVOT .GE. -0.5 .AND. NEWX .NE. 0
     1      .AND. FUNC .LT. 0.0) GO TO 60
      IF (PIVOT .GE. -0.5 .AND. FUNC .LT. 0.0) GO TO 50
      RATIO = FUNC / PIVOT
      IF (RATIO .LT. R .AND. NEWX .NE. 0) GO TO 60
      IF (RATIO .EQ. 0.0 .AND. PIVOT .GE. BESPIV) GO TO 60
      IF (RATIO .EQ. 0.0) BESPIV = PIVOT
      R = RATIO
      YAMINC = FUNC
      NEWX = J
      GO TO 60
   50 IF (PIVOT .GE. PIVMAX) GO TO 60
      PIVMAX = PIVOT
      YACP = FUNC
      JMAXP = J
   60 CONTINUE
      IF (NEWX .NE. 0) GO TO 70
      NEWX = JMAXP
      YAMINC = YACP
      IF (NEWX .NE. 0) R = YAMINC / PIVMAX
   70 RETURN
      END
```

21. SEEKY (seek y)

This routine is trivial in principle, but because of all the different cases under consideration appears very complex in practice. Having chosen, either in SEEKX or in ISOPT, which variable is to enter the basis, SEEKY determines which variable is to leave the basis. In the simplest form of primal Simplex this decision is made by the 'ratio test' between elements in the current x^P vector and the updated vector, g. In this more general situation we have to determine R, the maximum absolute value that the entering variable, NEWX, can take without violating any of the primal feasibility constraints which are currently satisfied, and simultaneously to determine NEWY, the constraint which limits R to that maximum value.

R starts at a very large value, BIG, and is successively reduced as more restrictive constraints are found. If at any stage during the search it emerges that R is zero control immediately returns to the calling routine, since R is essentially non-negative and there is no point in continuing the search.

The first limit on R is set by the upper bound on NEWX itself, if it has one. In this case, NEWY = −1.

The second limit considered applies only in the infeasible situation, and considers the value of R, RTRY, necessary to just eliminate the driving infeasibility in the row NEGINV. Note that by taking this row before the others we ensure that preference is given to pivoting in this row if there is a tie. The statements from 10 to 30 are complicated by the necessity of distinguishing what kind of infeasibility NEGINV is signalling, namely: a negative original variable; an original variable above its upper bound; a negative slack variable on a less-than-or-equal constraint or an equality; or a positive slack variable on a greater-than-or-equal constraint or an equality.†

'DO 90' considers next the other rows of XR(K), excluding the NEGINV row. It considers only constraints which are already satisfied. That is to say, a negative original variable is allowed to become more negative, or a variable exceeding its upper bound may exceed it even more, etc. But any variable which lies within its proper upper and lower limits is checked to see whether the new variable at the level R will take it outside its limits. If so, a new, lower, value of R is found, and a new value for NEWY. If the most restrictive constraint is set by the Kth basic variable, NEWY = K.

Finally, in 'DO 130', the effect on the SLACK array of introducing NEWX at the level R is considered and again any constraint currently satisfied may result in a reduction of R and the determination of a new value of NEWY. Since this calculation involves determining the effect on each new element of SLACK(I) of introducing NEWX at the unit level, this effect is recorded in G(I), so that in CHSLCK when R has been determined, SLACK(I) can be modified by subtracting R * G(I) * XKPOS. If the most restrictive constraint is the Ith, NEWY is set equal to SIZE + I.

COMMON variables altered in SEEKY

G(I)	NEWY
GR(K)	R

† Since the objective function may be increasing with NEWX, even in the infeasible situation, we might consider that in such a case the NEGINV constraint should not restrict R. However, the number of basis changes this is likely to save has not seemed worth the programming effort.

COMMON variables used in SEEKY

BIG	S(I)
BOUND(J)	SIZE
INBASE(J)	SIZE1
ISBND	SLACK(I)
ISEFF(I)	SMALL
MNOW	TOL(JK)
N	XBASIS(K)
NEGINV	XKPOS
NEWX	XR(K)

COMMON/AREF variables used in SEEKY

AA(LOOK)	JCOL(LOOK)
IROW(I)	

```
      SUBROUTINE SEEKY
********************** COMMON AND TYPE STATEMENTS ********************
********************** COMMON/AREF ***********************************
      SI = 1.0
      BOUNDJ = -1.0
      R = BIG
      NEWY = 0
      TOL5 = TOL(5)
      IF(ISBND.EQ.0.OR.NEWX.GT.N) GO TO 10
      IF(BOUND(NEWX).EQ.-1.0) GO TO 10
      R = BOUND(NEWX)
      NEWY = -1
   10 IF(NEGINV.EQ.0) GO TO 30
      XRNEG = XR(NEGINV)
      J = XBASIS(NEGINV)
      IF(J.GT.N) GO TO 20
      BOUNDJ = BOUND(J)
      IF(BOUNDJ.GE.XRNEG.OR.BOUNDJ.EQ.-1.0) GO TO 20
      XRNEG = XRNEG - BOUNDJ
   20 RTRY = XRNEG / (XKPOS * GR(NEGINV))
      IF(RTRY.GT.R) GO TO 30
      R = RTRY
      IF(R.LE.SMALL) R = 0.0
      NEWY = NEGINV
      IF(R.EQ.0.0) GO TO 140
   30 DO 90 K = 1,SIZE
      IF(K.EQ.NEGINV) GO TO 90
      GK = GR(K) * XKPOS
      IF(ABS(GK).LE.TOL5) GO TO 90
      J = XBASIS(K)
      IF(J.GT.N) SI = S(J-N)
      IF(J.LE.N) BOUNDJ = BOUND(J)
      XX = XR(K)
      IF(GK.LE.0.0) GO TO 70
      IF(XX.LT.0.0) GO TO 90
```

```
      IF(J.LE.N.AND.BOUNDJ.EQ.-1.0.OR.J.LE.N.AND.XX.LE.BOUNDJ) GO TO 40
      IF(J.GT.N.AND.SI.EQ.1.0) GO TO 40
      GO TO 90
   40 IF(XX.GE.GK * R) GO TO 90
   50 R = XX / GK
   60 IF(R.LE.SMALL) R = 0.0
      NEWY = K
      IF(R.EQ.0.0) GO TO 140
      GO TO 90
   70 IF(J.GT.N) GO TO 80
      IF(BOUNDJ.EQ.-1.0.OR.XX.LT.0.0.OR.XX.GT.BOUNDJ) GO TO 90
      IF((XX - GK * R) .LE. BOUNDJ) GO TO 90
      R = (BOUNDJ - XX) / (-1.0 * GK)
      GO TO 60
   80 IF(XX.GE.0.0.OR.S(J-N).GE.0.0) GO TO 90
      IF((XX - GK * R) .LE. 0.0) GO TO 90
      GO TO 50
   90 CONTINUE
      DO 130 I = 1,MNOW
      IF(ISEFF(I).EQ.0) GO TO 100
      G(I) = 0.0
      GO TO 130
  100 SLACKI = SLACK(I)
      SI = S(I)
      GI = 0.0
      ISTART = IROW(I)
      LAST = IROW(I+1) - 1
      DO 120 LOOK = ISTART,LAST
      J = JCOL(LOOK)
      INJ = INBASE(J)
      IF(INJ.LE.0) GO TO 110
      GI = GI - AA(LOOK ) * GR(INJ)
      GO TO 120
  110 IF(J.EQ.NEWX) GI = GI + AA(LOOK)
  120 CONTINUE
      G(I) = GI
      IF(ABS(GI).LE.TOL5) GO TO 130
      IF(SI.EQ.0.0.AND.SLACKI.NE.0.0) GO TO 130
      IF(SI * SLACKI .LT. 0.0) GO TO 130
      GI = GI * XKPOS
      T = SLACKI - GI * R
      IF(T.GE.0.0 .AND. SI.EQ.1.0 .OR. T.LE.0.0 .AND.SI.EQ.-1.0)GO TO130
      R = SLACKI / GI
      IF(R.LE.SMALL) R = 0.0
      NEWY = SIZE + I
      GR(SIZE1) = GI * XKPOS
      IF(R.EQ.0.0) GO TO 140
  130 CONTINUE
  140 RETURN
      END
```

22. SPRINT (small print)

This routine is called from IPRINT only when there are fewer than eight variables in the problem. Its sole purpose is for teaching, since it lays out the problem and its solution in a way which exactly corresponds to the natural blackboard presentation, with the A matrix bordered above and to the left by the x and y solution vectors; to the right by the b and slack $(b - Ax)$ vectors; and below by the c and $yA - c$ vectors.

It makes it simple to draw attention to the orthogonal relationship between y and $b - Ax$ and between x and $yA - c$. In the cutting plane and the QP algorithms the presence of constraints additional to those originally specified is readily apparent, and so is the zero dual value of the added constraints in the QP.

For larger problems, SPRINT is not used and the A matrix is printed in condensed form, and the vectors which are printed as columns in SPRINT (y, b, slack) are printed (in IPRINT) as rows for economy of space.

SPRINT can be removed if it is not required by simply deleting the first three executable statements in IPRINT, namely:

```
IF (N ·GE· 8) GO TO 90
CALL SPRINT
GO TO 400
```

Appendix 4, Section 3 contains an example of this print routine and of the same LP problem printed when these three statements are deleted.

It is possible that some compilers may mishandle the variable format statements; a simple solution to this problem is to remove SPRINT from the program and the three statements in IPRINT, as above, so that the A matrix and associated vectors are printed by IPRINT.

COMMON variables altered in SPRINT

PIV(J)

COMMON variables used in SPRINT

B(I)	OBJ
BOUND(J)	S(I)
C(J)	SLACK(I)
ISBND	X(J)
MNOW	Y(I)
N	YAC(J)

COMMON/AREF variables used in SPRINT

AA(LOOK)	JCOL(LOOK)
IROW(I)	

```
      SUBROUTINE SPRINT
*********************** COMMON AND TYPE STATEMENTS ********************
*********************** COMMON/AREF ***********************************
      DIMENSION  COLUMN(7),FMT1(20),FMT2(13),SI(3),FMT3(6)
      DATA  COLUMN(1)/1H1/,COLUMN(2)/1H2/,COLUMN(3)/1H3/,COLUMN(4)/1H4/,
     1      COLUMN(5)/1H5/,COLUMN(6)/1H6/,COLUMN(7)/1H7/
      DATA FMT1(1)/5H(1H ,/,FMT1(2)/8H5H I    ,/,FMT1(3)/8H5HY VEC,/,
     1     FMT1(4)/6H3HTOR,/,FMT1(5)/4H11X,/,
     2     FMT1(7)/6H(11X),/,FMT1(8)/7H1HB,8X,/,FMT1(9)/8H4HB-AX/1/,
     3     FMT1(10)/8H5X,2H--,/,
     4     FMT1(12)/8H(4H----,/,FMT1(13)/8H5H-----,/,
     5     FMT1(14)/8H2H--),16/,FMT1(15)/8HX,4H(SLA/,
     6     FMT1(16)/7H,3HCK)//,FMT1(17)/8H15X,1H(,/,
     7     FMT1(19)/6H(11X),/,FMT1(20)/4H1H))/
      DATA  FMT2(1)/8H(1H ,I2,/,FMT2(2)/8H1X,F10.4/,FMT2(3)/8H,1X,1H(,/,
     1      FMT2(5)/8H(F10.4,1/,FMT2(6)/8HX),2H) ,/,
     2      FMT2(8)/8HF8.2,1X,/,FMT2(9)/8HF10.4/15/,
     3      FMT2(10)/6HX,1H(,/,
     4      FMT2(12)/6H(11X),/,FMT2(13)/4H1H))/
      DATA  SI(1)/6H3HGE ,/,SI(2)/6H3H = ,/,SI(3)/6H3HLE ,/
      DATA  FMT3(1)/8H(1H ,14X/,FMT3(2)/6H,2H--,/,
     1      FMT3(4)/8H(4H----,/,FMT3(5)/8H5H-----,/,FMT3(6)/6H2H--))/
 9000 FORMAT(1H0,'OBJECTIVE ',F22.8)
 9004 FORMAT(1H0,15X,'J. . .    ',7(I1,10X))
 9008 FORMAT(1H0,10X,'BOUND VECTOR. . . .'/16X,7(F10.4,1X))
 9012 FORMAT(1H0,12X,'X VECTOR. . . .'/16X,7(F10.4,1X))
 9016 FORMAT(1H0,12X,'C VECTOR. . . .'/16X,7(F10.4,1X))
 9020 FORMAT(1H0,15X,12HY'A-C. . . ./16X,7(F10.4,1X))
      WRITE(6,9000) OBJ
      WRITE(6,9004)(J,J=1,N)
      IF(ISBND.EQ.0) GO TO 10
      WRITE(6,9008)(BOUND(J),J=1,N)
   10 WRITE(6,9012)(X(J),J=1,N)
      COL = COLUMN(N)
      FMT1(6)  = COL
      FMT1(11) = COL
      FMT1(18) = COL
      WRITE(6,FMT1)
      DO 40 I=1,MNOW
      DO 20 J= 1,8
   20 PIV(J) = 0.0
      ISTART = IROW(I)
      LAST = IROW(I+1) - 1
      DO 30 LOOK = ISTART, LAST
      J = JCOL(LOOK)
   30 PIV(J) = AA(LOOK)
      ISI = S(I) + 2
      FMT2(4)  = COL
      FMT2(7)  = SI(ISI)
      FMT2(11) = COL
      WRITE(6,FMT2) I,Y(I),(PIV(J),J=1,N),B(I),SLACK(I)
   40 CONTINUE
      FMT3(3) = COL
      WRITE(6,FMT3)
      WRITE(6,9016) (C(J),J=1,N)
      WRITE(6,9020) (YAC(J),J=1,N)
      RETURN
      END
```

CHAPTER 3

A Program to Solve QP

1. PROGRAM QP (quadratic programming)

The method used to solve QP problems is that of E.M.L. Beale[2] and of Land and Morton[9] and is discussed in Chapter 1.

The main routine calls QPDATA to read the data of a QP problem, then calls DOAQP (do a QP) to solve it. If DOAQP produces an optimum or an infeasible answer the accuracy of the solution is checked in CHACC, and if necessary a re-inversion is performed in REVERT. According to the value of MORE, the algorithm either stops or returns to statement 10 to read the data of another problem.

Subroutines called in QP

CHACC	QPDATA
DOAQP	REVERT
IEXIT	

COMMON variables altered in QP

ISTATE

COMMON variables used in QP

IR	ISDONE
IRMAX	MORE

```
      PROGRAM QP (INPUT,OUTPUT,TAPE5=INPUT,TAPE6=OUTPUT)
*********************** COMMON AND TYPE STATEMENTS ********************
   10 CALL QPDATA
      IF(ISDONE.EQ.1) GO TO 60
      ISTATE = 0
   20 CALL DOAQP
      IF (ISDONE .EQ. 1) GO TO 60
      IF (ISTATE .GT. 3 .AND. ISTATE .NE. 9) GO TO 40
      CALL CHACC
```

```
      IF(ISTATE.NE.7) GO TO 40
      IF(IR.GE.IRMAX) GO TO 40
      CALL REVERT
      ISTATE = 11
      GO TO 20
   40 CALL IEXIT(ISTATE)
   50 IF (MORE.NE.0) GO TO 10
   60 STOP
      END
```

2. DOAQP (do a QP)

This routine is basically very similar to DOANLP, but the linear function, c, is re-evaluated at each basis change, once feasibility has been attained, in the subroutine PRICE (after statement 40).

It is possible to add an auxiliary constraint at every basis change, once feasibility is reached, as Beale suggested. At the other extreme, one can make ordinary basis changes and only add an auxiliary constraint if the function falls from one basis change to the next. A limited amount of experimentation on some randomly generated problems, reported in [9], suggests that the version included in the listing provided here is more efficient that either of these. That is to say, no auxiliary constraints are added until the quadratic function falls from one basis change to the next, then the variable which has just left the basis is re-introduced and an auxiliary constraint is computed. Thereafter, auxiliary constraints are added at each iteration until the optimum is reached or until another extreme point of the feasible region is reached.

To apply an auxiliary constraint at every iteration (once feasibility has been attained) alter the listing as follows:

Alter the statement following 70 from

> IF (NEGROW ·EQ· O ·AND· NEGINV ·EQ· O ·AND· OBJ ·LT· PREOBJ ·OR· MNOW ·GT· M) CALL QCON

to:

> IF (NEGROW ·EQ· O ·AND· NEGINV ·EQ· O) CALL QCON

Note that Beale suggested that slack variables on auxiliary constraints should be given precedence in choosing the variable to enter the basis. The experience of 25 randomly generated QPs was that this gave a uniformly worse result (more iterations) than following the usual Simplex rule of choice, although proof of finiteness of the algorithm may be more difficult.

To choose auxiliary slack variables preferentially, alter ISOPT as follows:

Before 'DO 10' insert:

```
      YAM 2 = YAMINC
      NEWX2 = 0
```

In 'DO 10', replace IF (YRL ·GE· YAMINC) GO TO 10 by:

```
      IF (I ·GT· M) GO TO 5
      IF (YRL ·GE·YAM2) GO TO 10
      YAM2 = YRL
      NEWX2 = I + N
      GO TO 10
    5 IF (YRL ·GE· YAMINC) GO TO 10
```

After 'DO 10', insert:

```
      IF (NEWX ·NE· 0) RETURN
      NEWX = NEWX2
      YAMINC = YAM2
```

Subroutines called in DOAQP

ADDCON	PRICE
CHBSIS	PURGE
CHSLCK	QCON
FIRSTB	REDUCE
ISOPT	SEEKX
NEWVEC	SEEKY

COMMON variables altered in DOAQP

DRIVER	NEWX
ISTATE	NEWY
NEGINV	YAMINC

COMMON variables used in DOAQP

BIG	OBJ
INBASE(J)	R
ISDONE	S(I)
ITR	SIZE
ITRMAX	SIZE1
M	SLACK(I)
MNOW	XBASIS(K)
N	Y(I)
NEGROW	YAC(J)

```
      SUBROUTINE DOAQP
********************** COMMON AND TYPE STATEMENTS ********************
      PREOBJ = -BIG
      IF (ISTATE .EQ. 11) GO TO 20
      CALL FIRSTB
   10 CALL CHSLCK
      IF (ITR .LE. ITRMAX) GO TO 20
      ISTATE = 5
      GO TO 100
   20 IF (NEGROW .EQ. 0 .AND. NEGINV .EQ. 0) GO TO 40
      IF (NEGINV .NE. 0) GO TO 30
      NEWY = NEGROW + SIZE
      DRIVER = 1.0
      IF (SLACK(NEGROW) .GT. 0.0) DRIVER = -1.0
      NEGINV = SIZE1
      CALL ADDCON
      IF (ISTATE.EQ.4) GO TO 100
   30 CALL SEEKX
      IF (NEWX .NE. 0) GO TO 70
      ISTATE = 2
      GO TO 100
   40 CALL PURGE
      CALL PRICE
      IF (OBJ .GT. PREOBJ .OR. R .EQ. 0.0 .OR. MNOW .GT. M) GO TO 60
      NEWX = IXOUT
      IF (NEWX .GT. N) GO TO 50
      YAMINC = YAC(NEWX)
      IF (INBASE(NEWX) .EQ. -1) YAMINC = -YAMINC
      GO TO 70
   50 I = NEWX - N
      YAMINC = Y(I) * S(I)
      GO TO 70
   60 CALL ISOPT
      IF (NEWX .NE. 0) GO TO 70
      ISTATE = 9
      GO TO 100
   70 CALL NEWVEC
      IF (NEGROW .EQ. 0 .AND. NEGINV .EQ. 0 .AND. OBJ .LE. PREOBJ .OR.
     1      MNOW .GT. M) CALL QCON
      IF (ISDONE .EQ. 1) GO TO 100
      IF (NEGROW .EQ. 0 .AND. NEGINV .EQ. 0) PREOBJ = OBJ
      CALL SEEKY
      IF (NEWY .NE. 0) GO TO 80
      ISTATE = 3
      GO TO 100
   80 IF (NEWY .LE. SIZE) GO TO 90
      CALL ADDCON
      IF (ISTATE.EQ.4) GO TO 100
   90 IXOUT = NEWX
      IF (NEWY .NE. -1) IXOUT = XBASIS(NEWY)
      CALL CHBSIS
      CALL REDUCE
      GO TO 10
  100 RETURN
      END
```

3. PRICE

The name of this routine arises from the use of QP in the situation of a firm maximizing profit when the demand curves for its products have a downward slope, so that the price of a product is itself a function of the amount sold, and hence profit is a quadratic function of quantity produced and sold. Actually, 'price' is slightly a misnomer, since in that application it is marginal revenue rather than market price which is evaluated at each basis change.

In 'DO 20', $p = c + \bar{x}D$ is evaluated for $\bar{x}$, the present value of x, and put into the array C(J).

In 'DO 70', the y vector and $yA - c$ are computed from the new c vector. In the interests of efficiency, the computation of YAC(J) should really be removed from CHSLCK in this program, since it is only computed from the 'wrong' (previous) c vector there, and has to be recomputed here. But in order to minimize the changes to existing subroutines, it has not been so removed in this description of the program.

Since the auxiliary constraints must not remain effective if their dual values differ from zero, either positively or negatively, we must ensure that either a positive or a negative slack vector is available to be introduced, according to which move from the constraint will increase the function (they cannot both increase it). This is ensured by the statement (immediately preceding statement 50)

```
IF (S(I) * YRL ·GT· 0·0) S(I) = –S(I)
```

This converts an auxiliary constraint from a less-than-or-equal constraint to a greater-than-or-equal constraint, or vice versa.

Finally, the value of the quadratic function at the current point, $\bar{x}$, is computed by the relation OBJ $= \frac{1}{2}(c + p)\bar{x}$.

COMMON variables altered in PRICE

C(J)	Y(I)
OBJ	YAC(J)
S(I)	YR(L)

COMMON variables used in PRICE

INBASE(J)	SLACK(I)
INV(K,L)	SMALL
M	X(J)
MNOW	XBASIS(K)
N	YBASIS(L)
SIZE	

COMMON/AREF variables used in PRICE

AA(LOOK) JCOL(LOOK)
IROW(I)

COMMON/RETAIN variables altered in PRICE

KEEP(I)

COMMON/Q variables used in PRICE

D(ID, JD) KEYTOD(ID)
HOLDC(J) NUMQ

```
      SUBROUTINE PRICE
*********************** COMMON AND TYPE STATEMENTS ********************
*********************** COMMON/AREF ***********************************
*********************** COMMON/RETAIN *********************************
*********************** COMMON/Q **************************************
      DO 5 J = 1,N
      YAC(J) = 0.0
      IF (INBASE(J) .LE. 0) YAC(J) = -C(J)
    5 CONTINUE
      DO 20 ID = 1,NUMQ
      J = KEYTOD(ID)
      CJ = HOLDC(J)
      DO 10 JD = 1,NUMQ
      JJ = KEYTOD(JD)
      XJ = X(JJ)
      IF (XJ .EQ. 0.0) GO TO 10
      CJ = CJ + XJ * D(ID,JD)
   10 CONTINUE
      IF (ABS(CJ) .LE. SMALL) CJ = 0.0
      YAC(J) = 0.0
      IF (INBASE(J) .LE. 0) YAC(J) = -CJ
   20 C(J) = CJ
      DO 30 I = 1,MNOW
      IF (SLACK(I) .NE. 0.0) KEEP(I) = 0
   30 Y(I) = 0.0
      DO 70 L = 1,SIZE
      YRL = 0.0
      DO 40 K = 1,SIZE
      J = XBASIS(K)
      IF (J .GT. N) GO TO 40
      YRL = YRL + C(J) * INV(K,L)
   40 CONTINUE
      IF (ABS(YRL) .LE. SMALL) YRL = 0.0
      I = YBASIS(L)
      IF (I .LE. M) GO TO 50
      IF (S(I) * YRL .GT. 0.0) S(I) = -S(I)
   50 YR(L) = YRL
      Y(I) = YRL
      LAST = IROW(I+1) - 1
      ISTART = IROW(I)
```

```
      DO 60 LOOK = ISTART,LAST
      JJ = JCOL(LOOK)
      IF (INBASE(JJ) .GT. 0) GO TO 60
      AIJ = AA(LOOK)
      YAC(JJ) = YAC(JJ) + YRL * AIJ
   60 CONTINUE
   70 CONTINUE
      OBJ = 0.0
      DO 80 J = 1,N
      XJ = X(J)
      IF (XJ .EQ. 0.0) GO TO 80
      OBJ = OBJ + (C(J) + HOLDC(J)) * XJ
   80 CONTINUE
      OBJ = OBJ * 0.5
      RETURN
      END
```

4. PURGE

This routine removes from the A matrix, the b vector, and all the vectors associated with b, any constraints additional to the original M, which are neither currently effective, nor marked for retention in the array KEEP(I), which is in the labelled COMMON/RETAIN.

Rows to delete are searched for in 'DO 40'. If one is found, MNOW is reduced by one and the following row examined. If that is also to be deleted, MNOW is reduced again, and so on, until either it is established that there is no further row to be retained, or the next row to be retained is identified. In the former case there is a return from PURGE. In the latter case, the row to be retained is 'moved up' to fill the gap left by the one or more rows being deleted. Then control returns to 20 (immediately before 40 CONTINUE) and the next row to be retained is sought, and when found moved up, etc.

COMMON variables altered in PURGE

B(I)	SLACK(I)
ISEFF(I)	Y(I)
MNOW	YBASIS(I)
S(I)	

COMMON variables used in PURGE

M

COMMON/AREF variables altered in PURGE

AA(LOOK)	JCOL(LOOK)
IROW(I)	

COMMON/RETAIN variables altered in PURGE

KEEP(I)

```
      SUBROUTINE PURGE
*********************** COMMON AND TYPE STATEMENTS ********************
*********************** COMMON/AREF **********************************
*********************** COMMON/RETAIN ********************************
      MOVE = 0
      MSTART = MNOW
      M1 = M + 1
      IF (M1.GT.MSTART) GO TO 50
      DO 40 I = M1,MSTART
      I1 = I
      IF (ISEFF(I).NE.0 .OR. KEEP(I).NE.0) GO TO 40
      ILEFT = I - 1
   10 MNOW = MNOW - 1
   20 I1 = I1 + 1
      IF (I1.GT.MSTART) GO TO 50
      IF (ISEFF(I1).EQ.0 .AND. KEEP(I1).EQ.0) GO TO 10
      ILEFT = ILEFT + 1
      NEXT = IROW(I1)
      MOVE = NEXT - IROW(ILEFT)
      LASTIN = IROW(I1+1) - 1
      DO 30 IJ = NEXT,LASTIN
      IJNOW = IJ - MOVE
      AA(IJNOW) = AA(IJ)
   30 JCOL(IJNOW) = JCOL(IJ)
      LENGTH = LASTIN - NEXT + 1
      INEXT = ILEFT + 1
      IROW(INEXT) = IROW(ILEFT) + LENGTH
      B(ILEFT) = B(I1)
      Y(ILEFT) = Y(I1)
      SLACK(ILEFT) = SLACK(I1)
      S(ILEFT) = S(I1)
      KEEP(ILEFT) = KEEP(I1)
      ISEFF(ILEFT) = ISEFF(I1)
      L = ISEFF(ILEFT)
      IF(L.NE.0) YBASIS(L) = ILEFT
      GO TO 20
   40 CONTINUE
   50 RETURN
      END
```

5. QCON (quadratic constraint)

The A elements of the new auxiliary constraint are accumulated in PIV(J), which is first zeroed in 'DO 10'. The right-hand-side of the new auxiliary constraint is accumulated in BMNOW, which is assigned to B(MNOW) at the end. Finally, the SLACK of the new constraint = – YAMINC, the (positive) value of the function element of the entering variable. PIV(J) is copied into the array AA in the subroutine COPY. The new constraint is quite likely to have all zero coefficients in the A matrix, but the COPY routine is designed to deal with this eventuality. In such a case, the new auxiliary constraint will not be picked as the restraining constraint in SEEKY, and it will be eliminated by the following PURGE.

Subroutines called in QCON

COPY

COMMON variables altered in QCON

B(I)	S(I)
ISEFF(I)	SLACK(I)
MNOW	Y(I)
PIV(J)	

COMMON variables used in QCON

GR(K)	SMALL
N	XBASIS(K)
NEWX	XKPOS
SIZE	YAMINC

COMMON/RETAIN variables altered in QCON

KEEP(I)

COMMON/Q variables used in QCON

D(ID, JD)	KEYTOD(ID)
HOLDC(J)	NUMQ
ISQ(J)	

```
      SUBROUTINE QCON
********************** COMMON AND TYPE STATEMENTS ********************
********************** COMMON/RETAIN *********************************
********************** COMMON/Q **************************************
      MNOW = MNOW + 1
      DO 10 J = 1,N
   10 PIV(J) = 0.0
      BMNOW = 0.0
      IF (NEWX .GT. N) GO TO 30
      BMNOW = HOLDC(NEWX) * XKPOS
      IDNEWX = ISQ(NEWX)
      IF (IDNEWX .EQ. 0) GO TO 30
      DO 20 JD = 1,NUMQ
      J = KEYTOD(JD)
   20 PIV(J) = -D(IDNEWX,JD) * XKPOS
```

```
30 DO 50 K = 1,SIZE
   J = XBASIS(K)
   IF (J .GT. N) GO TO 50
   BMNOW = BMNOW - GR(K) * HOLDC(J) * XKPOS
   ID = ISQ(J)
   IF (ID .EQ. 0) GO TO 50
   DO 40 JD = 1,NUMQ
   J = KEYTOD(JD)
40 PIV(J) = PIV(J) + GR(K) * D(ID,JD) * XKPOS
50 CONTINUE
   DO 60 J = 1,N
   IF (ABS(PIV(J)) .LE. SMALL) PIV(J) = 0.0
60 CONTINUE
   IF (ABS(BMNOW) .LE. SMALL) BMNOW = 0.0
   B(MNOW) = BMNOW
   Y(MNOW) = 0.0
   SLACK(MNOW) = - YAMINC
   S(MNOW) = 1.0
   ISEFF(MNOW) = 0
   KEEP(MNOW) = 1
   CALL COPY
   RETURN
   END
```

6. QPDATA (QP data)

This subroutine reads in and initialises the data for the solution of a QP problem.

The quadratic program maximizes a quadratic function, $px + \frac{1}{2}xDx$, subject to linear constraints. The data required for this program are read in subroutine QPDATA and the information needed for the quadratic function is stored in COMMON/Q. MAXQ is the maximum number of variables which have quadratic coefficients in the function that the program can store. NUMQ is the number of such variables in a particular problem. The matrix D is stored in the array D(ID,JD). D is a symmetric matrix but this structure has not been used in its storage. KEYTOD(ID) is the number, J, of the original variable, x_j, which is associated with the ID row and column of the array D. MAXQ is the dimensions of the arrays KEYTOD and D. The array ISQ(J) indicates whether or not an original variable, x_j, enters the function non-linearly; ISQ(J) = 0 if x_j has no non-linear terms, otherwise ISQ(J) is the cross reference to the row and column of the array D in which the quadratic coefficients appear. HOLDC(J) contains the vector p of the quadratic function. MAXN is the dimension of the arrays ISQ and HOLDC.

The first executable statement of QPDATA initializes MAXQ (see Chapter 7, Section 4). Throughout this subroutine ISDONE has the value 0 unless an error condition occurs in which case ISDONE is set to 1 and control returns to the calling routine. The subroutine reads M, N and NUMQ, and checks that NUMQ satisfies $1 \leqslant \text{NUMQ} \leqslant \text{MAXQ}$. The arrays ISQ, KEYTOD and D are initialized to zero.

The statements from statement 50 to statement 120 are concerned with reading and checking the D matrix. Each card is read, listed and checked. A card contains up to four non-zero matrix coefficients. Also on the card are the variables associated with the row and column of the D matrix coefficient. The coefficients may be in any order, they do *not* have to be ordered either by rows or by columns. The D matrix is symmetric, $D_{ij} = D_{ji}$, and it is not necessary to specify to the program both coefficients; the subroutine assigns to D(ID, JD) and D(JD, ID) the same value. The subroutine checks that JD and ID, the variables associated with a column and a row respectively of D are within the range 1 to N and that the number of quadratic variables is not greater than NUMQ.

The linear part of the objective function, the p vector, and the linear constraints are read in by subroutine DATA. Subroutine QPDATA checks that the size of the problem specified in QPDATA and in DATA are the same, i.e., that M equals MHOLD and N equals NHOLD.

The statements from 140 until the statement before 170 print all the coefficients of the objective function. Then KEEP(I) is initialized to zero. A problem may be bounded with respect to the non-linear objective function but unbounded with respect to the linear part of the objective function, px. In order that the algorithm does not terminate prematurely with an unbounded solution, the variables that are unbounded are assigned a bound of BIG. If necessary ISBND is set to 1 as the problem is now one in bounded variables. Finally HOLDC(J) is set equal to the linear part of the objective function which has been read (in subroutine DATA) into C(J).

The format of the input data to QP is described in Appendix 3.2.

Subroutines called in QPDATA

DATA

COMMON variables altered in QPDATA

BOUND(J)	M
ISBND	N
ISDONE	

COMMON variables used in QPDATA

BIG
C(J)

COMMON/RETAIN variables altered in QPDATA

KEEP(I)

COMMON/Q variables altered in QPDATA

D(ID, JD)	KEYTOD(ID)
HOLDC(J)	MAXQ
ISQ(J)	NUMQ

```
      SUBROUTINE QPDATA
********************** COMMON AND TYPE STATEMENTS ********************
********************** COMMON/RETAIN *********************************
********************** COMMON/Q **************************************
      DIMENSION K1(4),K2(4),F(4)
 9000 FORMAT (8I10)
 9004 FORMAT (1H1,'M = ',I3,', N = ',I3, ', NUMBER OF VARIABLES WITH NON
     1-LINEAR COEFFICIENTS = ',I5,'.')
 9008 FORMAT (1H0,'CARD INPUT FOR THE NON-LINEAR COEFFICIENTS OF THE FUN
     1CTION. . . .')
 9012 FORMAT (4(2I5,F10.0))
 9016 FORMAT (1H ,4('(',I5,')(',I5,')(',F8.2,')  '))
 9020 FORMAT (1H0,'P VECTOR . . . .')
 9024 FORMAT (1H0,12(6X,I3,1X))
 9028 FORMAT (1H ,12(F9.2,1X))
 9032 FORMAT (1H0,11X,'THE D MATRIX OF NON-LINEAR COEFFICIENTS. . . .')
 9034 FORMAT (1H0,8X,'COLUMN',9(I3,8X))
 9036 FORMAT (1H ,'ROW',3X,'VARIABLE',9(I3,8X))
 9040 FORMAT (1H ,I3,1X,I4,1X,9(F10.4,1X))
 9050 FORMAT (1H0,'ROW',6X,'THE D MATRIX CONTINUES. . . .')
 9054 FORMAT (1H0,'IN THE FOLLOWING OUTPUT, THE C VECTOR CONTAINS THE PA
     1RTIAL DERIVATIVES OF THE QUADRATIC FUNCTION.  THERE MAY BE'/' MORE
     1 CONSTRAINTS PRESENT THAN THE M SPECIFIED ORIGINALLY, BUT THEY HAV
     2E ZERO DUAL VALUES.'/' ALL VARIABLES HAVE BEEN ASSUMED TO HAVE AN
     3UPPER BOUND OF 10E10 UNLESS OTHERWISE SPECIFIED.')
 9100 FORMAT (1H0,'THE NUMBER OF VARIABLES WITH QUADRATIC COEFFICIENTS M
     1UST BE BETWEEN 1 AND',I5,'  YOU HAVE SPECIFIED ',I5,'.')
 9104 FORMAT (1H0,'YOU HAVE SPECIFIED A QUADRATIC COEFFICIENT FOR A VARI
     1ABLE OUTSIDE THE RANGE 1 TO N, NAMELY ',I5,'.'/' IT HAS BEEN IGNOR
     1ED.')
 9108 FORMAT (1H0,'YOU HAVE SPECIFIED THAT THERE ARE ',I2,' VARIABLES WI
     1TH NON-LINEAR COEFFICIENTS, BUT HAVE NOW LISTED ',I5,'.')
 9112 FORMAT (1H0,'YOU HAVE SPECIFIED TWO DIFFERENT VALUES FOR M OR FOR
     1N.')
      MAXQ = **
      ISDONE = 0
   10 READ (5,9000) M,N,NUMQ
      WRITE (6,9004) M,N,NUMQ
      IF(NUMQ .GE. 1 .AND. NUMQ .LE. MAXQ) GO TO 20
      WRITE (6,9100) MAXQ,NUMQ
      ISDONE = 1
      GO TO 200
   20 DO 30 J = 1,N
   30 ISQ(J) = 0
      DO 40 I = 1,NUMQ
      KEYTOD(I) = 0
      DO 40 J = 1,NUMQ
   40 D(I,J) = 0.0
```

```
      WRITE (6,9008)
      NEXT = 0
   50 READ (5,9012)((K1(J),K2(J),F(J)),J=1,4)
      WRITE (6,9016)((K1(J),K2(J),F(J)),J= 1,4)
      IF (K1(1) .EQ. 99999) GO TO 130
      DO 120 K = 1,4
      ID = K1(K)
      IF (ID .GE. 1 .AND. ID .LE. N) GO TO 60
      IF (ID .LE. 0) GO TO 50
      WRITE (6,9104) ID
      GO TO 120
   60 KEYI = ISQ(ID)
      IF (KEYI .NE. 0) GO TO 80
      NEXT = NEXT + 1
      IF (NEXT .LE. NUMQ) GO TO 70
      WRITE (6,9108) NUMQ ,NEXT
      ISDONE = 1
      GO TO 200
   70 ISQ(ID) = NEXT
      KEYTOD(NEXT) = ID
      KEYI = NEXT
   80 JD = K2(K)
      IF (JD .GE. 1 .AND. JD .LE. N) GO TO 90
      WRITE (6,9104) JD
      GO TO 120
   90 KEYJ = ISQ(JD)
      IF (KEYJ .NE. 0) GO TO 110
      NEXT = NEXT + 1
      IF (NEXT .LE. NUMQ) GO TO 100
      WRITE (6,9108) NUMQ,NEXT
      ISDONE = 1
      GO TO 200
  100 ISQ(JD) = NEXT
      KEYTOD(NEXT) = JD
      KEYJ = NEXT
  110 COEFF = F(K)
      D(KEYI,KEYJ) = COEFF
      D(KEYJ,KEYI) = COEFF
  120 CONTINUE
      GO TO 50
  130 MHOLD = M
      NHOLD = N
      CALL DATA
      IF (ISDONE .EQ. 1) GO TO 200
      IF (M .EQ. MHOLD .AND. N .EQ. NHOLD) GO TO 140
      WRITE (6,9112)
      ISDONE = 1
      GO TO 200
  140 WRITE (6,9020)
      ISTART = 1
      IEND = ISTART + 11
  145 IF (N .LE. IEND) IEND = N
      WRITE (6,9024) (J,J=ISTART,IEND)
      WRITE (6,9028)(C(J),J=ISTART,IEND)
      IF(IEND .GE. N) GO TO 150
      ISTART = IEND + 1
      IEND = IEND + 12
```

```
      GO TO 145
  150 IEND = 9
      ISTART = 1
      WRITE (6,9032)
  155 IF(NUMQ .LE. IEND) IEND = NUMQ
      WRITE (6,9034) (JD,JD=ISTART, IEND)
      WRITE (6,9036) (KEYTOD(JD), JD = ISTART, IEND)
      DO 160 ID = 1,NUMQ
      WRITE (6,9040) ID, KEYTOD(ID), (D(ID,JD), JD = ISTART, IEND)
  160 CONTINUE
      IF(IEND .GE. NUMQ) GO TO 170
      ISTART = IEND + 1
      IEND = ISTART + 8
      WRITE(6,9050)
      GO TO 155
  170 DO 175 I = 1,M
  175 KEEP(I) = 0
      WRITE (6,9054)
      DO 180 J = 1,N
      IF (BOUND(J) .EQ. -1.0) BOUND(J) = BIG
  180 HOLDC(J) = C(J)
      IF(ISBND.EQ.0) ISBND = 1
  200 RETURN
      END
```

CHAPTER 4

Method of Integer Forms—MIF

1. INTRODUCTION

This program is designed to solve an integer LP, in which *all* the variables have to take integer values. The algorithm used in this program is based upon Gomory's cutting planes, described in Chapter 1.

The data for this program are the same as for an LP problem except that the elements of upper bound vector, the b vector and the A matrix must have integer values.

2. PROGRAM STRUCTURE

This program, MIF, uses a main routine, the LP subroutines of Chapter 2, subroutine PURGE of Chapter 3, and two additional subroutines, IFDATA (integer forms data) and INTCON (integer constraint). The main routine directs the algorithm by calling subroutines LP, INTCON and PURGE. The main routine is described in greater detail below and IFDATA and INTCON are described later in this chapter.

3. A COMMON STATEMENT FOR MIF

The datum needed for communication between the main routine and subroutine INTCON is stored in labelled COMMON/IF.

COMMON/IF/ISINT

ISINT (is integer) records whether an integer solution has (ISINT = 1), or has not (ISINT = 0), been found in subroutine INTCON.

4. PROGRAM MIF

The program starts by calling subroutine IFDATA which reads in and checks the problem data.

The statements from 30 to 60 form a loop. Ignoring the exits from it, the loop consists of three subroutines: LP, PURGE and INTCON. Subroutine LP finds an optimal solution to an LP problem starting from either no basis, ISTATE = 0, or from an infeasible basis, ISTATE = 11. Subroutine PURGE deletes from the A matrix and from the b vector any unwanted constraints. Subroutine INTCON checks whether a solution is integer and if it is not generates, if possible, a series of cutting planes that 'cut off' part of the feasible region including the current non-integer solution. If a new constraint is generated the value of MNOW is increased in INTCON so that on return from INTCON, MNOW is not equal to MHOLD, the previous value of MNOW.

The possible exits from the loop are:

1. ISTATE ≠ 1, subroutine LP cannot find an accurate optimal solution to an LP problem;
2. ISTATE = 5, the iteration count, ITR, is greater than its maximum, ITRMAX;
3. ISTATE = 7, the reinversion count, IR, is greater than its maximum, IRMAX;
4. ISDONE = 1, there is insufficient space in either of the arrays AA or B to store the coefficients of another constraint;
5. MNOW = MHOLD and ISINT = 0, the solution is non-integer but INTCON is unable to generate a new constraint (this is either because the tolerances have incorrect values or because the values of the constraint coefficients have become so large and the 'cuts' therefore so small that we believe it is not possible to solve the problem by this cutting plane algorithm);
6. MNOW = MHOLD and ISINT = 1, the optimal integer solution has been found.

Subroutines called in MIF

IEXIT	IPRINT
IFDATA	LP
INTCON	PURGE

COMMON variables altered in MIF

IR	ITR
ISTATE	

COMMON variables used in MIF

IRMAX	MNOW
ISDONE	MORE
ITRMAX	

COMMON/IF variables used in MIF
ISINT

```
      PROGRAM MIF (INPUT,OUTPUT,TAPE5=INPUT,TAPE6=OUTPUT)
*********************** COMMON AND TYPE STATEMENTS *********************
********************** COMMON/IF *************************************
 9000 FORMAT(1H0,'THE SOLUTION IS NON INTEGER BUT THE ALGORITHM IS UNABL
     1E TO GENERATE A NEW CONSTRAINT EITHER BECAUSE IT CANNOT SATISFY'/'
     2 THE TOLERANCE CONDITIONS OR BECAUSE THE ABSOLUTE VALUE OF THE RIG
     3HT HAND SIDE IS GREATER THAN 5000')
   20 CALL IFDATA
      IF (ISDONE .EQ. 1) GO TO 90
      ISTATE = 0
   30 IRHLD = IR
      ITRHLD = ITR
      CALL LP
      ITR = ITRHLD + ITR
      IR = IRHLD + IR
      IF (ISTATE .NE. 1) GO TO 70
      IF (ITR .LE. ITRMAX) GO TO 40
      ISTATE = 5
      GO TO 70
   40 IF (IR .LE. IRMAX) GO TO 50
      ISTATE = 7
      GO TO 70
   50 CALL PURGE
      MHOLD = MNOW
      CALL INTCON
      IF (ISDONE .EQ. 1) GO TO 80
      IF (MNOW .NE. MHOLD) GO TO 60
      ISTATE = 8
      IF(ISINT.EQ.1) GO TO 70
      WRITE(6,9000)
      CALL IPRINT
      GO TO 80
   60 ISTATE = 11
      GO TO 30
   70 CALL IEXIT(ISTATE)
   80 IF (MORE .NE. 0) GO TO 20
   90 STOP
      END
```

5. IFDATA (integer forms data)

The data for the Method of Integer Forms is the same as for an LP except that the coefficients of the BOUND and B arrays and of the A matrix must be integer. These coefficients are read and stored as real variables and it is necessary to check that they have integer values.

IFDATA starts by calling DATA which reads the problem specification. If the maximum number of iterations, ITRMAX, has been assigned its default value, it is multiplied by the number of variables, N. As a series of LPs are to be solved this should ensure that the maximum number of iterations is adequate.

In the 'DO 20' loop the array BOUND is checked to ensure that the coefficients have integer values. If there is a non-integer coefficient an error message is printed and ISDONE is set to 1 which indicates to the calling program that there is an error in the data. In the 'DO 30' loop the coefficients of the array AA, and in the 'DO 40' loop the coefficients of the array B, are similarly checked for non-integer values. Also in the 'DO 40' loop the array KEEP is initialized to zero.

The format of the input data to MIF is described in Appendix 3.3.

Subroutines called in IFDATA

DATA

COMMON variables altered in IFDATA

ISDONE
ITRMAX

COMMON variables used in IFDATA

B(I)	M
BOUND(J)	N
ISBND	

COMMON/AREF variables used in IFDATA

AA(LOOK)
IROW(I)

COMMON/RETAIN variables altered in IFDATA

KEEP(I)

```
      SUBROUTINE IFDATA
*********************** COMMON AND TYPE STATEMENTS ********************
*********************** COMMON/AREF ***********************************
*********************** COMMON/RETAIN *********************************
 9000 FORMAT(1H0,'YOU HAVE A NON INTEGER COEFFICIENT ',F12.3,' IN UPPER
     1BOUND ',I6,'.'/' THE ALGORITHM IS NOT APPLICABLE.')
 9004 FORMAT(1H0,'YOU HAVE A NON INTEGER COEFFICIENT ',F12.3,' IN CONSTR
     1AINT ',I6,'.'/' THE ALGORITHM IS NOT APPLICABLE.')
 9008 FORMAT(1H0,'YOU HAVE A NON INTEGER COEFFICIENT ',F12.3,' IN THE RI
     1GHT HAND SIDE OF CONSTRAINT ',I6,'.'/' THE ALGORITHM IS NOT APPLIC
     2ABLE.')
```

```
10 CALL DATA
   IJK = ISBND
   IF(IJK.EQ.-1) IJK = N
   IF(ITRMAX.EQ.3*(M+N+IJK)) ITRMAX = ITRMAX * N
   DO 20 J= 1,N
   BOUNDJ = BOUND(J)
   IB = BOUNDJ
   FIB = IB
   IF (FIB .EQ. BOUNDJ) GO TO 20
   WRITE(6,9000) BOUNDJ,J
   ISDONE = 1
20 CONTINUE
   LAST = IROW(M+1) - 1
   DO 30 LOOK = 1,LAST
   AIJ = AA(LOOK)
   IAIJ = AIJ
   FAIJ = IAIJ
   IF (FAIJ .EQ. AIJ) GO TO 30
   WRITE(6,9004) AIJ,I
   ISDONE = 1
30 CONTINUE
   DO 40 I = 1,M
   KEEP(I) = 0
   BI = B(I)
   IBI = BI
   FIBI = IBI
   IF (FIBI .EQ. BI) GO TO 40
   WRITE(6,9008) BI,I
   ISDONE = 1
40 CONTINUE
   RETURN
   END
```

6. INTCON (integer constraint)

The subroutine starts by initializing the tolerances, TOLIF1 which is used to test whether a coefficient has an integer value and TOLIF2 which is used to test whether the accuracy of a new constraint is adequate (see also Chapter 7, Section 2).

'DO 90' is the main loop of INTCON which computes a constraint from every row, K, of the inverse which has a non-integer XR(K). The statements at the beginning of the loop, to statement 10, are concerned with testing whether a basic variable has an integer value, i.e., whether XR(K) is integer. If it is integer then control passes to the end of the loop, otherwise ISINT is set to 0, and MNOW incremented by 1. The fractional part, or cut, of the new constraint is stored in DIF. The A matrix coefficients are accumulated in the array PIV, which is first zeroed in 'DO 20' and the b vector coefficient is accumulated in BMNOW which is initially zeroed.

In 'DO 60' each element of the selected row of the inverse is split into its integer part, ELINT, and its fractional part, FRAC. ELINT and FRAC are multiplied by SI, where SI equals S(I) in the case of an inequality constraint, while in the case of an equality constraint SI = 1·0 if the less-than-or-equal side of the equality is effective and SI = −1·0 if the greater-than-or-equal side is effective.

We have to calculate the vector t of coefficients of the new constraint in terms of the original variables (see Chapter 1). Note that $t = fP$ implies that the row t can be computed by multiplying the row of fractional parts in the basis (f) by the columns of the basis. However, it is also true that $t = (w - d)P = wP - dP = e_k - dP$. Since e_k, d, and P are entirely integer, an *exact* calculation of t, with no problems of rounding error, can be made by using the latter relationship for the part of t associated with the current basic variables t^R. For the non-basic part, t^U, however, d^U is not available, and hence the alternative calculation is used, $t^U = f^R U - f^U$ (i.e., $f^R U$ rounded down to the integers below).

Since t^R is calculated as $e_k - d^R R$, before 'DO 60' PIV(J) is zeroed and a 1·0 is put into the element of PIV which relates to x_k, the basic variable from whose row of the inverse the new constraint is being generated (i.e., PIV is set equal to e_k). The elements, AIJ, of the I (= YBASIS(L)) constraint through the A matrix are picked up in 'DO 50'. The basic variable elements, t^R, are computed by $e_k - d^R R$, i.e. ELINT * AIJ is subtracted from PIV(J) each time. The non-basic elements, $f^R U$, are computed by adding FRAC * AIJ into PIV(J). In 'DO 60' BMNOW is also accumulated as $f^R b^R$, i.e., FRAC * B(I).

In 'DO 80' the non-basic elements of t, t^U, are reduced to the greatest integers with a positive fractional part less-than-or-equal (or greater-than-or-equal) to the element of $f^R U$ (depending on whether the variables are non-basic at their lower or upper bounds respectively). Also the value of the slack of the new constraint at the current solution, $\bar{x}$, i.e., $t\bar{x}$, is accumulated in SLK.

BMNOW is rounded to the nearest integer with a positive fractional part. Theoretically SLK and the cut, DIF, should be identical in value though opposite in sign. The constraint is rejected if the sum of SLK and DIF is not within a tolerance or if the value of BMNOW is greater than 5000·0. In the latter case the values of the coefficients of the added constraints have become so large that a cutting plane will be of little or no use and thus it may well be that the problem cannot be solved by this cutting plane algorithm. A measure of the amount cut off the feasible region is the extent of the parallel shift of the new constraint from its position at the current basic point, $px \leqslant d_0 + f_0$ to its cutting position $px \leqslant d_0$. If f_0 is very small relative to d_0, the parallel shift is very small. Since f_0 is necessarily less than

1·0, constraints are rejected if d_0 is greater than 5000. If this restriction is not made it will be observed that the subsequent added constraints tend to have greater and greater values of the coefficients, and eventually the algorithm fails on some tolerance check or another due to the basic matrix becoming too ill-conditioned for the computer to handle.

If a new constraint is accepted, it is copied by subroutine COPY into the AA array, and the MNOW elements of the other associated arrays are updated and NEGROW computed. It is quite possible for the same new constraint to be added more than once. Although any constraints which are not explicitly effective will subsequently be removed in PURGE, it might be worth checking for each row that DIF is not the same (to a tolerance) as any previous new constraint before calculating the rest of the new constraint. This has not been done.

Subroutines called in INTCON

COPY

COMMON variables altered in INTCON

B(I)	PIV(J)
ISEFF(I)	S(I)
MNOW	SLACK(I)
NEGROW	Y(I)

COMMON variables used in INTCON

BOUND(J)	X(J)
INBASE(J)	XBASIS(K)
INV(K,L)	XR(K)
ISDONE	YBASIS(L)
N	YR(L)
SIZE	

COMMON/AREF variables used in INTCON

AA(LOOK)	JCOL(LOOK)
IROW(I)	

COMMON/RETAIN variables altered in INTCON

KEEP(I)

COMMON/IF variables altered in INTCON

ISINT

```
      SUBROUTINE INTCON
********************** COMMON AND TYPE STATEMENTS ********************
********************** COMMON/AREF ***********************************
********************** COMMON/RETAIN *********************************
********************** COMMON/IF *************************************
      TOLIF1 = 1.0E-5
      TOLIF2 = TOLIF1 * 10.0
      ISINT = 1
      NEGROW = 0
      BIGNEG = 0.0
      DO 90 K = 1,SIZE
      XRK = XR(K)
      ITX = XRK + TOLIF1
      XX = ITX
      DIF = XRK - XX
      IF (DIF .LT. TOLIF1) GO TO 90
      ISINT = 0
      MNOW = MNOW + 1
      BMNOW = 0.0
      DO 20 J = 1,N
   20 PIV(J) = 0.0
      J = XBASIS(K)
      PIV(J) = 1.0
      DO 60 L = 1,SIZE
      I = YBASIS(L)
      SI = S(I)
      IF (SI .NE. 0.0 ) GO TO 30
      SI = 1.0
      IF (YR(L) .LT. 0.0) SI = -1.0
   30 EL  = INV(K,L) * SI
      ELL = EL + TOLIF1
      IT = ELL
      ELINT = IT
      IF (ELL .LT. 0.0) ELINT = ELINT - 1.0
      FRAC = (EL - ELINT) * SI
      ELINT = ELINT * SI
      LAST = IROW(I+1) - 1
      ISTART = IROW(I)
      DO 50 LOOK = ISTART,LAST
      J = JCOL(LOOK)
      AIJ = AA(LOOK)
      IF (INBASE(J) .LE. 0) GO TO 40
      PIV(J) = PIV(J) - ELINT * AIJ
      GO TO 50
   40 PIV(J) = PIV(J) + FRAC * AIJ
   50 CONTINUE
      BMNOW = BMNOW + FRAC * B(I)
   60 CONTINUE
      SLK = 0.0
      DO 80 J = 1,N
      P = PIV(J)
      INJ  = INBASE(J)
      IF (INJ .LE. 0) GO TO 65
      SLK = SLK + P * X(J)
      GO TO 80
   65 PP = P + TOLIF1
      IT = PP
```

```
      PPP = IT
      IF (PP .LT. 0) PPP = PPP - 1.0
      IF (INJ .EQ. 0) GO TO 70
      IF(P - PPP .GE. TOLIF1) PPP = PPP + 1.0
      BMNOW = BMNOW + BOUND(J) * (PPP - P)
      SLK = SLK + PPP * X(J)
   70 PIV(J) = PPP
   80 CONTINUE
      IT = BMNOW
      TEMP = IT
      IF(BMNOW.LT.0.0) TEMP = TEMP - 1.0
      SLK = TEMP - SLK
      IF(ABS(SLK+DIF).LE.TOLIF2.AND.ABS(BMNOW).LE.5000.) GO TO 85
      MNOW = MNOW - 1
      GO TO 90
   85 CALL COPY
      IF (ISDONE .NE. 0) GO TO 100
      B(MNOW) = TEMP
      S(MNOW) = 1.0
      SLACK(MNOW) = SLK
      Y(MNOW) = 0.0
      ISEFF(MNOW) = 0
      KEEP(MNOW) = 0
      IF (DIF .LE. BIGNEG) GO TO 90
      BIGNEG = DIF
      NEGROW = MNOW
   90 CONTINUE
  100 RETURN
      END
```

CHAPTER 5

A Branch and Bound Algorithm for Discrete Programming

1. INTRODUCTION

The algorithm is described in broad terms in Chapter 1.

As well as the block of COMMON storage required for a simple LP, this algorithm uses a labelled COMMON, as follows:

```
COMMON/BBB/HLDBND(MAXN),JDISC(MAXN),
2 FUNCL(MAXD),FUNCR(MAXD),INTX(MAXD),IRIGHT(MAXD),LEFT(MAXD),
3 RATEL(MAXD),RATER(MAXD),VALUE(MAXD),
4 BEFORE,BEST,FIXOBJ,FUNC,IBEST,INTOBJ,IPRBB,IRBB,IRBBM,ITAIL
5 ITRBB,ITRBBM,KHERE,LEFORT,LEVEL,MAXD,NEWD,NEWUP,NEXNUM,NUMBES,
6 NUMD,PREOBJ,RATIOD,RATIOU,TOLBB1,TOLBB2,YACD,YACUP
```

MAXN, and MAXD (maximum number of discrete variables) must of course be replaced by the appropriate numbers for use in the program. HLDBND(J) is used to hold the values of the upper bounds of the variables, since as variables are fixed during the algorithm the values of BOUND(J) are set at zero. JDISC(J) indicates for each variable whether or not it is discrete (JDISC(J) = 0 indicates a continuous variable) and its step size (JDISC(J) = 1 for a simple integer variable). Note that a large step size is to be preferred to a large element in A.

The remaining arrays are used to record the chain from the current solution back to the LP solution, the origin of the tree of explorations. INTX(JJ) contains the identity of the variable fixed at each LEVEL, JJ; VALUE(JJ) contains the value at which INTX(JJ) is fixed.

LEFT(JJ) contains the next value remaining to be considered below that at which the variable INTX(JJ) is currently fixed. Initially this will be one discrete step lower than its current value. But at later stages it may be two or more steps lower, when the intermediate steps have already been examined.

FUNCL(JJ) contains the upper bound of the function if the variable INTX(JJ) is fixed at LEFT(JJ), and RATEL(JJ) contains the rate (per step) at which the function falls as INTX(JJ) is further reduced by one step.

Similarly, FUNCR(JJ) contains the upper bound of the function if the variable INTX(JJ) is fixed at IRIGHT(JJ), the next available value greater than VALUE(JJ). And RATER(JJ) contains the rate of decrease of the function as INTX(JJ) is further increased.

If the values to the left or the right are known to lead to infeasibility, FUNCL(JJ) or FUNCR(JJ) is set at −BIG. This is obviously the case if LEFT(JJ) is less than zero or IRIGHT(JJ) is greater than the upper bound of variable INTX(JJ). Thus this algorithm can be used, albeit somewhat clumsily, even if all the discrete variables are (0,1) variables.

BEST is the function value of the best discrete solution found so far. It is set initially at −BIG, and IBEST is the greatest integer in BEST.

FIXOBJ (fixed part of the objective) is that part of the function, FUNC, due to the variables currently at fixed values. FUNC = OBJ + FIXOBJ.

INTOBJ (integer objective) is read in the data input and is zero if the optimum function value may be non-integer and one if it must be integer.

IPRBB (I print in BB) controls the amount of information printed at each tail of the tree (see ISTAIL).

ITRBB is the total number of Simplex iterations, and ITRBBM the maximum number. Similarly IRBB is the total number of re-inversions and IRBBM the maximum number.

MAXD is the greatest number of discrete variables that the program will handle. Its value is set in BBDATA.

ITAIL = 0 if the current solution is not a tail of the tree; = 1 if it is a discrete solution; = 2 if the current has function lower than BEST; = 3 if the current solution is infeasible.

LEFORT (left or right) is −1 if the current move is being made to the left, and is +1 if the move is to the right. It is important to know this. For instance, if a solution proves to be an infeasible tail, all values of INTX(LEVEL) to the right of VALUE(LEVEL) also lead to infeasibility if LEFORT is +1, but it is the values to the left which are infeasible if LEFORT is −1.

The other variables in COMMON/BBB will be explained as they are used, and are also described in Appendix 2.

2. PROGRAM BB

The data for a branch and bound problem are read in BBDATA, and the variables controlling the calculation are initialized there. There is provision in the program for restarting the calculation with a record of the state of the tree carried over from a previous run of the program. If such a record has been read in, LEVEL will not be equal to zero after BBDATA.

At statement 20, LP is called, and so long as there is an optimal or an infeasible outcome the algorithm proceeds. If the calculation is restarting, a statement to that effect is printed, otherwise a statement of the LP solution is made, in more or less detail according to the value of IPRBB.

After statement 30, the routine ISTAIL determines whether the present solution is a tail of the tree. A check is made to see if the number of remaining iterations allowed (ITRBBM – ITRBB) is great enough (> MNOW) to make it almost certain that the program will be able to get round to this point again without violating the maximum. If not PNODE (punch a node) is called to punch out sufficient data to restart the program if required.

If the limit is not yet in sight and ITAIL = 0, the current solution is not a tail, and BRANCH is called to further partition the feasible region by fixing a new variable, and control returns to statement 20 to obtain the LP solution to the new main branch.

If the current solution is a tail, BACKUP is called to backtrack along the chain of left and right branches until one is found for which the upper bound on the function is better than the best solution found so far (if one has yet been found). In this case also, control returns to 20 to find the LP solution for the new branch. It is in BACKUP that it may be found that the exploration is complete: that no partition of the feasible region has a better feasible value of the function than a discrete solution already found.

If the restart facility is not required, the subroutines PNODE and RESTRT (restart, called in BBDATA) can be omitted and the three statements omitted which are immediately before statement 35, namely:

```
IF (ITRBBM – ITRBB·GT·MNOW·OR·LEVEL·EQ·O) GO TO 35
CALL PNODE
GO TO 60
```

Similarly in BBDATA, the two statements immediately before 120 may be removed, namely:

```
IF (IREST·EQ·O) GO TO 120
CALL RESTRT
```

Subroutines called in PROGRAM BB

BACKUP	IPRINT
BBDATA	ISTAIL
BRANCH	LP
IEXIT	PNODE

COMMON variables altered in PROGRAM BB

ISTATE

COMMON variables used in PROGRAM BB

ISDONE	N
IR	NEWX
ITR	OBJ
MNOW	X(J)
MORE	

COMMON/BBB variables altered in PROGRAM BB

FUNC	ITAIL
IRBB	ITRBB

COMMON/BBB variables used in PROGRAM BB

FIXOBJ	ITRBBM
IPRBB	LEVEL

```
      PROGRAM BB(INPUT,OUTPUT,PUNCH,TAPE5=INPUT,TAPE6=OUTPUT,
     1          TAPE7=PUNCH,TAPE8=INPUT)
********************** COMMON AND TYPE STATEMENTS ********************
********************** COMMON/BBB ***********************************
 9000 FORMAT (1H1,'THE LP OPTIMUM, WITH FUNCTION VALUE ',F20.7,', REACHE
     1D AT ITERATION ',I5,', IS AS FOLLOWS...')
 9004 FORMAT (8(1X,F14.7))
 9008 FORMAT(1H0,'THE FUNCTION VALUE AT THE LP OPTIMUM OF THE RESTART NO
     1DE IS ',F20.7,' REACHED AT ITERATION ',I5)
   10 CALL BBDATA
      IF(ISDONE.EQ.1) GO TO 70
      IREST = 0
      IF(LEVEL.NE.0) IREST = 1
      ISTATE = 0
   20 CALL LP
      ITRBB = ITRBB + ITR
      IRBB = IRBB + IR
      IF (ISTATE .GT. 2) GO TO 50
      IF(IREST.EQ.0) GO TO 25
      WRITE(6,9008) OBJ,ITR
      IREST = 0
      GO TO 30
   25 IF (LEVEL .NE. 0) GO TO 30
      IF(ISTATE.EQ.1) WRITE(6,9000) OBJ,ITR
      IF(ISTATE.EQ.1) WRITE(6,9004) (X(J),J=1,N)
      IF(IPRBB.GE.1) CALL IPRINT
   30 FUNC = OBJ + FIXOBJ
      ITAIL = 0
      CALL ISTAIL
      IF (ISDONE .EQ. 1) GO TO 60
      IF(ITRBBM ITRBB.GT.MNOW.OR.LEVEL.EQ.0) GO TO 35
      CALL PNODE
      GO TO 60
   35 IF (ITAIL .GT. 0) GO TO 40
      CALL BRANCH
```

```
      ISTATE = 2
      IF (NEWX .EQ. 0) GO TO 30
      ISTATE = 12
      GO TO 20
   40 CALL BACKUP
      IF (ISDONE .EQ. 1) GO TO 60
      ISTATE = 10
      GO TO 20
   50 CALL IEXIT(ISTATE)
   60 IF (MORE .NE. 0) GO TO 10
   70 STOP
      END
```

3. BACKUP (back up)

BACKUP is entered when ISTAIL has established that the present solution is a tail of the tree. The various arrays which describe the present state of the tree are currently of length LEVEL. Each vertex of the tree is described by a current fixed value of some variable (the 'central' value), a left-hand discrete value LEFT(JJ) with an upper bound on the function FUNCL(JJ) and a right-hand discrete value IRIGHT(JJ) with an upper bound on the function FUNCR(JJ). The central value of the LEVEL vertex has been disposed of by discovering that it corresponds to a tail.

BACKUP examines first the left-hand and right-hand branches at LEVEL. If INTOBJ = 1, the optimum function value must be an integer; and if any partition of the feasible region is to contain a better solution than has been obtained so far, it must have an upper bound at least an integer lower than that best solution. If INTOBJ = 0, the comparison is simply between the upper bound of the partition and BEST. If the upper bounds on the function for both branches are sufficiently low, LEVEL is reduced by one, the upper bound on the variable is restored to its original value from the value 0·0 which it had whilst fixed. Control then goes to 40 where the B(I) array is restored to its value before this variable was fixed and so also is FIXOBJ. Simultaneously, the vector of changes in that part of the B(I) array associated with the currently effective constraints is accumulated in GR(L) (which was zeroed in 'DO 5').

The statement 'IF (LEVEL ·EQ· LEVNOW) GO TO 60' eliminates the other cases, where LEVEL has not been reduced. If LEVEL is not yet zero, the whole routine is entered again at 10.

Eventually either LEVEL is reduced to zero, in which case the algorithm is complete, or a left-hand or right-hand value better than BEST is discovered, and control goes to 20. If FUNCR(LEVEL) is greater than or equal to FUNCL(LEVEL) the next move will be to the right and the updating of the tree vectors is done between 30 and 40. Otherwise the next move is to the left and the updating is carried out in the part of the subroutine before 30. In this case also, the B(I) array and FIXOBJ are corrected, but since LEVEL equals LEVNOW (i.e., it has not been reduced in this scan through BACKUP) a new vertex to be explored has been discovered. The B(I) array has been continuously corrected through the backtracking procedure, but XR(K) has not been corrected. If the current basis is to be used as a starting point for the next LP calculation, the XR(K) array will have to be recomputed by adding the product of the GR(L) array (which contains the accumulated changes to the currently effective B elements) and the rows of the inverse matrix, to the XR(K) elements. (Alternatively, the LP routine could be entered with ISTATE = 0, in which case this correction procedure would be unnecessary. Perhaps a criterion related to the change in LEVEL could be developed to determine whether to start the LP from the existing basis or from scratch.) As XR(K) is corrected, simultaneously the greatest infeasibility (in row NEGINV) is determined. It is not necessary to also update X(J) and SLACK(I), since the LP will be entered at CHSLCK.

Subroutines called in BACKUP

A(I, J)

COMMON variables altered in BACKUP

B(I)	ISDONE
BOUND(J)	NEGINV
DRIVER	OBJ
GR(K)	XR(K)
INBASE(J)	

COMMON variables used in BACKUP

BIG	N
C(J)	S(I)
INV(K,L)	SIZE
ISBIG	TOL(JK)
ISEFF(I)	XBASIS(K)
MNOW	

COMMON/BBB variables altered in BACKUP

BEFORE	LEFORT
FIXOBJ	LEFT(JJ)
FUNCL(JJ)	LEVEL
FUNCR(JJ)	PREOBJ
IRIGHT(JJ)	VALUE(JJ)

COMMON/BB variables used in BACKUP

BEST	JDISC(J)
HLDBND(J)	NUMBES
IBEST	RATEL(JJ)
INTOBJ	RATER(JJ)
INTX(JJ)	TOLBB2
ITRBB	

```
      SUBROUTINE BACKUP
*********************** COMMON AND TYPE STATEMENTS ********************
*********************** COMMON/BBB ************************************
 9000 FORMAT (1H0,'ALL BRANCHES OF THE TREE HAVE BEEN EXPLORED, AT ITERA
     1TION ',I5,', AND THE OPTIMUM DISCRETE SOLUTION IS NO.',I5)
 9004 FORMAT(1H0,'THERE IS NO FEASIBLE DISCRETE SOLUTION')
 9008 FORMAT (1H0,'(N.B., THE MAXIMUM SIZE OF THE INVERSE DURING THE CAL
     1CULATION WAS ',I4,')')
      DO 5 L = 1,SIZE
    5 GR(L) = 0.0
   10 J = INTX(LEVEL)
      VAL = VALUE(LEVEL)
      LEVNOW = LEVEL
      FUNL = FUNCL(LEVEL)
      FUNR = FUNCR(LEVEL)
      IF(NUMBES.EQ.0.OR.INTOBJ.EQ.0) GO TO 15
      FF = FUNL + TOLBB2
      IFUNL = FF
      IF (FF .LT. 0.0) IFUNL = IFUNL - 1
      FF = FUNR + TOLBB2
      IFUNR = FF
      IF (FF .LT. 0.0) IFUNR = IFUNR - 1
      IF (IFUNL .GT. IBEST .OR. IFUNR .GT. IBEST) GO TO 20
      GO TO 16
   15 IF (FUNL .GT. BEST .OR. FUNR .GT. BEST) GO TO 20
   16 LEVEL = LEVEL - 1
      DIF = VAL
      BOUND(J) = HLDBND(J)
      IF (INBASE(J) .EQ. -1) INBASE(J) = 0
      GO TO 40
   20 ISTEP = JDISC(J)
      STEP = ISTEP
      ISTEPL = LEFT(LEVEL)
      STEPL = ISTEPL
      ISTEPR = IRIGHT(LEVEL)
      STEPR = ISTEPR
      IF (FUNR .GE. FUNL) GO TO 30
      LEFORT = -1
      DIF = VAL - STEPL
      RATE = RATEL(LEVEL)
      BEFORE = STEPL + STEP
      PREOBJ = FUNL + RATE
      VALUE(LEVEL) = STEPL
      NEXT = ISTEPL - ISTEP
      LEFT(LEVEL) = NEXT
      FUNEXT = -BIG
```

```
      IF (NEXT .GE. 0) FUNEXT = FUNL - RATE
      FUNCL(LEVEL) = FUNEXT
      GO TO 40
   30 LEFORT = 1
      DIF = VAL - STEPR
      RATE = RATER(LEVEL)
      BEFORE = STEPR - STEP
      PREOBJ = FUNR + RATE
      VALUE(LEVEL) = STEPR
      NEXT = ISTEPR + ISTEP
      IRIGHT(LEVEL) = NEXT
      FUNEXT = -BIG
      BJ = HLDBND(J)
      IF (NEXT .LE. BJ .OR. BJ .LT. 0.0) FUNEXT = FUNR - RATE
      FUNCR(LEVEL) = FUNEXT
   40 DO 50 I = 1,MNOW
      DIFI = DIF * A(I,J)
      L = ISEFF(I)
      IF (L .EQ. 0) GO TO 50
      GR(L) = GR(L) + DIFI
   50 B(I) = B(I) + DIFI
      FIXOBJ = FIXOBJ - DIF * C(J)
      IF (LEVEL .EQ. LEVNOW) GO TO 60
      IF (LEVEL .GT. 0) GO TO 10
      WRITE (6,9000) ITRBB, NUMBES
      IF(NUMBES.EQ.0) WRITE(6,9004)
      WRITE(6,9008) ISBIG
      ISDONE = 1
      GO TO 140
   60 NEGINV = 0
      HOWNEG = 0.0
      TOL1 = TOL(1)
      DO 130 K = 1,SIZE
      J = XBASIS(K)
      DIFK = 0.0
      DO 100 L = 1,SIZE
  100 DIFK = DIFK + INV(K,L) * GR(L)
      XRK = XR(K) + DIFK
      IF (ABS(XRK) .LE. TOL1) XRK = 0.0
      XR(K) = XRK
      IF (J .GT. N) GO TO 110
      BOUNDJ = BOUND(J)
      IF (ABS(BOUNDJ - XRK) .LE. TOL1) XR(K) = BOUNDJ
      XRK = XR(K)
      OBJ = OBJ + DIFK * C(J)
      IF (XRK .LE. BOUNDJ .OR. BOUNDJ .EQ. -1.0) GO TO 120
      XRK = BOUNDJ - XRK
      GO TO 120
  110 I = J - N
      SI = S(I)
      IF (SI .EQ. 0.0 .AND. XRK .GT. 0.0 .OR. SI .EQ. -1.0) XRK = -XRK
  120 IF (XRK .GE. HOWNEG) GO TO 130
      HOWNEG = XRK
      NEGINV = K
      DRIVER = 1.0
      IF (XR(K) .GT. 0.0) DRIVER = -1.0
  130 CONTINUE
  140 RETURN
      END
```

4. BBDATA (BB DATA)

This routine reads in the data and initializes the constants for the branch and bound program. The routine starts by initializing MAXD, the maximum number of discrete variables, to match the dimensions of the variables in COMMON/BBB (see Chapter 7, Section 4). Then the tolerances, TOLBB1 and TOLBB2, are initialized; these tolerances are used to test the integrality of the function value and of the discrete variables (see Chapter 7, Section 2).

The first data card contains M; N; NUMD, the number of discrete variables; INTOBJ, which indicates whether the function must be integer; IPRBB, a variable to control the amount of printing; ITRBBM, the maximum number of iterations; IRBBM, the maximum number of re-inversions.

A check is made to ensure that NUMD is in the range −1 to MAXD. If NUMD = 0, the program will be solved as an LP. If NUMD = −1, the problem is solved with *all* variables as integers with a step size of 1. (If ISBND also is −1, the problem is an 0-1 integer problem.)

If NUMD is greater than zero, the following cards contain the discrete variables and their step sizes, eight to a card, in the standard data card form, i.e., three digits to identify the variable, one unused digit, and six digits to specify the length of the step. These cards (if they are used at all) are terminated by a 9999999999 card.

At statement 80 M and N are stored and subroutine DATA is called. DATA reads the usual data of the objective function and the constraints. A check is made that the same values of M and N have been read in both BBDATA and DATA. Then BOUND(J) is copied into HLDBND(J). If the value of ITRBBM is 0 then the default of ITRMAX * N is substituted. The program indicates that a variable has been 'fixed' by changing its upper bound to zero, so in anticipation of the creation of bounded variables ISBND is set to 1. Finally the controlling variables are initialized.

The format of the input data to BB is described in Appendix 3.4.

Subroutines called in BBDATA

DATA	RESTRT

COMMON variables altered in BBDATA

IRMAX	M
ISBND	N
ISDONE	

COMMON variables used in BBDATA

B(I)	BOUND(J)
BIG	ITRMAX

COMMON/BBB variables altered in BBDATA

BEST	JDISC(J)
FIXOBJ	LEFORT
HLDBND(J)	LEVEL
IBEST	MAXD
INTOBJ	NEXNUM
IPRBB	NUMBES
IRBB	NUMD
IRBBM	PREOBJ
ITRBB	TOLBB1
ITRBBM	TOLBB2

```
      SUBROUTINE BBDATA
*********************** COMMON AND TYPE STATEMENTS ********************
********************** COMMON/BBB ************************************
      DIMENSION K1(8),K3(8)
 9000 FORMAT (8I10)
 9004 FORMAT (8(I3,I1,I6))
 9100 FORMAT (1H0,'M (NO. OF CONSTRAINTS) = ',I5,', N (NO. OF VARIABLES)
     1 = ',I5,'.'/1X,I5,' OF THE VARIABLES ARE TO TAKE DISCRETE VALUES.'
     2)
 9104 FORMAT (1H0,'SINCE YOU HAVE SPECIFIED THAT THERE ARE NO DISCRETE V
     1ARIABLES, THE PROBLEM WILL BE SOLVED AS AN LP.'/' THE SECOND CARD
     2OF YOUR DATA MUST BE THE FIRST LP CARD.')
 9108 FORMAT (1H0,'YOU HAVE SPECIFIED THAT ALL THE VARIABLES MUST BE INT
     1EGERS.'/' THE SECOND CARD OF YOUR DATA MUST BE THE FIRST LP CARD.'
     3)
 9112 FORMAT (1H0,'YOU HAVE SPECIFIED TWO DIFFERENT VALUES EITHER FOR M
     1OR FOR N.')
 9116 FORMAT(1H0,'YOU HAVE SPECIFIED A PROBLEM THAT IS TOO BIG FOR THE
     1PROGRAM')
      MAXD = **
      TOLBB1 = 0.1E-5
      TOLBB2 = 0.1E-5
      ISDONE = 0
   10 READ (5,9000) M,N,NUMD,INTOBJ,IPRBB,ITRBBM,IRBBM,IREST
      IT = NUMD
      IF (IT .EQ. -1) IT = N
      WRITE (6,9100) M,N,IT
      IF(NUMD.GE.-1.AND.NUMD.LE.MAXD) GO TO 15
      WRITE(6,9116)
      ISDONE = 1
      GO TO 120
   15 IF (NUMD .EQ. 0) GO TO 20
      IF (NUMD .EQ. -1) GO TO 30
      GO TO 40
   20 WRITE (6,9104)
      GO TO 40
   30 WRITE (6,9108)
```

```
40 IT = 0
   IF (NUMD .EQ. -1) IT = 1
   DO 50 J = 1,N
50 JDISC(J) = IT
   IF (NUMD .LE. 0) GO TO 80
60 READ (5,9004)((K1(JK),KK,K3(JK)),JK=1,8)
   IF (K1(1) .EQ. 999) GO TO 80
   DO 70 JK = 1,8
   J = K1(JK)
   IF (J .LE. 0 .OR. J .GT. N) GO TO 70
   JDISC(J) = K3(JK)
70 CONTINUE
   GO TO 60
80 MHOLD = M
   NHOLD = N
   CALL DATA
   IF (ISDONE .EQ. 1) GO TO 120
   IF (ISBND .EQ. 0) ISBND = 1
   IF (M .EQ. MHOLD .AND. N .EQ. NHOLD) GO TO 90
   WRITE (6,9112)
   ISDONE = 1
   GO TO 120
90 DO 100 J = 1,N
100 HLDBND(J) = BOUND(J)
   IF(ITRBBM.LE.0) ITRBBM = ITRMAX * N
   IF (IRMAX .EQ. 0 .AND. IRBBM .GT. 3) IRMAX = 3
   IF (IRMAX .EQ. 0 .AND. (IRBBM.LE.3.AND.IRBBM.GT.0)) IRMAX = IRBBM
   ITRBB = 0
   IRBB = 0
   NUMBES = 0
   PREOBJ = 0.0
   FIXOBJ = 0.0
   LEFORT = 0
   NEXNUM = 0
   LEVEL = 0
   BEST = -BIG
   IBEST = BEST
   IF(IREST.EQ.0) GO TO 120
   CALL RESTRT
120 RETURN
   END
```

5. BRANCH

In this routine, the LEVEL of the tree is increased by one, the variable JMOVE is selected as the one to be fixed at this LEVEL. The function would fall by at least CMOST if JMOVE were fixed in one direction, but only by CPAIR if it is fixed in the other direction. The variable JMOVE is chosen to make CMOST as great as possible, but the variable is then fixed in the CPAIR direction.

Since this routine is only entered after ISTAIL and when ITAIL = 0, the selection of variables on which to branch need only be made from amongst those not already established as satisfying the discrete constraints, i.e., from KHERE to SIZE (KHERE having been determined in ISTAIL). The choice of JMOVE is carried out in 'DO 20'. Each basic variable is first checked to see if it satisfies its discrete constraint. If not, the amount it would have to be reduced to the discrete value below is recorded in DOWN (a positive amount) and the amount it would have to be raised to the discrete value above is recorded in UP (a negative amount). The subroutine DUAL is then called to find the two variables to enter the basis according to the dual Simplex criterion to alternatively raise or lower the Jth variable whilst maintaining optimality.

DUAL computes NEWUP, NEWD, YACUP, YACD, RATIOU, and RATIOD. The new variable to raise the Jth variable is NEWUP, with $yA - c$ element, YACUP, and the new variable to reduce the Jth variable is NEWD, with $yA - c$ element, YACD. RATIOD (ratio down) is the negative of the level at which NEWD would have to enter the basis to reduce the Jth variable by one unit, and RATIOU (ratio up), the negative of the level at which NEWUP would have to enter to increase the Jth variable by one unit.

Then YDOWN = –DOWN * RATIOD is the minimum possible cost (reduction in the function) of reducing the Jth variable to its discrete value below. YDOWN is BIG if there is no variable which will reduce the Jth variable (i.e., if NEWD = 0). Similarly, YUP is the minimum possible cost of raising the Jth variable to its discrete value above. According to which cost is greater, YDOWN or YUP, control now goes to 10 or continues. If YUP is the greater, it is compared to CMOST. Either if YUP is the greatest cost so far encountered for moving one of the basic variables to a discrete value (YUP is greater than CMOST) or if it is as great as the greatest cost and the cost of moving in the other direction is *less* than for the alternative CPAIR, the Jth variable is chosen as the best to branch on so far. JMOVE is set at J, CMOST at YUP, CPAIR at YDOWN, NEWX at NEWD, and YAMINC at YACD. Since this implies that the branch will be to the left (as always, in the CPAIR direction) LEFORT is set at –1. HDOWN (hold down) is the discrete level of J to the left, and HUP (hold up) the discrete level of J to the right.

From 10 to 20 is the parallel operation, *mutatis mutandi,* when the greater cost is encountered by the move to the left, and the branch is therefore to the right.

After the 'DO 20' loop, the arrays describing the current state of the tree are incremented by one element (since LEVEL has increased by one unit) and DRIVER is set at 1·0 or –1·0 according to whether the JMOVE variable is to be driven up or down.

At 140, the B array is reduced by subtracting the column of A coefficients of the JMOVE variable, times its newly-fixed value, from the present B(I) array. The upper bound of JMOVE is fixed at zero. In fact, the variable JMOVE is now really a new variable which is the divergence between JMOVE and its fixed value. Since this new variable is to be non-negative and have an upper bound of zero, feasibility will only be restored when it is either raised or lowered to zero, and the infeasibility is entirely indicated by the row NEGINV of the basis, which is now the new variable, either negative or above its upper bound. The contribution of the newly-fixed variable is removed from OBJ into FIXOBJ. Control now returns to the main program, where LP can be called with NEWX already known for the first basis change.

Subroutines called in BRANCH

A(I, J)	DUAL

COMMON variables altered in BRANCH

B(I)	OBJ
BOUND(J)	X(J)
DRIVER	XR(K)
NEGINV	YAMINC
NEWX	

COMMON variables used in BRANCH

BIG	N
C(J)	SIZE
INBASE(J)	XBASIS(K)
MNOW	

COMMON/BBB variables altered in BRANCH

BEFORE	LEFT(JJ)
FIXOBJ	LEVEL
FUNCL(JJ)	PREOBJ
FUNCR(JJ)	RATEL(JJ)
INTX(JJ)	RATER(JJ)
IRIGHT(JJ)	VALUE(JJ)
LEFORT	

COMMON/BBB variables used in BRANCH

FUNC	RATIOD
HLDBND(J)	RATIOU
JDISC(J)	TOLBB1
KHERE	YACD
NEWD	YACUP
NEWUP	

```
      SUBROUTINE BRANCH
*********************** COMMON AND TYPE STATEMENTS ********************
*********************** COMMON/BBB ************************************
      LEVEL = LEVEL + 1
      CMOST = 0.0
      CPAIR = 1.0
      JMOVE = 0
      DO 20 K = KHERE,SIZE
      J = XBASIS(K)
      IF (J .GT. N) GO TO 20
      XRK = XR(K)
      STEP = JDISC(J)
      IF(STEP.LE.0.0) GO TO 20
      IT = XRK / STEP + TOLBB1
      T1 = IT
      T1 = T1 * STEP
      DOWN = XRK - T1
      IF (DOWN .LE. TOLBB1 * STEP) GO TO 20
      UP = DOWN - STEP
      NEGINV = K
      CALL DUAL
      YDOWN = -DOWN * RATIOD
      IF (NEWD .EQ. 0) YDOWN = BIG
      YUP = UP * RATIOU
      IF (NEWUP .EQ. 0) YUP = BIG
      IF (YDOWN .GT. YUP) GO TO 10
      IF (YUP .LT. CMOST) GO TO 20
      IF (YUP .EQ. CMOST .AND. YDOWN .GE. CPAIR) GO TO 20
      CMOST = YUP
      CPAIR = YDOWN
      HDOWN = T1
      HUP = T1 + STEP
      JMOVE = J
      LEFORT = -1
      NEWX = NEWD
      YAMINC = YACD
      IF (YDOWN .EQ. BIG .AND. YUP .EQ. BIG) GO TO 21
      GO TO 20
   10 IF (YDOWN .LT. CMOST) GO TO 20
      IF (YDOWN .EQ. CMOST .AND. YUP .GE. CPAIR) GO TO 20
      CMOST = YDOWN
      CPAIR = YUP
      HDOWN = T1
      HUP = T1 + STEP
      JMOVE = J
      LEFORT = 1
      NEWX = NEWUP
      YAMINC = YACUP
   20 CONTINUE
   21 BNDJ = HLDBND(JMOVE)
      INTX(LEVEL) = JMOVE
      BEFORE = X(JMOVE)
      STEP = JDISC(JMOVE)
      IF (LEFORT .EQ. -1) GO TO 70
      VALUE(LEVEL) = HUP
      IF (CMOST .NE. BIG) GO TO 30
      RATEL(LEVEL) = BIG
```

```
      FUNCL(LEVEL) = -BIG
      GO TO 40
   30 DIF = BEFORE - HDOWN
      FUNCL(LEVEL) = FUNC - CMOST
      RATEL(LEVEL) = STEP * CMOST / DIF
   40 IF (CPAIR .NE. BIG) GO TO 50
      RATER(LEVEL) = BIG
      FUNCR(LEVEL) = -BIG
      GO TO 60
   50 DIF = HUP - BEFORE
      RATE = STEP * CPAIR / DIF
      RATER(LEVEL) = RATE
      FUNCR(LEVEL) = FUNC - CPAIR - RATE
   60 DRIVER = 1.0
      GO TO 120
   70 VALUE(LEVEL) = HDOWN
      IF (CMOST .NE. BIG) GO TO 80
      RATER(LEVEL) = BIG
      FUNCR(LEVEL) = -BIG
      GO TO 90
   80 DIF = HUP - BEFORE
      FUNCR(LEVEL) = FUNC - CMOST
      RATER(LEVEL) = STEP * CMOST / DIF
   90 IF (CPAIR .NE. BIG) GO TO 100
      RATEL(LEVEL) = BIG
      FUNCL(LEVEL) = -BIG
      GO TO 110
  100 DIF = BEFORE - HDOWN
      RATE = STEP * CPAIR / DIF
      RATEL(LEVEL) = RATE
      FUNCL(LEVEL) = FUNC - CPAIR - RATE
  110 DRIVER = -1.0
  120 VAL = VALUE(LEVEL)
      LEFT(LEVEL) = VAL - STEP
      VALUP = VAL + STEP
      IF(VALUP.LE.BNDJ.OR.BNDJ.EQ.-1.0)GO TO 130
      FUNCR(LEVEL) = -BIG
      RATER(LEVEL) = BIG
  130 IRIGHT(LEVEL) = VALUP
      IF (VAL .NE. 0.0) GO TO 140
      RATEL(LEVEL) = BIG
      FUNCL(LEVEL) = -BIG
  140 DO 150 I = 1,MNOW
  150 B(I) = B(I) - VAL * A(I,JMOVE)
      BOUND(JMOVE) = 0.0
      K = INBASE(JMOVE)
      XRK = XR(K) - VAL
      XR(K) = XRK
      X(JMOVE) = XRK
      CH = VAL * C(JMOVE)
      OBJ = OBJ - CH
      FIXOBJ = FIXOBJ + CH
      NEGINV = K
      PREOBJ = FUNC
      RETURN
      END
```

6. DUAL

This subroutine is basically similar to SEEKX, except that instead of a single new variable (NEWX) we are here seeking *two* new variables, one to increase the basic variable in the NEGINV row (NEWUP), and one to reduce it (NEWD). In the case of a multiply optimal solution, and hence of some RATIO elements (element in YAC(J) divided by corresponding element in NEGINV row) equal to zero, a secondary criterion is used to choose NEWUP or NEWD, namely that the pivot element be as large (absolute) as possible. Thus the initialization of the routine sets NEWD and NEWUP = 0; BESPUP (best pivot up) and BESPD (best pivot down) = 0·0; YACUP and YACD ($yA - c$ up and $yA - c$ down) = BIG, and RATIOD and RATIOU (ratio down and ratio up) = –BIG. Since the updated NEGINV row of the A matrix will be accumulated in PIV(J), this is first zeroed in 'DO 10'.

'DO 40' seeks the new variables in the slack vectors, and simultaneously 'DO 20' accumulates the updated row in PIV(J). If the element in the NEGINV row is negative it is a possible candidate for increasing the NEGINV variable. If it is positive it may reduce the variable and is so considered from 30 onwards.

'DO 60' continues the search for the two new candidates for entering the basis through the updated row of the A matrix, again distinguishing the positive and negative cases.

COMMON variables altered in DUAL

PIV(J)

COMMON variables used in DUAL

BIG	S(I)
BOUND(J)	SIZE
INBASE(J)	TOL(JK)
INV(K,L)	YAC(J)
N	YBASIS(L)
NEGINV	YR(L)

COMMON/AREF variables used in DUAL

AA(LOOK)	JCOL(LOOK)
IROW(I)	

COMMON/BBB variables altered in DUAL

NEWD	RATIOU
NEWUP	YACD
RATIOD	YACUP

```
      SUBROUTINE DUAL
*********************** COMMON AND TYPE STATEMENTS ********************
*********************** COMMON/AREF ***********************************
*********************** COMMON/BBB ************************************
      NEWD = 0
      NEWUP = 0
      BESPUP = 0.0
      BESPD = 0.0
      YACUP = BIG
      YACD = BIG
      RATIOD = -BIG
      RATIOU = -BIG
      TOL3 = TOL(3)
      TOL4 = TOL(4)
      TOL5 = TOL(5)
      DO 10 J = 1,N
   10 PIV(J) = 0.0
      DO 40 L = 1,SIZE
      RINVKL = INV(NEGINV,L)
      I = YBASIS(L)
      SI = S(I)
      ISTART = IROW(I)
      LAST = IROW(I+1) - 1
      DO 20 LOOK = ISTART,LAST
      J = JCOL(LOOK)
      IF (INBASE(J) .GE. 1 .OR. BOUND(J) .EQ. 0.0) GO TO 20
      AIJ = AA(LOOK)
      PIV(J) = PIV(J) + AIJ * RINVKL
   20 CONTINUE
      IF (SI .EQ. 0) GO TO 40
      PIVOT = RINVKL * SI
      YRL = YR(L) * SI
      IF (ABS(YRL) .LT. TOL3) YRL = 0.0
      IF (PIVOT .GE. -TOL5) GO TO 30
      RATIO = YRL / PIVOT
      IF (RATIO .LT. RATIOU) GO TO 40
      IF (RATIO .EQ. 0.0 .AND. PIVOT .GE. BESPUP) GO TO 40
      IF (RATIO .EQ. 0.0) BESPUP = PIVOT
      YACUP = YRL
      NEWUP = N + I
      RATIOU = RATIO
      GO TO 40
   30 PIVOT = -PIVOT
      IF (PIVOT .GE. -TOL5) GO TO 40
      RATIO = YRL / PIVOT
      IF (RATIO .LT. RATIOD) GO TO 40
      IF (RATIO .EQ. 0.0 .AND.PIVOT .GE. BESPD) GO TO 40
      IF (RATIO .EQ. 0.0) BESPD = PIVOT
      YACD = YRL
      NEWD = N + I
      RATIOD = RATIO
   40 CONTINUE
      DO 60 J = 1,N
      INJ = INBASE(J)
      IF (INJ .GE. 1 .OR. BOUND(J) .EQ. 0.0) GO TO 60
      SJ = 1.0
      IF (INJ .EQ. -1) SJ = -1.0
      PIVOT = PIV(J) * SJ
```

```
   FUN = YAC(J) * SJ
   IF (ABS(FUN) .LT. TOL4) FUN = 0.0
   IF (PIVOT .GE. -TOL5) GO TO 50
   RATIO = FUN / PIVOT
   IF (RATIO .LT. RATIOU) GO TO 60
   IF (RATIO .EQ. 0.0 .AND. PIVOT .GE. BESPUP) GO TO 60
   IF (RATIO .EQ. 0.0) BESPUP = PIVOT
   RATIOU = RATIO
   YACUP = FUN
   NEWUP = J
   GO TO 60
50 PIVOT = - PIVOT
   IF (PIVOT .GE. -TOL5) GO TO 60
   RATIO = FUN / PIVOT
   IF (RATIO .LT. RATIOD) GO TO 60
   IF (RATIO .EQ. 0.0 .AND. PIVOT .GE. BESPD) GO TO 60
   IF (RATIO .EQ. 0.0) BESPD = PIVOT
   RATIOD = RATIO
   YACD = FUN
   NEWD = J
60 CONTINUE
   RETURN
   END
```

7. ISTAIL (is it a tail)

This subroutine principally examines the current solution to see whether it is a *tail* of the tree, and prints the required information (in more or less detail, according to the value of IPRBB). However, it also adjusts the bounds on the function of adjacent nodes of the tree because a more accurate estimate of the bound is now available.

Up to statement 10, the subroutine is concerned with the case where ISTATE = 2, i.e., the current LP is infeasible. If LEVEL = 0, i.e., if this is the first LP solution, the algorithm terminates (statement 100) with a statement to that effect.

Otherwise the node to the left or the node to the right is marked as infeasible by setting its function bound as –BIG. If IPRBB = 0, control returns to the main program (at statement 110). Otherwise, the current state of the tree is printed out.

If, on the other hand, the current LP is feasible (statement 10) a more complex adjustment to the neighbouring nodes is carried out (omitting the case where LEVEL = 0). We shall describe this adjustment in terms of a node to the right of the current one, but the left-hand adjustment is much the same. When a branch is determined from a node, an estimate of the upper bound to the function for the nodes to the left and to the right is also made. Consider the functions max x_k and min x_k (see Land and Doig [8]), relating the maximum values of the function to increasing and decreasing values of the variable, x_k, see Figure 5.1.

A branch has been determined from A, where x_k took a non-discrete value. The estimate of the upper bound of the function at the first discrete value of x_k moving to the right was at C, and by extrapolation, was D for the next value, further to the right. Because C has a higher function value than J, the decision has been made to 'move to the right'. But when the LP is completed it turns out that the bound at C was too high, and that the value of the function is now given by B. But then D is also too high. The simplest adjustment would be to subtract the RATER(LEVEL) from FUNC, and obtain the estimate, E.

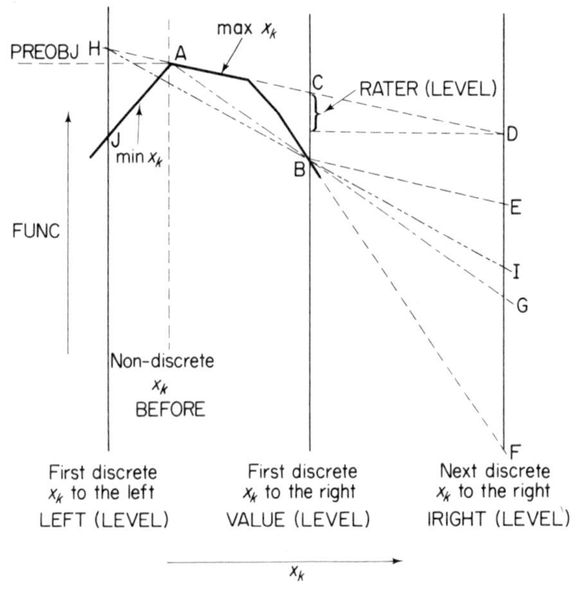

Figure 5.1.

The best estimate would be obtained from the slope of max x_k at B. This would give the estimate F, but it would involve extracting the information from the LP routine, and thus involve altering the existing routines. We therefore leave this refinement to the reader if he wishes to pursue it. A better estimate than E can be obtained by deducing the average rate of fall of max x_k between A and B, which yields G, and is the one used in this program. The values PREOBJ and BEFORE (the co-ordinates of A in figure 5.1) are set in the subroutine BRANCH.

If the point B has been reached from a backtracking operation, the values PREOBJ and BEFORE are not available (unless an additional element is stored with every node (i.e., and additional array is used). This has not been considered worth doing, but rather an extrapolation of C by applying RATER-(LEVEL) to C in BACKUP has set the value of PREOBJ and BEFORE as the co-ordinates of *H.* This yields a bound for the next right-hand value at *I,* worse than *G*, but better than *E.*

This is the calculation carried out from 10 to 30, only if the appropriate node is not already sufficiently low to exclude it from further consideration.

At 30 the current value of the function is checked against BEST (and/or IBEST), and if it is at least as low as BEST, a tail of type 2 is recognized and, if required, printed.

At 40, the test for a discrete solution is carried out. If the 'DO 50' loop is completed, the solution satisfies the discrete constraints, ITAIL = 1, BEST is increased, and the solution is printed (with more or less detail, as indicated by IPRBB). Otherwise the value KHERE indicates that all basic variables from 1 to KHERE – 1 satisfy the discrete constraints, i.e., that all non-discrete variables are to be found from KHERE to SIZE.

Finally, at statement 80, if the current solution is not a tail, the iteration and re-inversion counts are examined, and if the limits are exceeded the present state of the tree is printed, and ISDONE = 1. Note that if the restart option is being used, this exit should not occur.

COMMON variables altered in ISTAIL

ISDONE	PIV(J)

COMMON variables used in ISTAIL

BIG	SIZE
ISBIG	SLACK(I)
ISTATE	X(J)
MNOW	XBASIS(K)
N	XR(K)

COMMON/BBB variables altered in ISTAIL

BEST	KHERE
FUNCL(JJ)	NEXNUM
FUNCR(JJ)	NUMBES
IBEST	RATEL(JJ)
IPRBB	RATER(JJ)
ITAIL	

COMMON/BBB variables used in ISTAIL

BEFORE	JDISC(J)
FIXOBJ	LEFORT
FUNC	IRBBM
INTOBJ	IRIGHT(JJ)
INTX(JJ)	ITRBB
IRBB	ITRBBM

LEFT(JJ) TOLBB1
LEVEL TOLBB2
NUMD VALUE(JJ)
PREBOBJ

```
      SUBROUTINE ISTAIL
********************** COMMON AND TYPE STATEMENTS *******************
********************** COMMON/BBB ***********************************
 9000 FORMAT (1H0,'INFEASIBLE TAIL AT ITR. ',I5,'.')
 9010 FORMAT (17(1X,I6))
 9020 FORMAT (1H ,'FIXED AT VALUES...')
 9030 FORMAT (17(1X,F6.0))
 9040 FORMAT (1H ,'THE TREE VALUES TO THE LEFT ARE...')
 9050 FORMAT (1H ,'WITH UPPER BOUNDS ON THE FUNCTION...')
 9060 FORMAT (1H ,'AND THE TREE VALUES TO THE RIGHT ARE...')
 9070 FORMAT (1H0,'A TAIL WITH FUNCTION AT LEAST AS LOW AS THE BEST DISC
     1RETE SOLUTION SO FAR, AT ITR.',I5,/1H ,' WITH FUNCTION',F12.5,' AN
     2D FIXED VARIABLES...')
 9080  FORMAT  (1H0,'SOLUTION SATISFYING DISCRETE CONSTRAINTS, NO.',I5,'
     1, WITH FUNCTION VALUE,',F15.5,' AT ITERATION ',I5,20X,'*****')
 9090 FORMAT (1H ,'THE FIXED VARIABLES ARE...')
 9100 FORMAT (1H ,'THE RATEL (RATE OF FALL TO THE LEFT) VECTOR IS...')
 9110 FORMAT (1H ,'THE RATER (RATE OF FALL TO THE RIGHT) VECTOR IS...')
 9120 FORMAT (1H0,'THE LP OPTIMUM SATISFIES ALL THE DISCRETE CONSTRAINTS
     1.')
 9130 FORMAT (1H0,'THE LP SOLUTION IS INFEASIBLE EVEN WITHOUT THE DISCRE
     1TE CONSTRAINTS.')
 9140 FORMAT (1H0,'THE ALGORITHM HAS TERMINATED BY EXCEEDING THE ITERATI
     1ON LIMIT OR THE REINVERSION LIMIT.'/1H ,'ITERATIONS',I5,' AND REIN
     2VERSIONS',I5,'.  THE TREE IS AS FOLLOWS....')
 9150 FORMAT (1H0,'BEST = ',F15.5,', FIXOBJ = ',F15.5,', FUNC = ',F15.5,
     1', ITAIL = ',I5,', LEFORT = ',I5/1H ,'LEVEL = ',I5,', NUMD = ',I5)
 9160 FORMAT (1H ,'THE VALUES OF THE VARIABLES ARE...')
 9170 FORMAT (8(1X,F14.7))
 9180 FORMAT(1H ,'THE VALUES OF THE SLACK VARIABLES ARE...')
 9190 FORMAT (1H0,'(N.B., THE MAXIMUM SIZE OF THE INVERSE DURING THE CAL
     1CULATION WAS ',I4,')')
      IF (ISTATE .NE. 2) GO TO 10
      ITAIL = 3
      IF (LEVEL .EQ. 0) GO TO 120
      IF (LEFORT .EQ. -1) FUNCL(LEVEL) = -BIG
      IF (LEFORT .EQ. 1) FUNCR(LEVEL) = -BIG
      IF (IPRBB .LT. 1) GO TO 130
      WRITE (6,9000) ITRBB
      GO TO 95
   10 IF (LEVEL .EQ. 0) GO TO 40
      IF (LEFORT .EQ. -1 .AND. FUNCL(LEVEL) .LE. BEST .OR. LEFORT .EQ. 1
     1 .AND. FUNCR(LEVEL) .LE. BEST) GO TO 30
      FALL = PREOBJ - FUNC
      J = INTX(LEVEL)
      STEP = JDISC(J)
      VAL = VALUE(LEVEL)
      CHANGE = ABS(BEFORE - VAL)
      RATE = (FALL / CHANGE) * STEP
      IF (LEFORT .EQ. 1) GO TO 20
```

```
      FUNCL(LEVEL) = FUNC - RATE
      RATEL(LEVEL) = RATE
      GO TO 30
   20 FUNCR(LEVEL) = FUNC - RATE
      RATER(LEVEL) = RATE
   30 IF(NUMBES.EQ.0) GO TO 40
      IF(INTOBJ.EQ.0) GO TO 35
      FF = FUNC + TOLBB2
      IFUNC = FF
      IF (FF .LT. 0.0) IFUNC = IFUNC - 1
      IF (IFUNC .GT. IBEST) GO TO 40
      GO TO 36
   35 IF (FUNC .GT. BEST) GO TO 40
   36 ITAIL = 2
      IF (IPRBB .LT. 1) GO TO 130
      WRITE (6,9070) ITRBB,FUNC
      GO TO 100
   40 DO 50 K = 1,SIZE
      KHERE = K
      J = XBASIS(K)
      IF (J .GT. N) GO TO 50
      XRK = XR(K)
      STEP = JDISC(J)
      IF (STEP .LE. 0.0) GO TO 50
      IT = XRK / STEP + TOLBB1
      T1 = IT
      T2 = XRK/STEP - T1
      IF (T2 .GT. TOLBB1 .AND. T2 .LT. 1.0-TOLBB1) GO TO 60
   50 CONTINUE
      ITAIL = 1
      IF (LEVEL .EQ. 0) GO TO 110
      NEXNUM = NEXNUM + 1
      BEST = FUNC
      BST = BEST + TOLBB2
      IBEST = BST
      IF (BST .LT. 0.0) IBEST = IBEST - 1
      NUMBES = NEXNUM
      WRITE (6,9080) NEXNUM,FUNC,ITRBB
      GO TO 70
   60 IF(ITRBB.LE.ITRBBM.AND.IRBB.LE.IRBBM) GO TO 130
      WRITE (6,9140) ITRBB,IRBB
      WRITE (6,9150) BEST,FIXOBJ,FUNC,ITAIL,LEFORT,LEVEL,NUMD
      WRITE (6,9160)
      IPRBB = 3
      ISDONE = 1
   70 DO 80 J = 1,N
   80 PIV(J) = X(J)
      DO 90 JJ = 1,LEVEL
      J = INTX(JJ)
   90 PIV(J) = PIV(J) + VALUE(JJ)
      WRITE (6,9170)(PIV(J),J=1,N)
      WRITE(6,9180)
      WRITE(6,9170) (SLACK(I),I=1,MNOW)
      IF (IPRBB .LT. 1) GO TO 130
   95 WRITE (6,9090)
  100 WRITE (6,9010)(INTX(J),J=1,LEVEL)
      WRITE (6,9020)
```

```
      WRITE (6,9030)(VALUE(J),J=1,LEVEL)
      IF (IPRBB .LT. 2) GO TO 130
      WRITE (6,9040)
      WRITE (6,9010)(LEFT(J),J=1,LEVEL)
      WRITE (6,9050)
      WRITE (6,9030)(FUNCL(J),J=1,LEVEL)
      WRITE (6,9060)
      WRITE (6,9010)(IRIGHT(J),J=1,LEVEL)
      WRITE (6,9050)
      WRITE (6,9030)(FUNCR(J),J=1,LEVEL)
      IF (IPRBB .LT. 3) GO TO 130
      WRITE (6,9100)
      WRITE (6,9030)(RATEL(J),J=1,LEVEL)
      WRITE (6,9110)
      WRITE (6,9030)(RATER(J),J=1,LEVEL)
      GO TO 130
  110 WRITE (6,9120)
      ISDONE = 1
      GO TO 130
  120 WRITE (6,9130)
      ISDONE = 1
  130 IF(ISDONE.EQ.1) WRITE(6,9190) ISBIG
      RETURN
      END
```

8. PNODE (punch a node)

This subroutine saves the part of the branch and bound tree that has not yet been explored and a representation of the node from which the computation is to be restarted.

The first half of the subroutine prints (on channel 6) a description of the tree and of the node that are to be saved. The second half of the subroutine writes the data to be saved on to channel 7. Because of the field size in the format 9012 the value ±DUMBIG (±100000·0) is substituted for ±BIG in FUNCL(J), FUNCR(J), RATEL(J) and RATER(J) as appropriate.

Channel 7 can be a disc, a magnetic tape or a card punch. The FORMAT and WRITE statements in the subroutine are those that are needed to punch cards. If channel 7 is a disc or a magnetic tape then it would be advisable for accuracy and efficiency reasons, to replace the formatted WRITE statements by unformatted WRITE statements. The FORMAT statements numbered 9000, 9004, 9008 and 9012 will not be needed and a WRITE statement of the type

WRITE (7, 90xx) output list

should be replaced by

WRITE(7) output list

Channel 7 must correspond with channel 8 in subroutine RESTRT, that is a card punch and a card reader, or both magnetic tapes or both discs.

If channel 7 is a magnetic tape or a disc then there is no need to substitute DUMBIG for BIG in FUNCL(J), FUNCR(J), RATEL(J) and RATER(J). The statement initializing DUMBIG and the statements of the 'DO 10' loop may be deleted.

COMMON variables used in PNODE

B(I)	ISBIG
BIG	MNOW
BOUND(J)	N

COMMON/BBB variables altered in PNODE

FUNCL(JJ)	RATEL(JJ)
FUNCR(JJ)	RATER(JJ)

COMMON/BBB variables used in PNODE

BEST	LEFORT
FIXOBJ	LEFT(JJ)
IBEST	LEVEL
INTX(JJ)	NEXNUM
IRIGHT(JJ)	NUMBES
ITRBB	VALUE(JJ)

```
      SUBROUTINE PNODE
*********************** COMMON AND TYPE STATEMENTS ********************
*********************** COMMON/BBB **************************************
 9000 FORMAT(2F20.6,I15,4I5)
 9004 FORMAT(8F10.5)
 9008 FORMAT(8I10)
 9012 FORMAT(5F16.7)
 9016 FORMAT(1H0,'AT ITERATION',I6,'  A NODE HAS BEEN PUNCHED')
 9020 FORMAT(1H ,'THE FIXED VARIABLES ARE. . .')
 9024 FORMAT(17(1X,I6))
 9028 FORMAT(1H ,'FIXED AT VALUES. . .')
 9032 FORMAT(17(1X,F6.0))
 9036 FORMAT(1H ,'THE TREE VALUES TO THE LEFT ARE. . .')
 9040 FORMAT(1H ,'WITH UPPER BOUNDS ON THE FUNCTION. . .')
 9044 FORMAT(1H ,'AND THE TREE VALUES TO THE RIGHT ARE. . .')
 9048 FORMAT (1H0,'(N.B., THE MAXIMUM SIZE OF THE INVERSE DURING THE CAL
     1CULATION WAS ',I4,')')
      DUMBIG =  100000.0
      WRITE(6,9016) ITRBB
      WRITE(6,9020)
      WRITE(6,9024) (INTX(J),J=1,LEVEL)
      WRITE(6,9028)
      WRITE(6,9032) (VALUE(J),J=1,LEVEL)
```

```
      WRITE(6,9036)
      WRITE(6,9024)(LEFT(J),J=1,LEVEL)
      WRITE(6,9040)
      WRITE(6,9032) (FUNCL(J),J=1,LEVEL)
      WRITE(6,9044)
      WRITE(6,9024) (IRIGHT(J),J=1,LEVEL)
      WRITE(6,9040)
      WRITE(6,9032)(FUNCR(J),J=1,LEVEL)
      WRITE(6,9048) ISBIG
      WRITE(7,9000) BEST,FIXOBJ,IBEST,LEVEL,LEFORT,NEXNUM,NUMBES
      WRITE(7,9004)(B(I),I=1,MNOW)
      WRITE(7,9004)(BOUND(J),J=1,N)
      WRITE(7,9008)(INTX(J),J=1,LEVEL)
      WRITE(7,9004) (VALUE(J),J=1,LEVEL)
      WRITE(7,9008)(LEFT(J),J=1,LEVEL)
      WRITE(7,9008)(IRIGHT(J),J=1,LEVEL)
      DO 10 J=1,LEVEL
      IF(FUNCL(J).EQ.-BIG) FUNCL(J)=-DUMBIG
      IF(FUNCR(J).EQ.-BIG) FUNCR(J)=-DUMBIG
      IF(RATEL(J).EQ. BIG) RATEL(J)=DUMBIG
      IF(RATER(J).EQ. BIG) RATER(J)=DUMBIG
   10 CONTINUE
      WRITE(7,9012) (FUNCL(J),J=1,LEVEL)
      WRITE(7,9012) (FUNCR(J),J=1,LEVEL)
      WRITE(7,9012) (RATEL(J),J=1,LEVEL)
      WRITE(7,9012) (RATER(J),J=1,LEVEL)
      RETURN
      END
```

9. RESTRT (restart)

This subroutine retrieves the part of the branch and bound tree that is to be explored and a representation of the node from which the computation is to start.

The data representing the tree and a node are read in from channel 8. The right hand side and the bounds at the node are read into B(I) and BOUND(J). In 'DO 10' the value ±DUMBIG (±100000·0) is replaced by ±BIG in FUNCL(J), FUNCR(J), RATEL(J) and RATER(J) as appropriate.

In the second half of the subroutine a description of the node from which the computation is to start is printed (on channel 6).

Channel 8 can be a disc, a magnetic tape or a card reader. The FORMAT and READ statements are those that are needed to read from cards. If channel 8 is a disc or magnetic tape then it would be advisable for accuracy and efficiency reasons, to replace the formatted READ statements by unformatted READ statements. The FORMAT statements numbered 9000, 9004, 9008 and 9012 will not be needed and a READ statement of the type

READ(8, 90xx) input list

should be replaced by

READ(8) input list

Channel 8 must correspond with channel 7 in subroutine PNODE, that is a card reader and a card punch, or both magnetic tapes, or both discs.

If channel 8 is a magnetic tape or a disc there is no need to replace DUMBIG in FUNCL(J), FUNCR(J), RATEL(J) and RATER(J) by BIG. The statement initializing DUMBIG and the statements of the 'DO 10' loop may be deleted.

COMMON variables altered in RESTRT

B(I)	BOUND(J)

COMMON variables used in RESTRT

BIG	N
MNOW	

COMMON/BBB variables altered in RESTRT

BEST	LEFT(JJ)
FIXOBJ	LEVEL
FUNCL(JJ)	NEXNUM
FUNCR(JJ)	NUMBES
IBEST	RATEL(JJ)
INTX(JJ)	RATER(JJ)
IRIGHT(JJ)	VALUE(JJ)
LEFORT	

```
      SUBROUTINE RESTRT
*********************** COMMON AND TYPE STATEMENTS ********************
*********************** COMMON/BBB ************************************
 9000 FORMAT(2F20.6,I15,4I5)
 9004 FORMAT(8F10.5)
 9008 FORMAT(8I10)
 9012 FORMAT(5F16.7)
 9016 FORMAT(1H1,'THE BRANCH AND BOUND CALCULATION HAS BEEN RESTARTED')
 9020 FORMAT(1H ,'THE FIXED VARIABLES ARE. . .')
 9024 FORMAT(17(1X,I6))
 9028 FORMAT(1H ,'FIXED AT VALUES. . .')
 9032 FORMAT(17(1X,F6.0))
 9036 FORMAT(1H ,'THE TREE VALUES TO THE LEFT ARE. . .')
 9040 FORMAT(1H ,'WITH UPPER BOUNDS ON THE FUNCTION. . .')
 9044 FORMAT(1H ,'AND THE TREE VALUES TO THE RIGHT ARE. . .')
      DUMBIG =  100000.
      READ(8,9000)  BEST,FIXOBJ,IBEST,LEVEL,LEFORT,NEXNUM,NUMBES
      READ(8,9004) (B(I),I=1,MNOW)
      READ(8,9004) (BOUND(J),J=1,N)
```

```
      READ(8,9008)(INTX(J),J=1,LEVEL)
      READ(8,9004) (VALUE(J),J=1,LEVEL)
      READ(8,9008)(LEFT(J),J=1,LEVEL)
      READ(8,9008)(IRIGHT(J),J=1,LEVEL)
      READ(8,9012) (FUNCL(J),J=1,LEVEL)
      READ(8,9012) (FUNCR(J),J=1,LEVEL)
      READ(8,9012) (RATEL(J),J=1,LEVEL)
      READ(8,9012) (RATER(J),J=1,LEVEL)
      DO 10 J=1,LEVEL
      IF(FUNCL(J).EQ.-DUMBIG) FUNCL(J)=-BIG
      IF(FUNCR(J).EQ.-DUMBIG) FUNCR(J)=-BIG
      IF(RATEL(J).EQ.DUMBIG) RATEL(J)= BIG
      IF(RATER(J).EQ.DUMBIG) RATER(J)= BIG
   10 CONTINUE
      WRITE(6,9016)
      WRITE(6,9020)
      WRITE(6,9024) (INTX(J),J=1,LEVEL)
      WRITE(6,9028)
      WRITE(6,9032) (VALUE(J),J=1,LEVEL)
      WRITE(6;9036)
      WRITE(6,9024)(LEFT(J),J=1,LEVEL)
      WRITE(6,9040)
      WRITE(6,9032) (FUNCL(J),J=1,LEVEL)
      WRITE(6,9044)
      WRITE(6,9024) (IRIGHT(J),J=1,LEVEL)
      WRITE(6,9040)
      WRITE(6,9032)(FUNCR(J),J=1,LEVEL)
      RETURN
      END
```

CHAPTER 6

Parametric Linear Programming—PLP

1. INTRODUCTION

This program is designed to show the changes to the optimal solution of an LP that result from varying an element of b, b_i, or from varying an element of the objective function, c_j. The mathematical analysis upon which this program is based has been described in Chapter 1. In this algorithm it is only possible to vary the value of one parameter, whether b_i or c_j, at once; however, successive variations can be performed.

In the program there are three options as to which parameter is varied between which limits.

1. The value of a specified element of b (or c) may be varied between specified limits. The program evaluates the range of values of the parameter within which the initial LP basis is feasible and optimal and then increases the value of the parameter. When the specified upper limit is reached the value of the parameter is decreased to the specified lower limit. The values of the variables at the initial LP basis and at each corner point are printed.
2. A sensitivity analysis may be performed for a specified parameter. In this case the program evaluates the range of values of b_i (or c_j) within which the initial LP basis is feasible and optimal and prints the values of the variables at the initial LP basis and at either end of the range.
3. A range analysis may be performed for all elements of b (or c). In this case the range of values of each element of b (or c) within which the initial LP basis is feasible and optimal is evaluated and printed; the values of the variables are not printed. The range of each element of b (or c) is evaluated independently.

In the descriptions of the main routine, subroutines PDATA, PARAB and PARAC there are the details of how the program handles the different options. The printing options and the form of the printing are described in subroutine PPRINT.

2. PROGRAM STRUCTURE

The parametric program, PLP, consists of a main routine, the LP subroutines of Chapter 2, and the 'parametric' subroutines, CHAGY, CHXSL, MIDBI, MIDCJ, PARAB, PARAC, PDATA and PPRINT. Subroutine PDATA is concerned with the input of the parametric requests while subroutine PPRINT deals with the output of the parametric analysis. Subroutines CHXSL, MIDBI and PARAB are concerned with varying a specified element of b. The analysis is directed by PARAB which calls CHXSL and MIDBI. In an analogous fashion CHAGY, MIDCJ and PARAC are concerned with varying a specified element of c; the analysis is directed by PARAC which calls CHAGY and MIDCJ. The LP subroutines are called by the main routine and by the 'parametric' subroutines. The main routine handles the parametric requests and calls the appropriate routines having initialized the relevant markers so that the required parametric analysis is performed.

The main routine is described in greater detail below and the 'parametric' subroutines are described alphabetically later in this chapter.

3. A COMMON STATEMENT FOR PLP

The data needed for the parametric variations and communication between the subroutines are stored in labelled COMMON/PARA.

```
      COMMON/PARA/BMID,BOTOM(MAXP),CMID,DUMBIG,IJPARA(MAXP),IP,IPARAB,
     1            IPARAC,IPRPLP,IRANGB,IRANGC,ISENSB,ISENSC,JP,MAXP,
     2            NUMP,SBI,SBIN,SCJ,SCJN,TOP(MAXP),UBI,UBIN,UCJ,UCJN
```

The arrays BOTOM(MAXP), IJPARA(MAXP), TOP(MAXP) contain the data of the parametric requests. The dimension of these arrays, MAXP, is the maximum number of requests that the program can handle. MAXP must, of course, be replaced by the numerical value of MAXP for use in the program. NUMP is the number of parametric requests stored in the arrays. The relationship between MAXP, NUMP and the data stored in the arrays is described in PDATA.

The variables BMID, IP, IPARAB, IRANGB, ISENSB, SBI, SBIN, UBI and UBIN are concerned with varying the value of b_i and are described in subroutine PARAB. The variables CMID, IPARAC, IRANGC, ISENSC, JP, SCJ, SCJN, UCJ and UCJN are concerned with varying the value of c_j and are described in subroutine PARAC. DUMBIG and IPRPLP are described in subroutines PDATA and PPRINT respectively.

4. PROGRAM PLP

The program starts by calling PDATA to read in the parametric requests and the data for the associated LP. The optimal solution to the LP is obtained by calling subroutine LP. If IRANGB = 1 then the range of every element of B for which the LP optimal solution remains feasible is evaluated in the 'DO 20' loop. Similarly if IRANGC = 1 then the range of every element of C for which the LP optimal solution remains optimal is evaluated in the 'DO 30' loop.

If there are no further parametric requests, NUMP = 0, then the program considers the next problem, otherwise the program processes the NUMP requests. The data for the requests are contained in IJPARA(NP), BOTOM(NP) and TOP(NP). If IJPARA(NP) is positive then B(IP) is to be varied between SBI (= BOTOM(NP)) and UBI(= TOP(NP)), and IPARAB is set to 1. The program checks that $1 \leqslant \text{IP} \leqslant \text{M}$ and $\text{SBI} \leqslant \text{B(IP)} \leqslant \text{UBI}$. If SBI = UBI then a sensitivity analysis is to be performed and ISENSB is set to 1; otherwise ISENSB = 0.

If IJPARA(NP) is negative then C(JP) is to be varied between SCJ (= BOTOM(NP)) and UCJ (= TOP(NP)), and IPARAC is set to 1. The program checks that $1 \leqslant \text{JP} \leqslant \text{N}$ and $\text{SCJ} \leqslant \text{C(JP)} \leqslant \text{UCJ}$. If SCJ = UCJ then a sensitivity analysis is to be performed and ISENSC is set to 1; otherwise ISENSC = 0.

On returning from either PARAB or PARAC the program checks that the current basis is optimal, ISTATE = 1, and performs the next parametric request. Finally if there is not another problem the program finishes, otherwise it starts again.

Subroutines called in PLP

IEXIT	PARAC
LP	PDATA
PARAB	

COMMON variables altered in PLP

ISTATE

COMMON variables used in PLP

B(I)	M
C(J)	MORE
ISDONE	N

COMMON/PARA variables altered in PLP

IP	IPARAC
IPARAB	IRANGB

IRANGC	SBI
ISENSB	SCJ
ISENSC	UBI
JP	UCJ

COMMON/PARA variables used in PLP

BOTOM(JJ)	NUMP
IJPARA(JJ)	TOP(JJ)

```
      PROGRAM PLP (INPUT,OUTPUT,TAPE5=INPUT,TAPE6=OUTPUT)
*********************** COMMON AND TYPE STATEMENTS ********************
*********************** COMMON/PARA ***********************************
 9004 FORMAT(1H ,'ORIGINAL R.H.SIDE',F8.2,'MUST BE WITHIN LIMITS ',2(F8.
     12,1X))
 9008 FORMAT(1H ,'ORIGINAL OBJECTIVE FUNCTION ELEMENT ',F8.2,' MUST BE W
     1ITHIN THE LIMITS ',2(F8.2,1X))
 9012 FORMAT(1H ,'FAILED TO RESTORE ORIGINAL LP SOLUTION')
 9016 FORMAT(1H ,'INVALID REQUEST  CONSTRAINT',I6)
 9020 FORMAT(1H ,'INVALID REQUEST  VARIABLE',I6)
   10 CALL PDATA
      IF(ISDONE.EQ.1) GO TO 140
      ISTATE = 0
      CALL LP
      CALL IEXIT(ISTATE)
      IF(ISTATE.NE.1) GO TO 140
      IF(IRANGB.EQ.0) GO TO 30
      IPARAB = 1
      ISENSB = 0
      DO 20 I=1,M
      IP = I
      UBI = B(IP)
      SBI = UBI
      CALL PARAB
   20 CONTINUE
      IRANGB = 0
      IPARAB = 0
   30 IF(IRANGC.EQ.0) GO TO 50
      IPARAC = 1
      ISENSC = 0
      DO 40 J=1,N
      JP = J
      UCJ = C(JP)
      SCJ = UCJ
      CALL PARAC
   40 CONTINUE
      IRANGC = 0
      IPARAC = 0
   50 IF(NUMP.EQ.0) GO TO 140
      DO 120 NP = 1,NUMP
      IPARAB = 0
      IPARAC = 0
      ISENSB = 0
```

```
      ISENSC = 0
      IJ = IJPARA(NP)
      IF(IJ .LT.0) GO TO 80
      IPARAB = 1
      IP = IJ
      IF (IP .LE. M .AND. IP .GE. 1) GO TO 60
      WRITE(6,9016) IP
      GO TO 120
   60 SBI = BOTOM(NP)
      UBI = TOP(NP)
      IF(SBI.EQ.UBI) ISENSB = 1
      IF (B(IP) .GE. SBI .AND. B(IP) .LE. UBI) GO TO 70
      WRITE (6,9004) B(IP),SBI, UBI
      GO TO 120
   70 CALL PARAB
      GO TO 110
   80 IPARAC = 1
      JP = -IJ
      IF (JP .LE. N .AND. JP .GE. 1) GO TO 90
      WRITE (6,9020) JP
      GO TO 120
   90 SCJ = BOTOM(NP)
      UCJ = TOP(NP)
      IF(SCJ.EQ.UCJ) ISENSC = 1
      IF (C(JP) .GE. SCJ .AND. C(JP) .LE. UCJ) GO TO 100
      WRITE (6,9008) C(JP), SCJ, UCJ
      GO TO 120
  100 CALL PARAC
  110 IF (ISTATE .EQ. 1) GO TO 120
      WRITE (6,9012)
      GO TO 130
  120 CONTINUE
      GO TO 140
  130 CALL IEXIT(ISTATE)
  140 IF (MORE .NE. 0) GO TO 10
      STOP
      END
```

5. CHAGY (change y)

This subroutine changes the values of the dual variables of the effective constraints and of the function row variables, YR(L) and YAC(J), to correspond to a change, R, in the value of the parameter C(JP). The direction of change is expressed by the value of CUPDN. The change will make the value of either a dual variable of an effective constraint, or a function row variable, zero. The associated slack or original variable, NEWX, must be introduced into the implicit or explicit basis so that optimality can be maintained as the value of the parameter continues to change. The basis change to introduce NEWX into the implicit or explicit basis will be a zero dual basis change, thus YAMINC is set to zero.

The subroutine is entered with the data as to which variable, NEWX, is to enter the basis, the change, R, in C(JP), and the direction of change, CUPDN. If NEWX = 0 then no variable is to enter the basis, but the values of the variables are to be changed for printing purposes. If NEWX ≠ 0 and JP is non-basic then YAC(JP) is made equal to zero and NEWX, which is equal to JP, is introduced into the basis. If NEWX = 0 or the variable JP is basic then after statement 10 the objective, OBJ, is altered and in the loop 'DO 20' the dual variables of the effective constraints, YR(L), and hence Y(I), are altered. In the 'DO 30' loop the elements of the function row, YAC(J), corresponding to the non-basic variables are altered.

Finally if NEWX = 0 control is returned to the calling routine, otherwise, if NEWX ≠ 0, YAMINC is set to zero and DOANLP is called with ISTATE = 12 so that the variable NEWX is introduced into the basis.

Subroutines called in CHAGY

DOANLP

COMMON variables altered in CHAGY

ISTATE	YAC(J)
OBJ	YAMINC
R	YR(L)
Y(I)	

COMMON variables used in CHAGY

DRIVER ≡ CUPDN	PIV(J)
INBASE(J)	SIZE
INV(K,L)	TOL(JK)
N	XR(K)
NEWX	YBASIS(L)

COMMON/PARA variables used in CHAGY

JP

```
      SUBROUTINE CHAGY
*********************** COMMON AND TYPE STATEMENTS ********************
*********************** COMMON/PARA ***********************************
      EQUIVALENCE(CUPDN,DRIVER)
      IF (NEWX .EQ. 0) GO TO 10
      IF (INBASE(JP) .GE. 1) GO TO 10
      YAMINC = 0.0
      YAC(JP) = 0.0
      GO TO 40
```

```
10 K = INBASE(JP)
   R = R * CUPDN
   OBJ = OBJ + R*XR(K)
   DO 20 L = 1,SIZE
   I = YBASIS(L)
   T = YR(L) + INV(K,L) * R
   YR(L) = T
   Y(I) = T
20 CONTINUE
   TOL4 = TOL(4)
   DO 30 J = 1,N
   INJ = INBASE(J)
   IF (INJ .GE.1) GO TO 30
   T = YAC(J) + PIV(J) * R
   IF (ABS(T) .LE. TOL4) T = 0.0
   YAC(J) = T
30 CONTINUE
   IF (NEWX .EQ. 0) GO TO 50
   YAMINC = 0.0
40 ISTATE = 12
   CALL DOANLP
50 RETURN
   END
```

6. CHXSL (change *x* and slack)

This subroutine changes the values of the basic and slack variables, XR(K) and SLACK(I), to correspond with a change, R, in the value of the parameter, B(IP). The direction of change is expressed by the value of BUPDN. The change will either make the value of a basic variable either zero or equal to its upper bound, or make the value of a slack variable zero. This variable, NEWY, must be removed from the implicit or explicit basis so that feasibility can be maintained as the value of the parameter continues to change. The basis change to remove the NEWY variable will be a zero basis change.

The subroutine is entered with the data as to which variable, NEWY, is to leave the basis, the change, R, in B(IP) and the direction of change, BUPDN. If NEWY = 0 then no variable is to leave the implicit or explicit basis but the values of the variables are to be changed for printing purposes. If $0 < \text{NEWY} \leqslant \text{SIZE}$ then the basic variable XR(NEWY) is to leave the explicit basis; if NEWY > SIZE then the slack variable of the NEWY – SIZE constraint is to leave the implicit basis, thus making the NEWY – SIZE constraint effective.

Subroutine CHXSL determines in which direction either XR(NEWY) or SLACK(NEWY – SIZE) leaves the implicit basis, i.e., it determines the value of DRIVER. The sign of DRIVER is determined by the constraint that would become infeasible if the value of B(IP) continued to change. If it is a lower bound constraint, such that a basic or slack variable is above or at its lower bound and its value is changed (possibly by zero) to be equal to its lower bound, then DRIVER is set to 1·0. If it is an upper bound constraint, such that a basic or slack variable is below or at its upper bound and its value is changed to be equal to its upper bound, then DRIVER is set to −1·0. The process can be viewed as perturbing the value of the variable to be infeasible and then the sign of DRIVER indicates the direction, upwards (1·0) or downwards (−1·0), that the variable must be driven to restore feasibility. In the program the sign of DRIVER is determined by considering the direction of change of the NEWY variable XRK is used to store the initial value of XR(NEWY) or SLACK(NEWY − SIZE) depending upon whether NEWY refers to a basic or a slack variable.

NEWY will be less than or equal to SIZE if constraint IP is effective. If IP is an ineffective constraint only the value of SLACK(IP) has to be changed, and then the program goes to statement 150 to remove SLACK(IP) from the implicit basis; in this case NEWY has the value IP + SIZE. If IP is effective, the values of the basic variables, XR(K), and the value of the objective function, OBJ, are changed in the 'DO 30' loop; the values of the slack variables, SLACK(I) are changed in the 'DO 40' loop. At statement 50 if NEWY = 0 then the program goes to statement 90 and returns to the calling routine. If the NEWY variable is already basic (NEWY $\leqslant$ SIZE) then the sign of DIFF, the difference between the old and new values of XR(NEWY), is the sign of DRIVER and NEGINV is set equal to NEWY. If NEWY > SIZE then the value of SLACK(NEWY − SIZE) is zero and the sign of DRIVER is determined by considering the old value, XRK, and the sign of the NEWY − SIZE constraint, SI. In the case of an equality constraint, SI = 0·0, there will have been no change in the value of the slack and it is necessary to consider the direction of change, that is, the sign of BUPDN * G(NEWY − SIZE). Finally at statement 70 the NEWY − SIZE constraint is made effective, that is, SLACK(NEWY − SIZE) is made basic, and NEGINV is set equal to SIZE so pointing to SLACK (NEWY − SIZE) as the variable to be made non-basic.

AT statement 80 subroutine SEEKX is called to determine the variable, NEWX, that must enter the basis to remove from the basis the variable pointed to by NEGINV. If NEWX = 0, there is no such variable which means that any further change in the value of B(IP) will cause infeasibility; ISTATE is set to 2, NEGINV to zero and subroutine REDUCE is called to remove from the basis any slack variable that may have been added, and then the program goes to statement 90 to return to the calling routine. If NEWX $\neq$ 0 then subroutine NEWVEC is called, at statement 85. It is unnecessary to call subroutine SEEKY as there is to be a zero basis change hence R = 0·0, and the variable to leave the basis is pointed to by NEGINV, hence NEWY = NEGINV. The basis change is continued by calling subroutine CHBSIS, setting NEGINV to zero, calling subroutine REDUCE and CHSLCK and setting ISTATE = 1. Finally, the subroutine returns to the calling routine.

Subroutines called in CHXSL

ADDCON	NEWVEC
CHBSIS	REDUCE
CHSLCK	SEEKX

COMMON variables altered by CHXSL

DRIVER	R
ISTATE	SLACK(I)
NEGINV	X(J)
NEWY	XR(K)
OBJ	

COMMON variables used in CHXSL

BOUND(J)	NEWX
C(J)	S(I)
G(I)	SIZE
GR(K)	TOL(JK)
ISEFF(I)	XBASIS(K)
MNOW	XKPOS ≡ BUPDN
N	

COMMON/PARA variables used in CHXSL

IP

```
      SUBROUTINE CHXSL
*********************** COMMON AND TYPE STATEMENTS ********************
*********************** COMMON/PARA ***********************************
      EQUIVALENCE(BUPDN,XKPOS)
      IF (NEWY .EQ. 0) GO TO 20
      IF (NEWY .LE. SIZE) GO TO 10
      I = NEWY - SIZE
      SI = S(I)
      XRK = SLACK(I)
      IF (ISEFF(IP) .GT. 0) GO TO 20
      SLACK(IP) = SLACK(IP) - R * BUPDN
      GO TO 50
   10 XRK = XR(NEWY)
   20 R = R * BUPDN
      IF(R.EQ.0.0) GO TO 50
      TOL1 = TOL(1)
```

```
      DO 30 K = 1,SIZE
      XX = XR(K) - R * GR(K)
      IF (ABS(XX) .LE. TOL1) XX = 0.0
      J = XBASIS(K)
      IF (J .GT. N) GO TO 25
      BOUNDJ = BOUND(J)
      IF (BOUNDJ .NE. -1.0 .AND. ABS(BOUNDJ-XX).LE.TOL1) XX = BOUNDJ
      OBJ = OBJ + (XX - XR(K)) * C(J)
      X(J) = XX
   25 XR(K) = XX
   30 CONTINUE
      TOL2 = TOL(2)
      DO 40 I = 1,MNOW
      SLKI = 0.0
      IF (ISEFF(I) .GT. 0) GO TO 35
      SLKI = SLACK(I) - R * G(I)
      IF (ABS(SLKI) .LE. TOL2) SLKI = 0.0
   35 SLACK(I) = SLKI
   40 CONTINUE
   50 IF (NEWY .EQ. 0) GO TO 90
      IF (NEWY .GT. SIZE) GO TO 60
      J = XBASIS(NEWY)
      IF (J .GT. N) GO TO 60
      DIFF = XRK - XR(NEWY)
      DRIVER = 1.0
      IF(DIFF.LT.0.0.OR.DIFF.EQ.0.0.AND.XR(NEWY).EQ.BOUND(J))DRIVER=-1.0
      NEGINV = NEWY
      GO TO 80
   60 IF (SI .EQ. 0.0) GO TO 65
      DRIVER = 1.0
      IF (XRK.LT.0.0 .OR. XRK .EQ. 0.0 .AND. SI .EQ. -1.0) DRIVER = -1.0
      GO TO 70
   65 DRIVER = 1.0
      IF(BUPDN*G(NEWY-SIZE).LT.0.0) DRIVER = -1.0
   70 CALL ADDCON
      IF (ISTATE .EQ. 4) GO TO 90
      NEGINV = SIZE
   80 CALL SEEKX
      IF (NEWX .NE. 0) GO TO 85
      ISTATE = 2
      NEGINV = 0
      CALL REDUCE
      GO TO 90
   85 CALL NEWVEC
      R = 0.0
      NEWY = NEGINV
      CALL CHBSIS
      NEGINV = 0
      CALL REDUCE
      CALL CHSLCK
      ISTATE = 1
   90 RETURN
      END
```

7. MIDBI (mid b_i)

This subroutine returns to the optimal feasible basis associated with BMID, the initial value of B(IP). The subroutine is entered with the direction of change, BUPDN, from the current basis to the basis associated with BMID.

At the beginning of the subroutine the change, RATIO, in the value of the parameter is computed and B(IP) is set equal to BMID. T is a temporary store for the value of BUPDN. If the constraint IP is ineffective then SLACK(IP) is altered to correspond with the change in value of B(IP). SLACK(IP) is tested for feasibility; if it is feasible the program goes to statement 40 and subroutine LP is entered to check the accuracy of the solution, if it is not feasible NEGROW is set equal to IP and subroutine LP is entered with ISTATE = 11 to restore feasibility and check the accuracy of the solution.

If constraint IP is effective then, as in PARAB, the change, R, in the value of the parameter to the adjacent corner point and the variable NEWY, that would have to leave the basis to maintain feasibility, are computed. NEWY is temporarily stored in NEG, and R in RR. If the adjacent corner point is at a value of the parameter beyond or equal to BMID, that is R ⩾ RATIO, then the basis associated with BMID will be feasible and NEG is set to zero. Subroutine CHXSL is entered with R = RATIO and NEWY = 0 to change the values of the basic and slack variables to correspond to a change of the value of the parameter to BMID.

If the value of R (stored in RR), as found by subroutine SEEKY, is zero then the array G(I) may have not been computed, or been only partly computed. This means that the values of the slack variables after subroutine CHXSL will be wrong; the slack variables are corrected by setting INREV = 1 and calling subroutine CHSLCK.

At statement 20 if the basis is feasible, NEG = 0, then subroutine LP is entered with ISTATE = 11 to check the accuracy of the solution. But if it was necessary to overshoot beyond the adjacent feasible corner point, R < RATIO, then the basis will be infeasible. The program now deals with the known infeasibility. If the infeasibility is in a basic variable, NEGINV and DRIVER are set. If the infeasibility is in a slack variable then NEGROW is set. Finally subroutine DOANLP is entered with ISTATE = 11 to restore feasibility and the accuracy of the solution is checked by entering subroutine LP.

Subroutines called in MIDBI

CHSLCK CHXSL

DOANLP	NEWVEC
LP	SEEKY

COMMON variables altered in MIDBI

B(I)	NEWX
DRIVER	NEWY
INREV	R
ISTATE	SLACK(I)
NEGINV	XKPOS ≡ BUPDN
NEGROW	

COMMON variables used in MIDBI

BOUND(J)	SIZE
ISEFF(I)	XBASIS(K)
N	XR(K)
S(I)	

COMMON/PARA variables used in MIDBI

BMID	IP

```
      SUBROUTINE MIDBI
********************** COMMON AND TYPE STATEMENTS *******************
********************** COMMON/PARA **********************************
      EQUIVALENCE(BUPDN,XKPOS)
      T = BUPDN
      RATIO = ABS(B(IP) - BMID)
      B(IP) = BMID
      IF (ISEFF(IP) .GT. 0) GO TO 10
      SLACK(IP) = SLACK(IP) - RATIO * BUPDN
      IF(SLACK(IP)*S(IP).GE.0.0.AND.S(IP).NE.0.0) GO TO 40
      IF(S(IP).EQ.0.0.AND.SLACK(IP).EQ.0.0) GO TO 40
      NEGROW = IP
      GO TO 40
   10 NEWX = IP + N
      CALL NEWVEC
      BUPDN = T
      CALL SEEKY
      RR = R
      NEG = NEWY
      IF (R .GE. RATIO) NEG = 0
      R = RATIO
      NEWY = 0
      CALL CHXSL
      IF(RR.NE.0.0) GO TO 20
      INREV = 1
      CALL CHSLCK
   20 IF(NEG.EQ.0) GO TO 40
      IF (NEG .GT. SIZE) GO TO 30
```

```
      NEGINV = NEG
      J = XBASIS(NEGINV)
      DRIVER = 1.0
      IF(XR(NEGINV).GT.BOUND(J).AND.BOUND(J).NE.-1.0) DRIVER = -1.0
      GO TO 35
   30 NEGROW = NEG - SIZE
   35 ISTATE = 11
      CALL DOANLP
      IF(ISTATE.EQ.4) GO TO 50
   40 ISTATE = 11
      CALL LP
   50 RETURN
      END
```

8. MIDCJ (mid c_j)

This subroutine returns to the optimal feasible basis associated with CMID, the initial value of C(JP). The subroutine is entered with the direction of change, CUPDN, from the current basis to the basis associated with CMID.

At the beginning of the subroutine the change, RATIO, in the value of the parameter is computed and C(JP) is set equal to CMID. If the variable JP is non-basic then the function variable YAC(JP) is altered, and if JP is non-basic at its upper bound the objective is also altered, to correspond with the change in the objective function element from C(JP) to CMID. Then, at statement 20, subroutine LP is entered with ISTATE = 11 so that optimality is restored and the accuracy of the solution is checked.

If JP is basic then, as in PARAC, the change, R, in value of the parameter to the adjacent corner point and the variable, NEWX, that would have to enter the basis to maintain optimality, are computed. NEWX is temporarily stored in NONOPT. If the adjacent corner point is at a value of the parameter beyond or equal to CMID, that is $R \geqslant$ RATIO, then the basis associated with CMID will be optimal and so NONOPT is set to zero. Subroutine CHAGY is entered with R = RATIO and NEWX = 0 to change the values of the dual and function row variables to correspond to the change of the value of the parameter to CMID. If the basis is optimal, NONOPT = 0, then subroutine LP is entered with ISTATE = 11 to check the accuracy of the solution. But if it was necessary to overshoot beyond the adjacent optimal corner point, $R <$ RATIO, then the basis will be non-optimal. The program now introduces into the basis the variable that is known to be non-optimal; NEWX and YAMINC are set and subroutine DOANLP is entered with ISTATE = 12 so that NEWX will be introduced into the basis and optimality restored. Finally the accuracy of the solution is checked by calling subroutine LP.

Subroutines called in MIDCJ

CHAGY	LP
DOANLP	SEEKX

COMMON variables altered in MIDCJ

C(J)	OBJ
ISTATE	R
NEGINV	YAC(J)
NEWX	YAMINC

COMMON variables used in MIDCJ

BOUND(J)	ISEFF(I)
DRIVER ≡ CUPDN	N
INBASE(J)	YR(L)

COMMON/PARA variables used in MIDCJ

CMID	JP

```
      SUBROUTINE MIDCJ
*********************** COMMON AND TYPE STATEMENTS ********************
*********************** COMMON/PARA ************************************
      EQUIVALENCE(CUPDN,DRIVER)
      RATIO  = ABS(C(JP) - CMID)
      C(JP) = CMID
      IF (INBASE(JP) .GT. 0) GO TO 10
      YAC(JP) = YAC(JP) - RATIO * CUPDN
      IF(INBASE(JP).EQ.-1) OBJ = OBJ + RATIO * BOUND(JP) * CUPDN
      GO TO 20
   10 NEGINV = INBASE(JP)
      CALL SEEKX
      R = -R
      NEGINV = 0
      NONOPT = NEWX
      IF (R .GE. RATIO) NONOPT = 0
      R = RATIO
      NEWX = 0
      CALL CHAGY
      IF (NONOPT.EQ.0) GO TO 20
      NEWX = NONOPT
      IF (NEWX .LE. N) YAMINC = YAC(NEWX)
      IF (NEWX .GT. N) K = ISEFF(NEWX-N)
      IF (NEWX .GT. N) YAMINC = YR(K) * S(NEWX-N)
      ISTATE = 12
      CALL DOANLP
      IF (ISTATE .EQ. 4) GO TO 30
   20 ISTATE = 11
      CALL LP
   30 RETURN
      END
```

9. PARAB (parametrize b_i)

9.1. COMMON/PARA variables

IP is the constraint the value of whose right hand side is to be varied, i.e. B(IP) is the parameter. The initial value of B(IP) is stored in BMID. When the value of B(IP) is varied between specified limits, SBI, and UBI are the lower and upper limits respectively. When a sensitivity analysis of B(IP) is being performed, at the beginning of subroutine PARAB SBI and UBI have the same value as B(IP), and if IP is an effective constraint, then during the computation their values are changed to be the lower and upper values that B(IP) may take without causing the LP optimal basis to become infeasible. Throughout a range analysis SBI and UBI have the same value as the initial value of B(IP). SBIN and UBIN are the lower and upper values of B(IP) within which a particular basis is either feasible or infeasible; they are used for printing purposes.

ISENSB and IRANGB are used as markers to indicate the type of analysis that is being performed.

IRANGB = 1 ISENSB = 0	a range analysis of B(IP) is being performed.
IRANGB = 0 ISENSB = 1	a sensitivity analysis of B(IP) is being performed.
IRANGB = 0 ISENSB = 0	a parametric analysis of B(IP) between the limits, SBI and UBI is being performed.

The state of the parametric algorithm is contained in the values taken by IPARAB:

IPARAB = 0	parametric variations (of any type) of a b_i element are not being performed.
= 1	subroutine PARAB is entered and this indicates the beginning of the parametric variation of B(IP).
= 2	the initial basis is feasible between a lower, SBIN, and an upper, UBIN, value of B(IP).
= 3	the current basis is feasible between a lower and an upper, SBIN and UBIN, value of B(IP).
= 4	the current basis is feasible within the range SBIN to UBIN, but the constraint IP is ineffective, so only the value of SLACK(IP) will alter as B(IP) is varied.
= 5	the current basis is feasible between the limit SBIN and UBIN, one of which is either plus or minus infinity. Constraint IP is effective but the value of

B(IP) may be varied without causing the basis to become infeasible.

= 6 the current basis is infeasible within the range SBIN to UBIN.

= 7 the initial basis is feasible within SBIN and UBIN but the values of the variables and the objective function are not to be printed.

= 8 the end of the parametric variation of B(IP).

= 9 the variables at the specified limit, either SBI or UBI, are to be printed.

= 10 an equality constraint cannot be made effective so no parametric, sensitivity or range analysis can be performed.

9.2. Subroutine PARAB

The algorithm starts by evaluating the initial range of values of B(IP) within which the initial LP basis is feasible. It then explores the sequence of bases that results as the value of B(IP) is increased. Having reached the upper limit the algorithm returns to the initial value of B(IP) and then explores the sequence of bases as the value of B(IP) is decreased until the lower limit is reached. Finally, the algorithm returns to the optimal feasible basis associated with the initial value of B(IP). In a range analysis the computation ceases as soon as the initial range has been evaluated. In a sensitivity analysis there are no basis changes but the basic variables and the slack variables are altered to correspond to the values of B(IP) at either end of the range.

A message indicating the beginning of the analysis is not printed if a range analysis is being performed. The initial value of B(IP) is stored in BMID. SBIN and UBIN are initially set to BMID. NEWYDN and NEWYUP (NEWY down and NEWY up) point to the element of XR(K) or SLACK(I) that must leave the explicit or implicit basis in order to preserve feasibility as B(IP) decreases or increases. If either NEWYDN or NEWYUP have a value of 0 then no variable is to leave the explicit or implicit basis and a value of −1 indicates that no computation is to be carried out either decreasing or increasing B(IP). MIDPR (mid print) is a printing control variable that is initially at zero.

The beginning of the subroutine, to statement 50, is concerned with the situation when IP is an ineffective constraint. If IP is not an equality constraint then the range SBIN to UBIN within which B(IP) can vary is evaluated. NEWYUP and NEWYDN, as appropriate, are set equal to IP + SIZE to indicate that SLACK(IP) will have to leave the implicit basis. IPARAB is set to 2 and the range SBIN to UBIN, is printed. This is the finish of the computation if a range analysis is being conducted, IRANGB = 1, or if the initial range is beyond the specified range. Otherwise R, the change in the value of B(IP), is set and control passes to statement 90 if the value of B(IP) is to be increased or to statement 130 if the value of B(IP) is to be decreased.

It is only possible to parametrize the right hand side of an equality constraint if the constraint is effective. Statements 30 to the statement before 45 are concerned with making the IP equality constraint effective by adding the constraint to the explicit basis and then forcing the associated slack out of the basis. If it is not possible to force the slack out of the basis, having tried both DRIVER equal to 1·0 and to −1·0, then control passes to statement 45 where an error message is printed. The slack variable is removed from the basis and the computation finishes.

Statements 50 to 80 are concerned with evaluating and printing the initial range of values of B(IP) when IP is an effective constraint at the initial LP optimum solution. The amount by which the value of B(IP) can alter, R, is evaluated in subroutine SEEKY after the array GR has been computed in subroutine NEWVEC. The direction of change is contained in BUPDN (*b* up and down); BUPDN = 1·0, B(IP) is being decreased and BUPDN = −1·0, B(IP) is being increased. NEWY is the variable that must leave either the explicit or the implicit basis in order to preserve feasibility. If NEWY equals 0 then the value of B(IP) can change to plus or minus infinity, depending on the sign of BUPDN, without causing infeasibility. At statement 50 the program inspects downwards, BUPDN = 1·0, and sets SBIN equal to the lower end of the range. At statement 70 the program inspects upwards, BUPDN = 1·0, and sets UBIN equal to the upper end of the range. If the value of UBIN is above UBI then R is set equal to the change in B(IP) needed to increase it to UBI. At statement 80 the range, SBIN to UBIN, of the initial feasible basis is printed. The computation is finished if a range analysis, IRANGB = 1, is being performed. UBINA is a temporary storage for the upper limit of the initial feasible range. If a sensitivity analysis is being performed, ISENSB = 1, and the upper limit is not infinity IUP ≠ 5, R is set equal to the change needed to increase B(IP) to the upper limit, UBI. NEWY is set to NEWYUP.

Statements 100 to the IF statement after 115 are the loop that explores the optimal bases as B(IP) increases. The possible exits from the loop are:

1. ISTATE = 4, the inverse is too big for the program;
2. IPARAB = 4, IP is ineffective;
3. ISTATE = 2 and IPARAB = 6, the basis is infeasible;
4. IPARAB = 9, the upper limit of the range is reached.

If the upper limit of the range for a basis is plus infinity IPARAB is set to 5. Until one of the above conditions occurs IPARAB is equal to 3 throughout the loop.

The statements following 100 update B(IP) and SBIN. Subroutine CHXSL updates the basic variables and the slack variables to correspond to B(IP), and removes the NEWY variable from the explicit or implicit basis by a zero basis change. If the upper limit has been reached the basis is printed, otherwise control passes to statement 105. If the basis is feasible and constraint IP is effective, the upper limit on the value of B(IP) for which the basis remains feasible is evaluated and stored in UBIN. If UBIN is greater than UBI R is set equal to UBI – B(IP). The feasible range is printed and control returns to the beginning of the loop. In a sensitivity analysis the loop is entered at statement 100 with UBIN equal to UBI and NEWY equal to 0.

Subroutine MIDBI returns to the basis associated with the initial value of B(IP), BMID. It is necessary to recompute the arrays GR and G in order to be able to change the basic and slack variables to correspond to the value of B(IP) at the lower limit of the initial feasible range. In the case of a sensitivity analysis this is not necessary as no basis changes have taken place so that the contents of GR and G are unaltered.

Statements 130 to 150 are the loop that explore the optimal bases as B(IP) decreases. The computation is analogous to the loop that increases B(IP). A sensitivity analysis enters the loop with SBIN equal to SBI and NEWY equal to 0. A parametric analysis enters the loop at statement 135 in order to recompute the lower limit of the initial feasible range. As it is not necessary to print the basis associated with BMID again, MIDPR is used as a marker to indicate whether or not the basis being printed is the initial basis.

The subroutine finishes by calling subroutine MIDBI to return to the basis associated with BMID, and by calling PPRINT to print the final message.

Subroutines called in PARAB

ADDCON	NEWVEC
CHBSIS	PPRINT
CHSLCK	REDUCE
CHXSL	SEEKX
MIDBI	SEEKY

COMMON variables altered in PARAB

B(I)	NEWX
DRIVER	NEWY
ISTATE	R
NEGINV	XKPOS ≡ BUPDN

COMMON variables used in PARAB

ISEFF(I)	SIZE
N	SLACK(I)
S(I)	XBASIS(K)

COMMON/PARA variables altered in PARAB

BMID	SBIN
IPARAB	UBI
SBI	UBIN

COMMON/PARA variables used in PARAB

DUMBIG	IRANGB
IP	ISENSB

```
      SUBROUTINE PARAB
*********************** COMMON AND TYPE STATEMENTS ********************
*********************** COMMON/PARA ***********************************
      EQUIVALENCE (BUPDN,XKPOS)
      IF(IRANGB.NE.1) CALL PPRINT
      BMID = B(IP)
      NEWYUP = -1
      NEWYDN = -1
      UBIN = BMID
      SBIN = BMID
      MIDPR = 0
      IF (ISEFF(IP) .GT. 0) GO TO 50
      SI = S(IP)
      SLACKI = SLACK(IP)
      BIN = BMID - SLACKI
      IF (SI .EQ. 0.0) GO TO 30
      IF (SI .EQ. 1.0) GO TO 10
      SBIN = -DUMBIG
      UBIN = BIN
      NEWYUP = IP + SIZE
      GO TO 20
   10 UBIN = DUMBIG
      SBIN = BIN
      NEWYDN = IP + SIZE
   20 IPARAB = 2
      CALL PPRINT
      IF(IRANGB.EQ.1) GO TO 200
      IF(SBIN.EQ.SBI.AND.UBIN.EQ.UBI) GO TO 160
      R = ABS(SLACKI)
      IUP = 3
      IF (NEWYUP .NE. -1) GO TO 90
      IPARAB = 3
      NEWY = NEWYDN
      GO TO 130
   30 NEWY = IP + SIZE
      CALL ADDCON
      IF(ISTATE.EQ.4) GO TO 200
      NEGINV = SIZE
      DRIVER = 1.0
   40 CALL SEEKX
      IF(NEWX.NE.0) GO TO 42
      IF(DRIVER.EQ.-1.0) GO TO 45
      DRIVER = -1.0
      GO TO 40
```

```
42 CALL NEWVEC
   R = 0.0
   NEWY = NEGINV
   CALL CHBSIS
   NEGINV = 0
   CALL REDUCE
   CALL CHSLCK
   ISTATE = 1
   GO TO 50
45 IPARAB = 10
   CALL PPRINT
   NEGINV = 0
   CALL REDUCE
   ISTATE = 1
   GO TO 200
50 NEWX = IP + N
   BI = B(IP)
   CALL NEWVEC
   BUPDN = 1.0
   CALL SEEKY
   NEWYDN = NEWY
   SBIN = BI - R
   IF(NEWY.EQ.0.AND.ISENSB.EQ.1) NEWYDN = -1
   IF(NEWY.EQ.0) NEWYDN = -1
   IF(ISENSB.EQ.1) SBI = SBIN
70 BUPDN = -1.0
   IUP = 3
   CALL SEEKY
   IF (NEWY .EQ. 0 .OR. BI + R .GE. UBI) GO TO 75
   UBIN = BI + R
   NEWYUP = NEWY
   GO TO 80
75 UBIN = BI + R
   IF(NEWY.EQ.0) UBIN = DUMBIG
   R = UBI - BI
   NEWYUP = 0
   IF (NEWY .EQ. 0) IUP = 5
80 IPARAB = 2
   CALL PPRINT
   IF(IRANGB.EQ.1) GO TO 200
   UBINA = UBIN
   IF(ISENSB.EQ.0) GO TO 90
   UBI = UBIN
   IF(IUP.EQ.5) GO TO 120
   R = UBIN - BI
90 NEWY = NEWYUP
   IPARAB = IUP
100 BUPDN = -1.0
   B(IP) = UBIN
   IF(UBIN.GT.UBI) B(IP) = UBI
   SBIN = UBIN
   CALL CHXSL
   IF (ISTATE .EQ. 4) GO TO 200
   BUPDN = -1.0
   IF(UBIN.LT.UBI) GO TO 105
   IPARAB = 9
   CALL PPRINT
   GO TO 120
```

```
105 IF (ISEFF(IP) .EQ. 0) IPARAB = 4
    IF(SIZE.EQ.1.AND.XBASIS(1).EQ.IP+N) IPARAB = 4
    IF (ISTATE .EQ. 2) IPARAB = 6
    IF (IPARAB .NE. 3) GO TO 110
    NEWX = IP + N
    CALL NEWVEC
    BUPDN = -1.0
    CALL SEEKY
    IF (NEWY .EQ. 0) IPARAB = 5
    IF (B(IP) + R .GE. UBI) GO TO 110
    UBIN = B(IP) + R
    GO TO 115
110 UBIN = DUMBIG
    IF(IPARAB.EQ.3) UBIN = B(IP) + R
    R = UBI - B(IP)
    NEWY = 0
115 CALL PPRINT
    IF (IPARAB .EQ. 3 .OR. IPARAB .EQ. 5) GO TO 100
120 IF (NEWYDN .EQ. -1) GO TO 155
    IF(ISENSB.EQ.1) GO TO 125
    BUPDN = 1.0
    CALL MIDBI
    IF (ISTATE .EQ. 4) GO TO 200
    BI = B(IP)
    UBIN = UBINA
    IPARAB = 3
    GO TO 135
125 R = UBI - SBI
    NEWY = 0
    SBIN = SBI
130 BUPDN = 1.0
    UBIN = SBIN
    B(IP) = UBIN
    IF(SBIN.LT.SBI) B(IP) = SBI
    BI = B(IP)
    CALL CHXSL
    IF (ISTATE .EQ. 4) GO TO 200
    BUPDN = 1.0
    IF(SBIN.GT.SBI) GO TO 135
    IPARAB = 9
    CALL PPRINT
    GO TO 155
135 IF (ISEFF(IP) .EQ. 0) IPARAB = 4
    IF(SIZE.EQ.1.AND.XBASIS(1).EQ.IP+N) IPARAB = 4
    IF (ISTATE .EQ. 2) IPARAB = 6
    IF (IPARAB .NE. 3) GO TO 140
    NEWX = IP + N
    CALL NEWVEC
    BUPDN = 1.0
    CALL SEEKY
    IF (NEWY .EQ. 0) IPARAB = 5
    IF (BI - R .LE. SBI) GO TO 140
    SBIN = BI - R
    GO TO 145
140 SBIN = -DUMBIG
    IF(IPARAB.EQ.3) SBIN = B(IP) - R
    R = BI - SBI
    NEWY = 0
```

```
145 IF(MIDPR.EQ.1) CALL PPRINT
    IF(MIDPR.EQ.1) GO TO 150
    IUP = IPARAB
    IPARAB = 7
    CALL PPRINT
    IPARAB = IUP
    MIDPR = 1
150 IF (IPARAB .EQ. 3 .OR. IPARAB .EQ. 5) GO TO 130
155 BUPDN = -BUPDN
    CALL MIDBi
    IF (ISTATE .EQ. 4) GO TO 200
160 IPARAB = 8
    CALL PPRINT
200 RETURN
    END
```

10. PARAC (parametrize c_j)

10.1. COMMON/PARA variables

JP is the variable whose objective function element is to be varied. C(JP) is the parameter. The initial value of C(JP) is stored in CMID. When the value of C(JP) is varied between specified limits SCJ and UCJ are the lower and upper limits respectively. When a sensitivity analysis of C(JP) is being performed, as the beginning of subroutine PARAC SCJ and UCJ have the same value as C(JP). If JP is a basic variable, then during the computation their values are changed to be the lower and upper values that C(JP) may take without causing the LP basis to become non-optimal. Throughout a range analysis SCJ and UCJ have the same value as the initial value of C(JP). SCJN and UCJN are the lower and upper values of C(JP) within which a particular basis is either optimal or non-optimal; they are used for printing purposes.

ISENSC and IRANGC are used as markers to indicate the type of analysis that is being performed.

IRANGC = 1, ISENSC = 0 } a range analysis of C(JP) is being performed.

IRANGC = 0, ISENSC = 1 } a sensitivity analysis of C(JP) is being performed.

IRANGC = 0, ISENSC = 0 } a parametric analysis of C(JP) between the limits of SCJ and UCJ is being performed.

The state of the parametric algorithm is contained in the values taken by IPARAC:

IPARAC = 0 parametric variations (of any type) of a c_j element are not being performed.

= 1 subroutine PARAC is entered and this indicates the beginning of the parametric variation of C(JP).

= 2 the initial basis is optimal between a lower, SCJN, and an upper, UCJN, value of C(JP).

= 3 the current basis is optimal between a lower, SCJN, and an upper, UCJN, value of C(JP).

= 4 the current basis is optimal between the limits, SCJN and UCJN, but the variable JP is non-basic, so only the value of YAC(JP) will alter as C(JP) is varied.

= 5 the current basis is optimal between the limits SCJN and UCJN, one of which is plus or minus infinity. Variable JP is basic but the value of C(JP) may be varied without causing the basis to become non-optimal.

= 6 the current basis is non-optimal within the range SCJN and UCJN.

= 7 the initial basis is optimal within SCJN and UCJN but the values of the dual variables, the function row variables and the objective function are not to be printed.

= 8 the end of the parametric variation of C(JP).

= 9 the variables at the specified limit, either SCJ or UCJ, are to be printed.

10.2. Subroutine PARAC

The algorithm starts by evaluating the range of values of C(JP) within which the initial LP solution is optimal. It then explores the sequence of bases that results as the value of C(JP) is increased. Having reached the upper limit the algorithm returns to the initial value of C(JP) and then explores the sequence of bases as the value of C(JP) is decreased until the lower limit is reached. Finally the algorithm returns to the optimal basis associated with the initial value of C(JP). In a range analysis the computation ceases as soon as the initial range has been evaluated. In a sensitivity analysis there are no basis changes but the values of the dual variables and the function row variables are altered to correspond to the values of C(JP) at either end of the initial range.

A message indicating the beginning of the analysis is not printed if a range analysis is being performed. The initial value of C(JP) is stored in

CMID. SCJN and UCJN are initially set to C(JP). NEWXUP and NEWXDN (NEWX up and NEWX down) point to original or slack variables that must enter the explicit or implicit basis in order to preserve optimality as the value of C(JP) increases or decreases. If either NEWXUP or NEWXDN have a value of 0 then no variable is to enter the explicit or implicit basis and a value of −1 indicates that no computation is to be carried out either increasing or decreasing C(JP). MIDPR (mid print) is a printing control variable that is initially at zero.

The beginning of the subroutine to statement 20 is concerned with the situation when JP is non basic, INBASE(JP) $\leqslant 0$. The range of values, SCJN to UCJN, for which the initial LP solution remains optimal are computed and printed. If a range analysis is being performed, IRANGB = 1, or if the limits SCJN and UCJN are beyond the specified limits SCJ and UCJ, the computation finishes. Otherwise, in order to continue increasing or decreasing the value of C(JP), JP must be made basic and either NEWXUP or NEWX, as appropriate, are set equal to JP.

From statement 20 to just beyond statement 40 is concerned with the situation when JP is a basic variable at the initial LP optimum. The change in the value of C(JP) is evaluated in subroutine SEEKX, having set NEGINV to refer to the row of the basis associated with variable JP. The change is contained in R and the direction of change in CUPDN (C up and down). CUPDN = −1·0 means that the value of C(JP) is being decreased and CUPDN = 1·0 that C(JP) is being increased. NEWX is the variable that must enter either the explicit or the implicit basis. If NEWX equals 0 then C(JP) can change to plus or minus infinity, depending on the sign of CUPDN, without causing non-optimality. The program starts by considering decreasing C(JP), CUPDN = −1·0, and stores the lower end of the range in SCJN and the variable that must enter the basis in NEWXDN. It then considers increasing C(JP), CUPDN = 1·0, and stores the upper end of the range in UCJN and the variable to enter in NEWXUP. If the upper end of the range, UCJN, is beyond the specified limit, UCJ, then R is altered to the change needed to increase C(JP) to UCJ.

At statement 40 the range of values of C(JP) for which the initial LP solution is optimal is printed. If a range analysis is being performed the computation ceases. UCJNA is a temporary store of the upper limit of the initial basis. If a sensitivity analysis is being performed, ISENSC = 1, then R is set to the change needed to increase C(JP) to the upper limit, UCJ, and NEWX is set to NEWXUP.

Statements 60 to the IF statement after 75 are the loop that explores the optimal bases as C(JP) increases. The possible exits from this loop are:

1. ISTATE = 4, the inverse is too big for the program;
2. IPARAC = 4, JP is non basic;

3. IPARAC = 6, the basis is non-optimal;
4. IPARAC = 9, the upper limit of the range is reached;

If the upper limit of the range for a basis is plus infinity IPARAC is set to 5. Until one of these conditions occurs IPARAC is equal to 3 throughout the loop.

The statements following statement 60 update C(JP) and SCJN. Subroutine CHAGY updates the dual variables and the function row variables to correspond to C(JP), and performs a dual zero basis change to bring the NEWX variable into the explicit or implicit basis. Then if the upper limit has been reached the basis is printed, otherwise control passes to statement 65. If the basis is optimal and the variable JP basic the upper limit of the value of C(JP) for which the basis remains optimal is evaluated and stored in UCJN. If UCJN is greater than UCJ R is set equal to UCJ – C(JP). The optimal range is printed and control returns to the beginning of the loop. In a sensitivity analysis, the loop is entered at statement 60 with UCJN equal to UCJ and NEWX equal to 0.

Subroutine MIDCJ returns to the basis associated with the initial value of C(JP), CMID. It is necessary to recompute the array PIV in order to be able to change the dual variables to correspond to the value of C(JP) at the lower limit of the initial optimal range. This is performed by recomputing the lower limit of the initial range. In the case of a sensitivity analysis this is not necessary as no basis changes have occurred so that the contents of PIV have not been altered.

Statements 60 to 110 are the loop that explores the optimal bases as C(JP) decreases. The computation is analogous to the loop that increases C(JP). A sensitivity analysis enters the loop with SCJN equal to SCJ and NEWX equal to 0. A parametric analysis enters the loop at statement 95 in order to recompute the lower limit of the initial optimal range. As it is not necessary to print the basis associated with CMID again, MIDPR is used as a marker to indicate whether or not the basis being printed is the initial basis.

The subroutine finishes by calling subroutine MIDCJ to return to the basis associated with CMID, and by calling PPRINT to print the final message.

Subroutines called in PARAC

CHAGY	PPRINT
MIDCJ	SEEKX

COMMON variables altered in PARAC

C(J)	NEWX
DRIVER ≡ CUPDN	OBJ
NEGINV	R

COMMON variables used in PARAC

BOUND(J)	ISTATE
INBASE(J)	YAC(J)

COMMON/PARA variables altered in PARAC

CMID	SCJN
IPARAC	UCJ
SCJ	UCJN

COMMON/PARA variables used in PARAC

DUMBIG	ISENSC
IRANGC	JP

```
      SUBROUTINE PARAC
*********************** COMMON AND TYPE STATEMENTS ********************
*********************** COMMON/PARA ***********************************
      EQUIVALENCE(CUPDN,DRIVER)
      IF(IRANGC.NE.1) CALL PPRINT
      CMID = C(JP)
      NEWXUP = -1
      NEWXDN = -1
      SCJN = C(JP)
      UCJN = C(JP)
      MIDPR = 0
      IF (INBASE(JP) .GT. 0) GO TO 20
      IF (INBASE(JP) .EQ. -1) GO TO 10
      SCJN = -DUMBIG
      UCJN = YAC(JP) + C(JP)
      IPARAC = 2
      CALL PPRINT
      IF(IRANGC.EQ.1) GO TO 200
      IF (UCJN .GE. UCJ) GO TO 120
      IUP = 3
      NEWXUP = JP
      GO TO 50
   10 UCJN = DUMBIG
      SCJN = YAC(JP) + C(JP)
      IPARAC = 2
      CALL PPRINT
      IF(IRANGC.EQ.1) GO TO 200
      IF (SCJN .LE. SCJ) GO TO 120
      OBJ = OBJ - (C(JP)-SCJN) * BOUND(JP)
      NEWX = JP
      IPARAC = 3
      GO TO 90
   20 NEGINV = INBASE(JP)
      CJ = C(JP)
      CUPDN = -1.0
```

```
      CALL SEEKX
      R = -R
      NEWXDN = NEWX
      SCJN = CJ - R
      IF(NEWX.EQ.0) SCJN = -DUMBIG
      IF(NEWX.EQ.0.AND.ISENSC.EQ.1) NEWXDN = -1
      IF(ISENSC.EQ.1) SCJ = SCJN
   30 CUPDN = 1.0
      CALL SEEKX
      R = -R
      IUP = 3
      IF (NEWX .EQ. 0 .OR. CJ + R .GE. UCJ) GO TO 35
      UCJN = CJ + R
      NEWXUP = NEWX
      GO TO 40
   35 UCJN = CJ + R
      IF(NEWX.EQ.0) UCJN = DUMBIG
      R = UCJ - CJ
      NEWXUP = 0
      IF (NEWX .EQ. 0) IUP = 5
   40 NEGINV = 0
      IPARAC = 2
      CALL PPRINT
      IF(IRANGC.EQ.1) GO TO 200
      UCJNA = UCJN
      IF(ISENSC.EQ.0) GO TO 50
      UCJ = UCJN
      IF(IUP.EQ.5) GO TO 80
      R = UCJN - CJ
   50 NEWX = NEWXUP
      IPARAC = IUP
   60 CUPDN = 1.0
      C(JP) = UCJN
      IF(UCJN.GT.UCJ) C(JP) = UCJ
      SCJN = UCJN
      CALL CHAGY
      IF (ISTATE .EQ. 4) GO TO 200
      CUPDN = 1.0
      IF (UCJN .LT. UCJ) GO TO 65
      IPARAC = 9
      CALL PPRINT
      GO TO 80
   65 IF (INBASE(JP) .EQ. -1) IPARAC = 4
      IF (ISTATE .EQ. 3) IPARAC = 6
      IF (IPARAC .NE. 3) GO TO 70
      NEGINV = INBASE(JP)
      CALL SEEKX
      R = -R
      NEGINV = 0
      IF (NEWX .EQ. 0) IPARAC = 5
      IF (C(JP) + R .GE. UCJ) GO TO 70
      UCJN = C(JP) + R
      GO TO 75
   70 UCJN = DUMBIG
      IF(IPARAC.EQ.3) UCJN = C(JP) + R
      R = UCJ - C(JP)
      NEWX = 0
```

```
 75 CALL PPRINT
    IF (IPARAC .EQ. 3 .OR. IPARAC .EQ. 5) GO TO 60
 80 IF (NEWXDN .EQ. -1) GO TO 115
    IF(ISENSC.EQ.1) GO TO 85
    CUPDN = -1.0
    CALL MIDCJ
    IF (ISTATE .EQ. 4) GO TO 200
    UCJN = UCJNA
    IPARAC = 3
    GO TO 95
 85 R = C(JP) - SCJ
    NEWX = 0
    SCJN = SCJ
 90 CUPDN = -1.0
    UCJN = SCJN
    C(JP) = UCJN
    IF(SCJN.LT.SCJ) C(JP) = SCJ
    CALL CHAGY
    IF (ISTATE .EQ.4) GO TO 200
    CUPDN = -1.0
    IF (SCJN .GT. SCJ) GO TO 95
    IPARAC = 9
    CALL PPRINT
    GO TO 115
 95 IF (INBASE(JP) .EQ. 0) IPARAC = 4
    IF (ISTATE .EQ. 3) IPARAC = 6
    IF (IPARAC .NE. 3) GO TO 100
    CUPDN = -1.0
    NEGINV = INBASE(JP)
    CALL SEEKX
    R = -R
    NEGINV = 0
    IF (NEWX .EQ. 0) IPARAC = 5
    IF (C(JP) - R .LE. SCJ) GO TO 100
    SCJN = C(JP) - R
    GO TO 105
100 SCJN = -DUMBIG
    IF(IPARAC.EQ.3) SCJN = C(JP) - R
    NEWX = 0
    R = C(JP) - SCJ
105 IF(MIDPR.EQ.1) CALL PPRINT
    IF(MIDPR.EQ.1) GO TO 110
    IUP = IPARAC
    IPARAC = 7
    CALL PPRINT
    IPARAC = IUP
    MIDPR = 1
110 IF (IPARAC .EQ. 3 .OR. IPARAC .EQ. 5) GO TO 90
115 CUPDN = -CUPDN
    CALL MIDCJ
    IF (ISTATE .EQ. 4) GO TO 200
120 IPARAC = 8
    CALL PPRINT
200 RETURN
    END
```

11. PDATA (parametric data)

This subroutine reads the data for the parametric variations, if any.

The maximum number of parametric variations that can be made is MAXP. Each parametric request is made upon a separate card; the first data card contains the number of parametric request cards, NUMP, that follow the first card. The requests are of three types:

1. To vary the value of either b_i or c_j between two specified values. The lower limit is stored in BOTOM(NP) and the upper in TOP(NP) and the variable is stored in IJPARA(NP). The value of i is read and stored as positive if an element of b_i is varied, while the value of j is read as positive and stored as negative if a value of c_j is being varied.
2. To perform a sensitivity analysis upon either b_i or c_j. As in case (1) the variable to be varied is stored in IJPARA(NP) and the limits in BOTOM(NP) and TOP(NP). However, the limits have exactly the same value as each other and are equal to the value of b_i or c_j as appropriate.
3. To perform a range analysis of either all elements of b or all elements of c. In this case IRANGB (all elements of b) or IRANGC (all elements of c) is set to 1.

MAXP, which is initialized at the beginning of subroutine PDATA, is the dimension of the arrays used to store the parametric requests. NUMP must not be greater than MAXP. At the end of the subroutine NUMP is set equal to the sum of the number of valid requests of types (1) and (2).

DUMBIG is a large value that is used to represent infinity for printing purposes. It must have a value larger than any element of the arrays B or C. It is initialized at the end of subroutine PDATA.

Subroutine PDATA is concerned with reading the parametric requests and checking their validity. Erroneous requests are printed with an error message and ignored. The first card has the number of parametric requests, NUMP, and the printing control variable, IPRPLP, in the first two 10 digit fields. The program checks that $0 < \text{NUMP} \leqslant \text{MAXP}$. In the 'DO 35' loop the NUMP parametric requests are read. A request has the TYPE of request, B or C, in column 1, the variable to be parametrized in columns 2–10 and the limits in the following two 10-digit fields. The parametric request data cards are listed. The program checks that the TYPE is valid, and that the lower limit is less than or equal to the upper limit. If the variable to be parametrized is negative then either IRANGC or IRANGB is set to 1 depending upon TYPE; while if the variable to be parametrized is positive, it is stored either positively or negatively depending upon TYPE. The limits are stored in BOTOM(NP) and TOP(NP).

Finally, PDATA initializes DUMBIG and prints it, and then calls DATA to read in the LP data.

The format of the input data to PLP is described in Appendix 3.5.

Subroutines called in PDATA

DATA

COMMON variables altered in PDATA

ISDONE

COMMON/PARA variables altered in PDATA

BOTOM(JJ)
DUMBIG
IJPARA(JJ)
IPARAB
IPARAC
IPRPLP
IRANGB
IRANGC
MAXP
NUMP
TOP(JJ)

```
      SUBROUTINE PDATA
*********************** COMMON AND TYPE STATEMENTS ********************
*********************** COMMON/PARA ************************************
      DATA BI/1HB/,CJ/1HC/
 9000 FORMAT (2I10)
 9004 FORMAT (A1,I9,2F10.0)
 9008 FORMAT (1H ,A1,I9,2F15.3)
 9012 FORMAT (1H ,'CARD IGNORED, INVALID TYPE ',A1)
 9016 FORMAT (1H0,'INVALID LOW ',F12.6,' AND HIGH ',F12.6,' LIMITS. CASE
     1IGNORED')
 9020 FORMAT (1H1,'NUMBER OF PARAMETRIC REQUESTS',I6,' PRINT VARIABLE ',
     1I4)
 9024 FORMAT(1H0,'THE VALUE',F13.3,' WILL REPRESENT PLUS INFINITY AND TH
     2E VALUE',F13.3,' WILL REPRESENT MINUS INFINITY.')
 9028 FORMAT(1H1,'THE MAXIMUM NUMBER OF PARAMETRIC REQUESTS IS',I6,' YOU
     1 HAVE REQUESTED',I6)
      MAXP = **
      IPARAB = 0
      IPARAC = 0
      READ(5,9000) NUMP,IPRPLP
      WRITE (6,9020) NUMP,IPRPLP
      IF (NUMP .EQ. 0) GO TO 40
      IF(NUMP.LE.MAXP.AND.NUMP.GT.0) GO TO 10
      WRITE(6,9028) MAXP,NUMP
      ISDONE = 1
      GO TO 45
```

```
10 NP = 0
   IRANGB = 0
   IRANGC = 0
   DO 35 IJP = 1,NUMP
   READ (5,9004) TYPE,IT,TLOW,THIGH
   WRITE (6,9008) TYPE,IT,TLOW,THIGH
   IF (TYPE .EQ. BI .OR. TYPE .EQ. CJ) GO TO 20
   WRITE (6,9012) TYPE
   GO TO 35
20 IF (TLOW .LE. THIGH) GO TO 25
   WRITE (6,9016) TLOW, THIGH
   GO TO 35
25 IF(IT.GE.1) GO TO 30
   IF(TYPE.EQ.CJ) IRANGC = 1
   IF(TYPE.EQ.BI) IRANGB = 1
   GO TO 35
30 NP = NP + 1
   IF (TYPE .EQ. CJ) IT = -IT
   IJPARA(NP) = IT
   BOTOM(NP) = TLOW
   TOP(NP) = THIGH
35 CONTINUE
   NUMP = NP
   DUMBIG = 1000000.0
   TT = -DUMBIG
   WRITE(6,9024) DUMBIG,TT
40 CALL DATA
45 RETURN
   END
```

12. PPRINT (parametric print)

This subroutine prints the results of the parametric analysis. In the case of parametrizing an element of b, B(IP), the printing depends upon the values of IPARAB, ISENSB, IRANGB and IPRPLP. The range of values of B(IP) for a basis are contained in SBIN and UBIN, and the state of the range is expressed by the value of IPARAB.

When the value of B(IP) is parametrized between specified limits, at each feasible and optimal corner point, SBIN and UBIN, the value of the objective function, OBJ, and the values of the original and slack variables, X(J) and SLACK(I) are printed. If IPRPLP = 1 the values of the dual and function row variables, Y(I) and YAC(J), also are printed. The precise form of the printing is determined by the value of IPARAB.

When a sensitivity analysis of the value of B(IP) is performed, ISENSB = 1, in general three sets of solution values are printed: the solution values at the basis associated with the initial value of B(IP), and the solution values associated with the corner point at either limit of the feasible range. The solution values are not printed if they correspond to a value of B(IP) of either plus or minus infinity. Also, as above, the printing depends upon the value of IPRPLP. When a range analysis of all elements of b is performed, IRANGB = 1, only the limits SBIN and UBIN of each element of b for which the initial basis is feasible are printed; the values of the solution variables at either end of the range or at the initial LP basis are not printed.

Similarly when parametrizing an element of c, C(JP), the printing depends upon the values of IPARAC, ISENSC, IRANGC and IPRPLP. The range of values of C(JP) are contained in SCJN and UCJN, and the state of the range is expressed by the value of IPARAC.

When the value of C(JP) is parametrized between specified limits, at each feasible and optimal corner point, SCJN and UCJN, OBJ, the values of the dual and function row variables, Y(I) and YAC(J), are printed. If IPRPLP = 1 the values of the original and slack variables, X(J) and SLACK(I) are also printed. The form of the printing is determined by the value of IPARAC.

When a sensitivity analysis of C(JP) is performed, ISENSC = 1, in general, three sets of solution values are printed: the solution values at the basis associated with the initial value of C(JP), and the solution values associated with the corner point at either limit of the optimal range. The solution values are not printed if they correspond to the value of C(JP) of plus or minus infinity. Also, as above, the printing depends upon the value of IPRPLP. When a range analysis of all elements of c is performed, IRANGC = 1, only the limits SCJN and UCJN, of each element of c for which the initial basis is optimal are printed; the values of the solution variables at the limits of the optimal range are not printed.

COMMON variables used in PPRINT

B(I)	SLACK(I)
C(J)	X(J)
MNOW	Y(I)
N	YAC(J)
OBJ	

COMMON/PARA variables used in PPRINT

IP	ISENSC
IPARAB	JP
IPARAC	SBIN
IPRPLP	SCJN
IRANGB	UBIN
IRANGC	UCJN
ISENSB	

```
      SUBROUTINE PPRINT
*********************** COMMON AND TYPE STATEMENTS ********************
*********************** COMMON/PARA ***********************************
 9011 FORMAT(1H1,'PARAMETRIC VARIATION ON THE RIGHT HAND SIDE OF CONSTRA
     1INT',I6)
 9012 FORMAT(///1X,'INITIAL BASIS FEASIBLE BETWEEN ',F12.3,' AND ',F12.3
     1)
 9013 FORMAT(///1X,'BASIS FEASIBLE BETWEEN ',F12.3,' AND ',F12.3)
 9014 FORMAT(1H ,'CONSTRAINT',I6,'  IS INEFFECTIVE')
 9015 FORMAT(1H ,'CONSTRAINT',I6,'  IS EFFECTIVE')
 9016 FORMAT(///1X,'BASIS INFEASIBLE BETWEEN ',F12.3,' AND ',F12.3)
 9018 FORMAT(1H0,'END OF PARAMETRIC VARIATION OF CONSTRAINT',I6)
 9019 FORMAT (1H0,'CONSTRAINT',I6,' CANNOT BE MADE EFFECTIVE.  NO PARAME
     1TRISATION OR SENSITIVITY ANALYSIS CAN BE MADE.')
 9021 FORMAT(1H1,'PARAMETRIC VARIATION ON THE OBJECTIVE FUNCTION ELEMENT
     1 OF VARIABLE',I6)
 9022 FORMAT(///1X,'INITIAL BASIS OPTIMAL BETWEEN ',F12.3,' AND ',F12.3)
 9023 FORMAT(///1X,'BASIS OPTIMAL BETWEEN ',F12.3,' AND ',F12.3)
 9024 FORMAT(1H ,'VARIABLE',I6,' IS NON BASIC')
 9025 FORMAT(1H ,'VARIABLE',I6,' IS BASIC')
 9026 FORMAT(///1X,'BASIS NON OPTIMAL BETWEEN ',F12.3,' AND ',F12.3)
 9028 FORMAT(1H0,'END OF PARAMETRIC VARIATION OF VARIABLE',I6)
 9030 FORMAT(1H0,'OBJECTIVE',F16.3,' VALUE OF RIGHT HAND SIDE ',F12.3)
 9031 FORMAT(1H0,'OBJECTIVE',F16.3,' VALUE OF OBJECTIVE FUNCTION ELEMENT
     1 ',F10.3)
 9032 FORMAT(1H ,'VALUE OF REAL VARIABLES')
 9034 FORMAT(1H ,'VALUE OF SLACK VARIABLES')
 9036 FORMAT(1H ,10F12.4)
 9042 FORMAT(1H ,'VALUE OF DUAL VARIABLES')
 9044 FORMAT(1H ,23HVALUE OF Y'A-C ELEMENTS)
 9111 FORMAT(1H ,/////1X,'SENSITIVITY ANALYSIS OF THE RIGHT HAND SIDE OF
     1 CONSTRAINT',I6)
 9118 FORMAT(1H0,'END OF SENSITIVITY ANALYSIS OF CONSTRAINT',I6)
 9121 FORMAT(1H ,/////1X,'SENSITIVITY ANALYSIS OF THE OBJECTIVE FUNCTION
     1 ELEMENT OF VARIABLE',I6)
 9128 FORMAT(1H0,'END OF SENSITIVITY ANALYSIS OF VARIABLE',I6)
 9212 FORMAT(1H ,'THIS IS THE RANGE FOR THE RIGHT HAND SIDE OF CONSTRAIN
     1T',I6)
 9222 FORMAT(1H ,'THIS IS THE RANGE FOR OBJECTIVE FUNCTION ELEMENT',I6)
      IF (IPARAC .GT. 0) GO TO 20
      IF (IPARAB .GT. 0) GO TO 10
      GO TO 50
   10 GO TO (11,12,13,14,15,16,17,18,30,19),IPARAB
   11 IF(ISENSB.EQ.0) WRITE(6,9011) IP
      IF(ISENSB.EQ.1) WRITE(6,9111) IP
      GO TO 50
   12 WRITE (6,9012) SBIN,UBIN
      IF(IRANGB.EQ.0) GO TO 30
      WRITE(6,9212) IP
      GO TO 50
   13 WRITE (6,9013) SBIN,UBIN
      GO TO 30
   14 WRITE (6,9013) SBIN,UBIN
      WRITE (6,9014) IP
      GO TO 30
   15 WRITE (6,9013) SBIN,UBIN
      WRITE (6,9015) IP
      GO TO 30
```

```
16 WRITE (6,9016) SBIN,UBIN
   GO TO 30
17 WRITE(6,9012) SBIN,UBIN
   GO TO 50
18 IF(ISENSB.EQ.0) WRITE(6,9018) IP
   IF(ISENSB.EQ.1) WRITE(6,9118) IP
   GO TO 50
19 WRITE(6,9012) SBIN,UBIN
   WRITE(6,9019) IP
   GO TO 50
20 GO TO (21,22,23,24,25,26,27,28,40),IPARAC
21 IF(ISENSC.EQ.0) WRITE(6,9021) JP
   IF(ISENSC.EQ.1) WRITE(6,9121) JP
   GO TO 50
22 WRITE (6,9022) SCJN,UCJN
   IF(IRANGC.EQ.0) GO TO 40
   WRITE(6,9222) JP
   GO TO 50
23 WRITE (6,9023) SCJN,UCJN
   GO TO 40
24 WRITE (6,9023) SCJN,UCJN
   WRITE (6,9024) JP
   GO TO 40
25 WRITE (6,9023) SCJN,UCJN
   WRITE (6,9025) JP
   GO TO 40
26 WRITE (6,9026) SCJN,UCJN
   GO TO 40
27 WRITE(6,9022) SCJN,UCJN
   GO TO 50
28 IF(ISENSC.EQ.0) WRITE(6,9028) JP
   IF(ISENSC.EQ.1) WRITE(6,9128) JP
   GO TO 50
30 WRITE (6,9030) OBJ,B(IP)
35 WRITE (6,9032)
   WRITE (6,9036) (X(J),J = 1,N)
   WRITE (6,9034)
   WRITE (6,9036) (SLACK(I),I=1,MNOW)
   IF(IPRPLP.EQ.1.AND.IPARAB.GT.0) GO TO 45
   GO TO 50
40 WRITE (6,9031) OBJ,C(JP)
45 WRITE (6,9042)
   WRITE (6,9036) (Y(I), I = 1,MNOW)
   WRITE (6,9044)
   WRITE (6,9036) (YAC(J),J = 1,N)
   IF(IPRPLP.EQ.1.AND.IPARAC.GT.0) GO TO 35
50 RETURN
   END
```

CHAPTER 7

Modifications

1. MODIFICATION FOR DIFFERENT COMPUTERS

The programs as presented are suitable without modification for the CDC 6600 computer. IBM machines and others with a smaller word length require modifications to the programs.

We suggest, for computers with less than a 48-bit word, that all real variables and functions be declared double precision. This is not essential but the accuracy of the solution values is much better if the computation has been done in double precision (see Section 7.2 on Tolerances). On an IBM 360 the easiest method of doing this is to insert at the beginning of all the subroutines the statement

```
IMPLICIT REAL*8(A-H,O-Z)
```

Note that the array INV has to be declared double precision with the statement (on an IBM 360):

```
REAL*8 INV
```

If his problem coefficients do not need more storage than single precision, the user can save space by declaring the arrays BOUND, B, C and S to be single precision. On an IBM 360 the statement is

```
REAL*4 BOUND,B,C,S
```

Storage can also be saved by declaring the arrays INBASE, ISEFF, XBASIS and YBASIS to be half-words. On an IBM 360 the statement is

```
INTEGER*2 INBASE, ISEFF, XBASIS, YBASIS
```

Similarly in COMMON/AREF the array AA may be declared single precision and the arrays JCOL and IROW may be half words. On an IBM 360 the statements are

```
REAL*4 AA
INTEGER*2 JCOL,IROW
```

In COMMON/BBB the array HLDBND may be single precision and the arrays INTX, IRIGHT, JDISC and LEFT may be half-words. In COMMON/PARA the arrays BOTOM and TOP may be single precision and the array IJPARA may be half-words. In COMMON/Q the arrays HOLDC and D may be single precision and the arrays ISQ and KEYTOD may be half-words. But in program QP, AA should be double precision, like INV. Finally in COMMON/RETAIN the array KEEP may be half-words.

On an IBM 360 when the variables are a mixture of types the arrays and variables in COMMON will have to be 'aligned', that is, specified in the COMMON statements in the order REAL*8, REAL*4, INTEGER*4, INTEGER*2.

Throughout the suite of programs the only Fortran library function that is used is ABS, and there is one function subprogram, A(I, J). If the real variables are declared to be double precision then ABS must be changed to DABS and FUNCTION A(I, J) must be double precision. Below is a list of subroutines where ABS is used. The number in brackets after the subroutine name is the number of separate places that ABS is used within the subroutine.

BACKUP (1)	MIDBI (1)
CHACC (4)*	MIDCJ (1)
CHAGY (1)	PARAB (1)
CHBSIS (3)	PRICE (2)
CHSLCK (2)	QCON (2)
CHXSL (3)	REVERT (7)
DUAL (2)	SEEKX (2)
INTCON (2)	SEEKY (2)
ISOPT (1)	
ISTAIL (1)	

(* If the arrays B and C are single precision then only two of the ABS's must be changed to DABS.)

On an IBM 360 the statement to declare FUNCTION A(I, J) to be double precision is

REAL FUNCTION A*8(I, J)

FUNCTION A(I, J) must be double precision if the real variables in COMMON are so, even if the array AA is single precision.

For the ICL 1900 computers, the statement IBEST = BEST in BBDATA should be replaced by IBEST = 8.0E6 since the integer word length is very limited. These computers, and others, may also require explicit character-handling routines in place of the four logical IF statements concerned with TYPE in subroutine PDATA.

1.1 Storage management when computer core size is limited

These programs are made up from a fairly large number of individual subroutines, and the size of problem which may be handled is limited due to the retention of the data in core throughout execution.

When core space is limited it is desirable to reduce the space given to the program itself in order to allow more space for the problem. This is unlikely to arise on a CDC 6600, but these programs have also been used on IBM 360 and ICL System 4 computers where these difficulties can and do occur.

One technique for breaking up a program so that the minimum core store is required is to use overlays, where the relevant portion of the program is brought into core only when required and over written by another portion when the need arises. It is clear that there are many ways in which a program or an operating system could do this, but the internal logical structure of the program itself plays a central role. In view of the wide currency of IBM 360 machines and the similar conventions employed on ICL System 4 computers we shall present an overlay structure in IBM terms.

Definitions

Segment: a set of program modules (subroutines or functions) treated as a unit when copying parts of programs to core during execution.

Overlay Tree: a graph of segments connected by nodes that show all the permissible patterns of storage used by a program during execution.

Using IBM conventions, all segments in a given path through the tree must be capable of being held in store at once; this means that the longest chain through the tree formed by adding up the storage demands of each module in the chain defines the minimum core storage requirement of the overlaid program.

An efficient overlay for the whole set of programs is shown in Figure 7.1. Here we have assumed that all the different main programs have been named as subroutines invoked by a simple driver routine, called GENERAL, whose function is solely to select and transfer control to the desired program (LP, QP, etc). To deal with each program on its own, the part of the tree containing the relevant modules comprises an effective overlay for that program. As presented, all the programs are present in the tree.

The routines in the text are well adapted to an overlaid design; most of the routines are mutually exclusive and therefore need not be in core at the same time. CHBSIS, SEEKX, NEWVEC, REDUCE, SEEKY and ADDCON form such a set. The chains of segments AEF and ABCD are the two longest chains and are of nearly the same length. So it is more efficient to group these subroutines together in the same segment, segment D, as illustrated. This philosophy has been followed wherever possible. Each subroutine only appears on the tree once, so the commonly used subroutines, e.g. ISOPT, are placed high on the tree with the calling subroutines, e.g. LP, below them.

This ensures that the minimum amount of copying of segments to core will occur at run time. The logical structure of the overlay is in no way constrained by the logical hierarchy of calls in the program; a 'call' may be issued by QP at the bottom of the tree to QCON at the top. All the subroutines required by QCON before return to QP are in the chain of segments loaded to bring QCON into core.

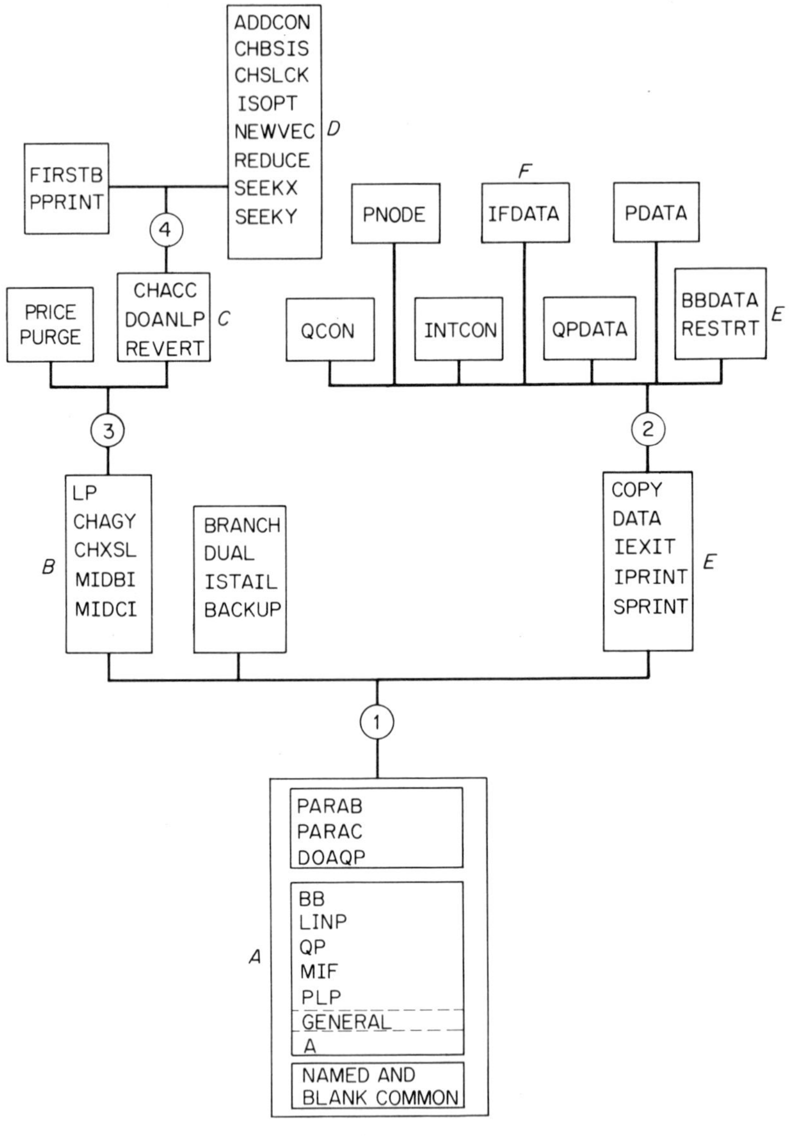

Figure 7.1

The storage requirement saved by this type of overlay is quite significant. On an ICL 4/70 for a program which handles problems up to (20 × 50), the amount of core store required to run the program is cut from 150 Kb (1000 bytes) without overlays to 96 Kb with this particular overlay.

The requirements of the IBM-oriented overlay structure are stricter than is necessary, and other machines may not require the same detail.

The overlay illustrated is only one of many possible overlay structures. It is possible to store and solve larger problems if each of the separate programs has its own overlay tree. The disadvantage of this is that such overlay trees use more backing store than one tree. In any overlay structure a balance must be struck between the size of problem that the user wishes to solve and the extra time needed to copy segments into core at run time. For instance space could be saved by overlaying the subroutines in segment D at the cost of the time taken to load each of these subroutines at every LP iteration.

2. TOLERANCES

Throughout the suite of programs each tolerance is used for a specific purpose. Thus, for instance, the same tolerance is used throughout to test the feasibility of the primal basic variables while another is used to test the feasibility of the slack variables. These two tolerances may or may not have the same values depending upon the numerical range of the coefficients in a problem that is being solved, but they both have a clearly defined use. All the tolerances are initialized in the data subroutine or in the only subroutine that uses them and, with only one exception (see below, SMALL), they have the same values throughout the computation.

The tolerances are described below in the order that they have appeared throughout the text.

2.1. LINP

The tolerances in COMMON are BIG, SMALL and an array, TOL(8).

BIG: This variable has a large value and it is treated as a representation of infinity. It must be larger than any individual coefficient or ratio that will occur throughout the computation.

Used in BACKUP, BBDATA, BRANCH, DOAQP, DUAL, IPRINT, ISTAIL, PNODE, QPDATA, RESTRT, SEEKX, SEEKY.

Initialized in DATA.

SMALL: This variable has a very small value, sufficiently small that a variable with a value less than it can be treated as 0·0 without introducing any error. However, in order to ensure that no error is introduced in the re-inversion procedure SMALL is temporarily set to 0·0 in REVERT. After the basis has been re-inverted SMALL is returned to its previous value.

Used in CHBSIS, IPRINT, PRICE, QCON, SEEKY.
Initialized in DATA; temporarily changed in REVERT.

TOL(1): Tests the feasibility of the basic primal variables in XR(K) at both their lower and upper bounds.
Used in BACKUP, CHBSIS, CHXSL, IPRINT.
Initialized in DATA.

TOL(2): Tests the feasibility of the slack variables, SLACK(I), of the ineffective constraints.
Used in CHACC, CHSLCK, CHXSL, IPRINT.
Initialized in DATA.

TOL(3): Tests the optimality of the dual variables, YR(L), of the effective constraints.
Used in DUAL, IPRINT, ISOPT, SEEKX.
Initialized in DATA.

TOL(4): Tests the optimality of the function row variables, YAC(J), of the non-basic variables.
Used in CHACC, CHAGY, DUAL, IPRINT, ISOPT, SEEKX.
Initialized in DATA.

TOL(5): Tests whether or not a proposed pivot, GR(K) or G(I), should be regarded as zero.
Used in DUAL, IPRINT, SEEKX, SEEKY.
Initialized in DATA.

TOL(6): Tests the relative error, (B(I) − SLACK(I) − Σ A(I,J) * X(J))/B(I) of the primal variables of a solution on the Ith constraint.
Used in CHACC, IPRINT.
Initialized in DATA.

TOL(7): Tests the relative error, (C(J) − YAC(J) − Σ Y(I) * A(I,J))/C(J), of the dual variables of a solution on the Jth variable.
Used in CHACC, IPRINT.
Initialized in DATA.

TOL(8): Tests the size of a proposed pivot during a re-inversion of the basis. The value of this tolerance is related to the value of TOL(5). TOL(8) is larger than TOL(5) to ensure that at the end of the re-inversion the basis is not singular.
Used in IPRINT, REVERT.
Initialized in DATA.

Note that the exact upper or lower bounds of the basic variables, XR(K), the slack variables, SLACK(I), and the function row variables, YAC(J), are substituted for the computed values when the latter are within the relevant tolerances. This does *not* happen to the dual basic variables, YR(L), as these variables are used to compute the function row, YAC(J), of the non basic variables. This is because any error that might be introduced by the substitution of values would accumulate and possibly cause further inaccuracies to be introduced. The correction of the basic variables XR(K) takes place in subroutine CHBSIS, and of the slack variables SLACK(I), in subroutine CHSLCK. The correction of the function row variables YAC(J) is for printing purposes only and so takes place in subroutine ISOPT only and not in subroutine SEEKX.

2.2. MIF

The tolerances are TOLIF1 and TOLIF2.

TOLIF1: Tests whether or not a coefficient has an integer value.
Used and initialized in INTCON.

TOLIF2: The slack variable on the new constraint is computed by two different means. The difference between these two values within the tolerance, TOLIF2, is used as a criterion to decide whether or not the coefficients of the new constraint are accurate.

TOLIF2 should be larger than TOLIF1.
Used and initialized in INTCON.

2.3. QP

No special tolerances are used.

2.4. BB

The tolerances in COMMON/BBB, are TOLBB1 and TOLBB2.

DUMBIG is a local variable that is used in the restart procedure.

DUMBIG: (dummy BIG) This variable has a large value, but it is less than the value of BIG. It is used as a substitute for BIG in the restart procedure in order that a large value can be punched. DUMBIG must have a value greater than any value of the objective function that will be encountered in course of solving an integer program. However, if the value of the objective function has more than eight digits to the left of the decimal place FORMAT 9012 in both subroutines PNODE and RESTRT must be altered. DUMBIG must be set to the same value in subroutines PNODE and RESTRT.

DUMBIG is only used if the restart procedure uses punched cards (see Chapter 5).

Initialized and used in PNODE and RESTRT.

TOLBB1: Tests whether or not a variable has an integer value.
Used in BRANCH, ISTAIL.
Initialized in BBDATA.

TOLBB2: Tests whether or not the total objective function, FUNC, has an integer value. This is only tested in the situation when the optimal objective function must have an integer value, i.e. INTOBJ = 1.
Used in BACKUP, ISTAIL.
Initialized in BBDATA.

2.5. PLP

The tolerance in COMMON/PARA is DUMBIG.

DUMBIG: (dummy BIG) This variable has a large value that is used to represent infinity. Its value must be greater than the value of any element of the arrays B or C, but if it has more than seven places to the left of the decimal point it is necessary, for printing purposes, to alter FORMATs 9012, 9013, 9016, 9022, 9023, 9026 in subroutine PPRINT.
Used in PARAB, PARAC.
Initialized in PDATA.

2.6. To determine the values of the tolerances

The values of the tolerances are determined heuristically; they are decided by what the user considers is an acceptable level of accuracy given the size of the coefficients in his problem data and the word length of the computer that he is using. A method of determining the values of the tolerances is for the user to solve some test problems of which he knows the solution, using the maximum print options, and to closely inspect the computational results and then to decide whether or not the results are acceptable. If the results are unacceptable then the appropriate tolerance must be altered. A particular point to inspect is whether infeasible tails in BB are truly infeasible.

The size of non-zero coefficients in the A matrix may very from 10^{-5} to 10^{6} without violating the input formats. However, a range as great as this is not to be recommended. It is desirable to scale a problem so that coefficients of A lie between 0·1 and 10·0 if this can be readily achieved, particularly for BB.

Note that mixed integer problems frequently involve a 'very large' number as a coefficient of an integer variable. It is preferable to use a large step size for the variable, instead of a unit step, and thus reduce the magnitude of the element in A.

As the iterative computation proceeds the errors do tend to accumulate and it may be necessary to recompute the inverse. The re-inversion will 'clean up' the basis and improve the accuracy of the solution. However, if the tolerance values are too small no number of re-inversions will achieve the required accuracy. The values of the tolerances need to be set at an achievable level of accuracy. In our experience we have found, for problems with similar orders of magnitude of the problem coefficients, that the tolerances, once set, do not need to be altered.

The following discussion is a guideline for determining the values of each tolerance.

2.6.1. LINP

TOL(1) and TOL(2): The values of these tolerances are what the user regards as acceptable levels of accuracy for the feasibility of the basic, XR(K), and slack, SLACK(I), variables. If the tolerances are too small then LINP will terminate a feasible problem with an infeasible solution, or if the tolerances are too big LINP will accept as feasible a variable that is really infeasible. There are two separate feasibility tolerances because the magnitude of the coefficients of the A matrix and b vector may result in the values of the original and slack variables being of a different order of magnitude.

The values of TOL(1) and TOL(2) can be determined by printing out and inspecting the values of the coefficients of the arrays XR and SLACK.

TOL(2) and TOL(3): The values of these tolerances are what the user regards as acceptable levels of accuracy for the optimality of the dual variables of the effective constraints, YR(K), and of the function row variables, YAC(J). If the tolerances are too small then LINP will terminate, having used the maximum number of iterations, with a non-optimal solution. Only in very exceptional circumstances will a problem require more than 3 * (M + N + number of bounded variables) iterations to evaluate an optimal solution. Similarly if the tolerances are too large the program will terminate with a solution that it considers optimal but which is really suboptimal. There are two separate optimality tolerances because the magnitude of the coefficients of the A matrix and c vector may result in the values of the dual variables of the effective constraints and the function row variables being of a different order of magnitude.

The values of TOL(3) and TOL(4) can be determined by printing and inspecting the values of the coefficients of the arrays YR and YAC.

TOL(5): The value of this tolerance is critical because if it is too small the program will accept as a pivot a value that is only non-zero because of round-off errors. The use of such a pivot will cause the basis to become singular. This singularity will be detected when the accuracy of the solution is checked. The printed error will be a large number, negative or positive, in which the digits appear as a string of random numbers. A well-defined error, e.g. 1·500000, probably arises because there is an error in the code, while a small error, e.g. ·0000623, probably arises because of round-off error, especially if many iterations have been performed. If the error is large and random in appearance then it is necessary to track down the unacceptable small pivot by calling subroutine IPRINT after each return from subroutine CHSLCK and at the same time printing the arrays GR(K) and G(I). The value of TOL(5) must be chosen so that the small elements of GR(K) and G(I) are not considered as pivots.

However if TOL(5) is too big then the program may terminate with an infeasible or unbounded solution because the pivots that would enable it to achieve feasibility or optimality are being rejected as too small. This may not be obvious in the BB case where the 'infeasibility' merely results in a partition of the feasible region being rejected.

TOL(6) and TOL(7): The value of these tolerances are what the user regards as acceptable levels of relative accuracy for the primal and dual variables respectively. As in the case of TOL(1), TOL(2), TOL(3) and TOL(4) if the values are too small LINP will terminate, having used the maximum number of re-inversions, while trying unsuccessfully to achieve the desired level of accuracy. The user must determine the values of these tolerances knowing the size of the coefficients of the A matrix and of the b and c vectors in his problems.

TOL(8): The value of this tolerance must be larger than that of TOL(5) so that at the end of the re-inversion the basis is not singular. The basis may not be the same basis as at the beginning of the re-inversion. It does not matter if at the end of the re-inversion the solution is infeasible or non-optimal as the program subsequently will re-optimize.

2.6.2. MIF

TOLIF1: The most critical use of this tolerance is in deciding whether or not an element of XR(K) has an integer value. If the tolerance is too small subroutine INTCON will treat a variable that has an integer value as having a non-integer value and subsequently may generate an invalid constraint that removes a feasible integer solution from the feasible region. If the tolerance is too big a non-integer element of XR(K) will be accepted as integer. The method of determining the value of the tolerance is for the user to solve a few problems to which the solution is known. If the problems are solved then the tolerance is probably satisfactory. However, if the problem is solved with an incorrect integer solution and a lower value of the objective function or the problem is infeasible then the tolerance needs altering. To determine the value of the tolerance:

1) call the subroutine IPRINT with MOREPR equal to 1 or 2 after every return from the subroutine INTCON,

2) substitute the known solution, $\bar{x}$, into each generated constraint, i.e. evaluate $\Sigma_j a_{ij}\bar{x}_j$, and compare the result with b_i. The constraint for which $\Sigma_j a_{ij}\bar{x}_j > b_i$ is the invalid constraint.

3) inspect the basis from which the invalid constraint was generated. One or more of the elements of XR(K) will have integer values that have been treated as non-integer. The value of the tolerance must be chosen so that if XR(K) has an integer value then

XR(K)-[XR(K) + TOLIF1] < TOLIF1,

where [Z] means the greatest integer less than or equal to Z.

TOLIF2: This tolerance is used to decide whether or not a new constraint is acceptable. If this tolerance is too small an invalid constraint may be added to the A matrix while if it is too big valid constraints may be rejected. We suggest that TOLIF2 be bigger than TOLIF1. If invalid constraints are accepted then it is necessary to inspect the difference between the SLACK(I) variable of the invalid constraint and the fractional part of the element of XR(K) from which the constraint was generated.

2.6.3. BB

DUMBIG: The user has to determine the value of this tolerance only if the restart procedure uses punched cards. In that case it must have a value greater than any value of the objective function that will be encountered in solving the problem.

TOLBB1: This tolerance tests whether or not the ratio XR(K)/STEP(J) has an integer value. If the tolerance is too small then the program will branch more than is necessary while if the value is too large a non-integer value will be accepted as integer. The user can determine the value of this tolerance by inspecting the elements of XR(K) at a number of bases and deciding upon the level of accuracy that he finds acceptable.

TOLBB2: This tolerance tests whether or not the variable FUNC has an integer value in the case when INTOBJ = 1. If the tolerance is too large then the program will branch more than is necessary while if the value is too small the program will reject nodes that might lead to a better integer solution. The user has to decide what he regards as an acceptable level of accuracy for the value of the objective function in the situation when he knows, from the nature of the problem, that the optimal value of the objective function will be integer.

2.6.4. PLP

DUMBIG: This tolerance must be larger than any element of the arrays B or C. The user can determine its value by inspecting the coefficients in his problems.

2.7. Suggested values of the tolerances

We have used the program, as given in the text, on computers with a 48, 60 and 64 (double precision) bit word and we have used the following values for the tolerances. BIG = 1·0E11, SMALL = 1·0E-9, TOL(1) = TOL(3) = 1·0E-6, TOL(2) = TOL(4) = TOL(5) = TOL(6) = TOL(7) = 1·0E-5, TOL(8) = 1·0E-4, TOLIF1 = 1·0E-5, TOLIF2 = 1·0E-4, DUMBIG(in BB) = 1·0E5, TOLBB1 = 1·0E-6, TOLBB2 = 1·0E-6, DUMBIG(in PLP) = 1·0E6. Also the program has been used in single precision on a computer with a 32 bit word and the following values were used for the tolerances. BIG = 1·0E8, SMALL = 1·0E-8, TOL(1) = TOL(2) = TOL(3) = TOL(4) = TOL(5) = TOL(6) = TOL(7) = 1·0E-3, TOL(8) = 1·0E-2, TOLIF1 = 1·0E-3, TOLIF2 = 1·0E-2, DUMBIG (in BB) = 1·0E5, TOLBB1 = 1·0E-3, TOLBB2 = 1·0E-4, DUMBIG (in PLP) = 1·0E6.

3. STORAGE REQUIRED

The total number of Fortran cards required for each of these programs is as follows:

LINP	1337
QP	1640
MIF	1554
BB	2072
PLP	2137

Of course, 1366 cards are common to two or more of these programs.

Every computer and every compiler is different, so the following is a rough guide only. If each program is compiled on the CDC 6600 using the MNF compiler and with the dimension of every array being one only, the field length of each program is as follows:

LINP	13200
QP	14460

MIF	13792
BB	16018
PLP	15784

These storage requirements give us a base line from which to compute the storage requirements for various sizes of problem dimensions. These requirements can be expressed as functions of the problem dimensions as follows.

3.1. LINP

MAXN = the maximum number of variables; MAXM = the maximum number of constraints; MAXA = the maximum number of non-zero elements in A; MXSIZE = the maximum number of *effective* constraints.

COMMON arrays BOUND, C, INBASE, PIV, X and YAC	6 * MAXN
Arrays B, G, ISEFF, S, SLACK and Y	6 * MAXM
Array INV	MXSIZE * MXSIZE
Arrays XBASIS, XR, YBASIS, YR and GR	5 * MXSIZE
COMMON/AREF	
Arrays AA and JCOL	2 * MAXA
Array IROW	MAXM + 1

The storage required for the arrays in LINP is 6* MAXN + 7 * MAXM + 2 * MAXA + 5 * MXSIZE + $(\text{MXSIZE})^2$.

3.2. QP

MAXQ = the maximum number of variables with quadratic coefficients in the objective function.

COMMON and COMMON/AREF	As LINP
COMMON/RETAIN	
Array KEEP	MAXM
COMMON/Q	
Array D	MAXQ * MAXQ
Array KEYTOD	MAXQ
Arrays HOLDC and ISQ	2 * MAXN

The storage required for the arrays in QP is the storage required for LINP + 2 * MAXN + MAXM + MAXQ + $(\text{MAXQ})^2$.
Note that MAXM includes the constraints generated by the program.

3.3. MIF

MIF requires the same storage for the arrays as LINP (bearing in mind that MAXM includes constraints generated by the program).

3.4. BB

MAXD = maximum number of variables that must take discrete values.

COMMON and COMMON/AREF	As LINP
COMMON/BBB	
Arrays HLDBND and JDISC	2 * MAXN
Arrays FUNCL, FUNCR, INTX, IRIGHT, LEFT, RATEL, RATER and VALUE	8 * MAXD

The storage required for the arrays in BB is the storage required for LINP + 2 * MAXN + 8 * MAXD.

3.5. PLP

MAXP = the maximum number of parametric requests

COMMON and COMMON/AREF	As LINP
COMMON/PARA	3 * MAXP

The storage required for the arrays in PLP is the storage required for LINP + 3 * MAXP.

We have found it convenient to store our source language programs on tape and on permanent file in an 'update' file on the CDC 6600. Those subroutines which are used in two or more programs are recorded in common decks which are then called as required. Furthermore the COMMON statements are not listed in each subroutine, but rather in a series of common decks. Their place in the subroutines is taken by a call to the appropriate common deck, as for instance:

```
* CALL BLANK
* CALL AREF
```

These nested calls to common decks are possible within the system. This facility is obviously valuable as it enables us to alter the dimensions of the arrays only once in the common decks rather than having to alter them through every subroutine. We would certainly recommend any user to utilize a similar editing facility if it is available.

4. CHANGING DIMENSIONS

In the suite of programs the arrays that are used are of two types.

1. The dimension of the array is independent of the size of problem that the program is intended to solve. There is one such array in COMMON. It is TOL(JK), whose dimension is 8. The other arrays

of this type are local arrays, e.g. the arrays K1(JK), K2(JK) and K3(JK) in subroutine DATA; these arrays are of dimension 8.
2. The dimension of the array is determined by the maximum size of problem that the program is intended to solve. This section is about the changes that are necessary in order to alter the dimensions of these arrays.

Many of the arrays must have the same dimension as each other, e.g. BOUND(J), C(J) and INBASE(J). Throughout we have attempted to indicate this by always using the same subscript, e.g. J, for such arrays. The dimension of some arrays is related to the dimension of other arrays e.g. the dimension of XR(K) is not more than the minimum of BOUND(J) and B(I). The values of the dimensions of these arrays are stored in 'size variables'. These 'size variables' check that the arrays are not overflowed. Thus it is essential when the dimensions of the arrays are altered that the values assigned to the associated 'size variables' are correspondingly altered.

4.1. LINP

The dimensions of the arrays in program LINP are determined by:

1. The maximum number of variables.
2. The maximum number of constraints.
3. The maximum number of constraints that will be effective at any iteration in the computation.
4. The maximum number of non-zero elements in the A matrix.

The user, knowing the problems that he intends to solve, can simply determine the maximum number of variables, the maximum number of constraints, and the maximum number of non-zero elements in A. In order to illustrate the changes to the program, we have taken as an example that the maximum number of variables be 100, the number of constraints, 60, and the non-zero elements of A, 500. Without any prior knowledge the user has to guess the maximum number of effective constraints, which will be not more than the minimum of the number of variables and the number of constraints. If the user overestimates then the program will use more store than necessary while if he underestimates then the program will terminate prematurely, with the problem unsolved, because it has run out of space. The safest dimension to choose would be the minimum of the variables and the constraints; however, this is very likely to be extravagant on space. So if the user has no previous experience, as a compromise between safety and extravagance, we suggest three-quarters of the minimum of the variables and the constraints. In the example, $\frac{3}{4}$ of minimum (100, 60) is 45. The program prints the maximum number of effective constraints so the user will have some guidance for the future.

The alterations of the array dimensions in LINP mean that changes have to be made in three places

1. COMMON
2. COMMON/AREF
3. Subroutine DATA.

For the illustration we have assumed that the COMMON statements are as described in the text.

1. COMMON

a. Delete the first line of the statement

```
COMMON BOUND(50),C(50),INBASE(50),PIV(50),X(50),YAC(50),
```

and insert the line

```
COMMON BOUND(100),C(100),INBASE(100),PIV(100),X(100),YAC(100),
```

This line dimensions all the arrays that store data concerned with the problem variables.

b. Delete the COMMON continuation line

```
2  B(25),G(25),ISEFF(25),S(25),SLACK(25),Y(25),
```

and insert the line

```
2  B(60),G(60),ISEFF(60),S(60),SLACK(60),Y(60),
```

This continuation line dimensions all the arrays that store data concerned with the problem constraints.

c. Delete the COMMON continuation line

```
3  INV(25,25),XBASIS(25),XR(25),YBASIS(25),YR(25),GR(25),
```

and insert the line

```
3  INV(45,45),XBASIS(45),XR(45),YBASIS(45),YR(45),GR(45),
```

This continuation line dimensions all the arrays that store data concerned with the effective constraints, i.e., the inverse.

2. COMMON/AREF

Delete the statement

```
COMMON/AREF/AA(1000),JCOL(1000),IROW(26),MAXA
```

and insert the statement

```
COMMON/AREF/AA(500),JCOL(500),IROW(61),MAXA
```

This statement dimensions all the arrays that store data concerned with the A matrix. Note that the dimension of the array IROW is the number of constraints plus one.

3. Subroutine DATA

a. Delete the assignment statement

MAXN = 50

and insert the statement

MAXN = 100

MAXN is the 'size variable' whose value is the dimension of the arrays BOUND, C, INBASE, PIV, X and YAC.

b. Delete the assignment statement

MAXM = 25

and insert the statement

MAXM = 60

MAXM is the 'size variable' whose value is the dimension of the arrays B, G, ISEFF, S, SLACK and Y. The value of MAXM is related to the dimension of array IROW.

c. Delete the assignment statement

MXSIZE = 25

and insert the statement

MXSIZE = 45

MXSIZE is the 'size variable' whose value is the dimension of the arrays INV, XBASIS, XR, YBASIS, YR and GR.

d. Delete the assignment statement

MAXA = 1000

and insert the statement

MAXA = 500

MAXA is the 'size variable' whose value is the dimension of the arrays AA and JCOL.

4.2. QP

The dimensions of the arrays in program QP are determined by:

1. The maximum number of variables, the maximum number of constraints, the maximum number of effective constraints and the maximum number of non-zero elements of matrix A.
2. The maximum number of variables with quadratic coefficients in the objective function.

The considerations for determining the maximum number of variables, constraints, effective constraints and non-zero elements of A are the same as in LINP except that the number of constraints and non-zero elements of A include the generated constraints that are added to the A matrix and b vector during the calculation. For example 100, 60, 45 and 500 could be the maximum number of variables, constraints, effective constraints and non-zero elements of A. Also, knowing his problems, the user can determine the maximum number of variables with quadratic coefficients, which may be less than the total number of variables, for example 30.

The alterations of the array dimensions in QP mean that changes have to be made in four places:

1. COMMON, COMMON/AREF and subroutine DATA
2. COMMON/RETAIN
3. COMMON/Q
4. Subroutine QPDATA.

1. COMMON, COMMON/AREF and subroutine DATA

These changes are the same as those for program LINP above.

2. COMMON/RETAIN

Delete the statement

```
COMMON/RETAIN/KEEP(MAXM)
```

and insert the statement

```
COMMON/RETAIN/KEEP(60)
```

This statement dimensions the array KEEP that stores data concerned with the constraints.

3. COMMON/Q

Delete the statement

```
COMMON/Q/D(MAXQ,MAXQ),HOLDC(MAXN),ISQ(MAXN),KEYTOD(MAXQ),MAXQ,NUMQ
```

and insert the statement

COMMON/Q/D(30,30),HOLDC(100),ISQ(100),KEYTOD(30),MAXQ,NUMQ

This statement dimensions the arrays D and KEYTOD that store the quadratic coefficients and the arrays HOLDC and ISQ that store data for all the variables concerning the quadratic objective function.

4. Subroutine QPDATA

Delete the statement

MAXQ = **

and insert the statement

MAXQ = 30

MAXQ is the 'size variable' whose value is the dimension of the arrays D and KEYTOD.

4.3. MIF

As in LINP, the dimensions of the arrays in MIF are determined by the maximum number of variables, the maximum number of constraints, the maximum number of effective constraints and the maximum number of non-zero elements of A. The considerations for determining these dimensions are the same as in LINP except that the number of constraints and the number of non-zero elements of A include the generated constraints that are added to the A matrix and b vector during the calculation.

The alterations of the array dimensions in MIF mean that changes have to be made in two places:

1. COMMON, COMMON/AREF and subroutine DATA

These changes are the same as those for program LINP above.

2. COMMON/RETAIN

This change is the same as that for program QP section 2 above.

4.4. BB

The dimensions of the arrays in program BB are determined by:

1. The maximum number of variables, the maximum number of constraints, the maximum number of effective constraints and the maximum number of non-zero elements of the A matrix.
2. The maximum number of variables that must have discrete values in the solution.

As in LINP, the user, knowing the problems that he intends to solve, can determine the maximum number of variables, constraints, effective constraints and non-zero elements of A; for example 100, 60, 45 and 500 respectively. Also, knowing his problems, the user can determine the maximum number of discrete variables, which may be less than the total number of variables; for example 80.

The alterations of the array dimensions in BB mean that changes have to be made in three places:

1. COMMON, COMMON/AREF and subroutine DATA
2. COMMON/BBB
3. Subroutine BBDATA.

1. COMMON, COMMON/AREF and subroutine DATA

These changes are the same as those for program LINP above.

2. COMMON/BBB

a. Delete the first line of the statement

```
COMMON/BBB/HLDBND(MAXN),JDISC(MAXN),
```

and insert the line

```
COMMON/BBB/HLDBND(100),JDISC(100),
```

This line dimensions the arrays HLDBND and JDISC that store data concerning all the variables.

b. Delete the continuation lines

```
2   FUNCL(MAXD),FUNCR(MAXD),INTX(MAXD),IRIGHT(MAXD),
3   LEFT(MAXD),RATEL(MAXD),RATER(MAXD),VALUE(MAXD),
```

and insert the lines

```
2   FUNCL(80),FUNCR(80),INTX(80),IRIGHT(80),
3   LEFT(80),RATEL(80),RATER(80),VALUE(80),
```

These lines dimension the arrays that store the data associated with discrete variables as they are fixed at integer values.

3. Subroutine BBDATA

Delete the statement

```
MAXD = **
```

and insert the statement

```
MAXD = 80
```

MAXD is the 'size variable' whose value is the dimension of the arrays FUNCL, FUNCR, INTX, IRIGHT, LEFT, RATEL, RATER and VALUE.

4.5. PLP

The dimensions of the arrays in program PLP are determined by:

1. The maximum number of variables, the maximum number of constraints, the maximum number of effective constraints and the maximum number of non-zero elements of the A matrix.
2. The maximum number of parametric variations that the user wishes to perform on an LP solution.

As in LINP, the user, knowing the problems that he intends to solve can determine the maximum number of variables, constraints, effective constraints and non-zero elements of A; for example 100, 60, 45 and 50 respectively. Also the user can determine the maximum number of parametric variations, for example 40.

The alteration of the array dimensions in PLP means that changes have to be made in three places:

1. COMMON, COMMON/AREF and subroutine DATA
2. COMMON/PARA
3. Subroutine PDATA.

1. COMMON, COMMON/AREF and subroutine DATA

These changes are the same as those for program LINP above.

2. COMMON/PARA

a. Delete the first line of the statement

```
COMMON/PARA/BMID, BOTOM(MAXP),CMID,DUMBIG,IJPARA(MAXP),IP,IPARAB,
```

and insert the line

```
COMMON/PARA/BMID,BOTOM(40),CMID,DUMBIG,IJPARA(40),IP,IPARAB,
```

This line dimensions the arrays BOTOM and IJPARA.

b. Delete the continuation line

```
2  NUMP,SBI,SBIN,SCJ,SCJN,TOP(MAXP),UBI,UBIN,UCJ,UCJN
```

and insert the line

```
2  NUMP,SBI,SBIN,SCJ,SCJN,TOP(40),UBI,UBIN,UCJ,UCJN
```

This line dimensions the array TOP.

3. Subroutine PDATA

Delete the statement

```
MAXP = **
```

and insert the statement

MAXP = 40

MAXP is the 'size variable' whose value is the dimension of the arrays BOTOM, IJPARA and TOP.

5. EXTENDING THE PROGRAMS

Our objective in writing these programs has been to make them as flexible as possible. In particular, we wanted to be able to solve, or partly solve, an LP, and then to add extra constraints and delete redundant constraints. We have presented one such algorithm in Chapter 4, but it was chosen as a standard and familiar algorithm rather than as a particularly successful algorithm. We have experimented with very many alternative cutting plane procedures for integer LP, and shall continue to do so, although our present interest is rather in various combinations of cutting planes with branch and bound.

One may also wish to add constraints to an LP for other reasons than to cut off non-integer solutions to an ILP. Some types of problem have potentially combinatorial numbers of constraints (e.g., travelling salesman, scheduling) and one possible approach is to solve the problem with a limited number of constraints, examine the solution and if necessary generate additional constraints. Another use we have made of the programs is in a standard (dual) decomposition algorithm.

We should feel that the publication of these programs has been worth while if readers found it possible to add their own routines to generate constraints and use our routines to reach LP feasibility and optimality. PROGRAM MIF could be used, but instead of calling INTCON it could call any constraint-generating routine required. Such a routine must be restricted as follows:

1. The new constraint must be in the form $\Sigma_j a_{ij} x_j \left(\begin{smallmatrix}\leq\\=\\\geq\end{smallmatrix}\right) b_i$, where the a_{ij} are the coefficients of the *original* x variables, and the sign may be $\leqslant$, $\geqslant$, or $=$, and b_i may be positive, negative or zero.
2. The value of the slack variable, $b_i - \Sigma_j a_{ij} \bar{x}_j$, at the current solution, $\bar{x}$, must be known, if necessary by direct computation.
3. If the LP routine is to be re-entered with one or more added constraints which are not feasible at the current solution, $\bar{x}$, NEGROW must point to at least one of the infeasible constraints. It is not essential that NEGROW should point to the *greatest* violation of feasibility.

To add the new constraint:

1. Put the coefficients a_{ij} of the new constraint into the array PIV(J).
2. Increase MNOW by 1.

3. Call COPY. This will transfer the non-zero elements of the new constraint into the AA array. Since COPY may fail because you have tried to add more constraints than you have room for, after CALL COPY you must check if ISDONE = 1, indicating that the algorithm is finished.
4. Set S(MNOW) = 1·0 if the new constraint is $\Sigma_j a_{ij} x_j \leqslant b_i$; S(MNOW) = –1·0 for $\geqslant b_i$; S(MNOW) = 0·0 for $= b_i$
5. Set NEGROW = MNOW if appropriate
6. Set B(MNOW) = b_i
7. Set SLACK(MNOW) = $b_j - \Sigma_j a_{ij} \bar{x}_j$
8. Set Y(MNOW) = 0·0
9. Set ISEFF(MNOW) = 0
10. Set KEEP(MNOW) = 0 if you are quite happy to have the constraint disappear the next time you call PURGE, if it is not effective. Otherwise set KEEP(MNOW) at some non-zero value.

6. PERFORMANCE OF THE ALGORITHMS ON SOME TEST PROBLEMS

To give some measure of the performance of the algorithms, we have used MIF (Method of Integer Forms) and BB (branch and bound) for each of the problems presented by C. A. Trauth and R. E. Woolsey [11].

Briefly, the problems are as follows:

A1–A9, nine allocation problems of the form

$$\begin{aligned}&\text{Max } 20x_1 + 18x_2 + 17x_3 + 15x_4 + 15x_5 + 10x_6 + 5x_7 + 3x_8 + x_9 + x_{10}\\ &\text{s.t. } 30x_1 + 25x_2 + 20x_3 + 18x_4 + 17x_5 + 11x_6 + 5x_7 + 2x_8 + x_9 + x_{10} \leqslant b\\ &\text{and } x_j = 0 \text{ or } 1, \text{ all } j.\end{aligned}$$

In the nine different problems b takes the values 55, 60, 65, 70, 75, 80, 85, 90 and 100 respectively (not 35, 60, 65 etc, as printed in [11]). B1–B10 are fixed charge problems originated by Dr John Haldi and presumably part of the set presented in his own working paper, No. 43 [6].

C1–C4 are graph-theoretic problems to determine a two-valued (0,1) colouring of the edges of a graph with N vertices, in such a way that there is not a complete sub-graph of k_1 vertices in red (0), or a complete subgraph of k_2 vertices in blue (1). Since the problem is purely one of finding a feasible solution (or of establishing that there is no feasible solution) we have used a zero function rather than a minimization of the number of edges coloured blue. The four problems are:

1. C1: $N = 4$, $k_1 = k_2 = 3$; which results in a problem with 8 constraints on 6 (0,1) variables. (The LP solution turns out to be also an integer solution.)

2. C2: $N = 5$, $k_1 = k_2 = 3$; 20 constraints on 10 (0,1) variables.
3. C3: $N = 6$, $k_1 = 3$, $k_2 = 4$; 35 constraints on 15 (0,1) variables. N.B. Trauth and Woolsey use 65 constraints by using constraints which prevent quadrilaterals, rather than complete 4-graphs (of which there are, of course, fewer).
4. C4: $N = 7$, $k_1 = 3$, $k_2 = 4$; 70 constraints on 21 (0,1) variables.

	Simplex iterations		
Problem	MIF	BB	ILP2-2
A1	17	19	51
A2	42	35	77
A3	52	20	59
A4	26	23	48
A5	13	13	32
A6	47	22	54
A7	>140†	44	119
A8	226	38	57
A9	12	12	34
B1	28	19	36
B2	9	20	47
B3	23	10	104
B4	38	8	18
B5	>558†	15	>7000
B6	330	11	311
B7	>424†	13	>7000
B8	>445†	10	306
B9	80	9	298
B10	>133†	64	>7000
C1	12	12	4
C2	>415†	89	74
C3	>156†	230	29
C4	>542†	357‡	>7000
D1	20	9	11
D2	49	19	15
D3	27	16	14
D4	30	60	18
D5	16	16	842
D6	>558†	767	1105

† These problems failed to reach a solution on the method of Integer Forms as presented here, not by exceeding an iteration limit (which was set at 7000) but by failing to find new acceptable constraints as described in INTCON.

‡ C4 proved to have no feasible integer solution, which is presumably why no cutting plane algorithm reached a conclusion.

D1– D6: 'IBM' test problems 1– 5 and Number 9 from Haldi. (It is assumed in the last, D6, that there should be a 1 in row 5 of column 10, not in row 15 of column 10, as printed in [11].) D6 is run as 35 constraints on 15 upper bounded variables.

Trauth and Woolsey's paper compares the performance of five codes on the problems, of which we have here presented one only, to give a very rough comparison. One of their codes, LIP1, solved all but one of the problems, but the iteration count for that code is not the number of Simplex pivots†. We have therefore included for our comparison the iteration counts for ILP2– 2, which solved all but four of the problems. It was, however, the code using the fewest Simplex iterations in only eight of the problems.

We are offering no conclusions drawn from calculations performed on these small problems. We are very conscious of the unpredictability of codes for the solution of integer and mixed integer problems. The largest integer problem, in terms of dimensions, which we have solved, is one based on a school timetabling problem, with 285 constraints on 280(0,1) variables [4]. This type of problem seemed to be very easy to solve on BB (it was not tried on MIF) in about 400 iterations. Another (0,1) type of problem, only 36 x 59, concerned with selection of investment projects with a threshold level of investment in each geographical area, took about 16,000 iterations to solve on BB,

The main limitation on the practical application of these routines (as opposed to research into methods of solution) is presented by their storage requirements. One of us is working towards adapting more modern methods of handling the pivoting in the Simplex algorithm to the requirements of these programs. The other line of development being pursued is in the direction of special purpose algorithms for various classes of problem.

† It has also had doubt cast on it by Briskin [1].

APPENDIX 1

Index of Programs and Subroutines

1. PROGRAMS

PROGRAM LINP (see Chapter 2) solves linear programming problems with an accuracy check and reinversion.

Subroutines required:

A(I,J)	IPRINT
ADDCON	ISOPT
CHACC	LP
CHBSIS	NEWVEC
CHSLCK	REDUCE
COPY	REVERT
DATA	SEEKX
DOANLP	SEEKY
FIRSTB	SPRINT
IEXIT	

PROGRAM BB (see Chapter 5) is a branch and bound algorithm for discrete programming.

Subroutines required:

As PROGRAM LINP, and:

BACKUP	ISTAIL
BBDATA	PNODE
BRANCH	RESTRT
DUAL	

PROGRAM MIF (see Chapter 4)—Method of Integer Forms—is a cutting plane algorithm for all-integer programming problems.

Subroutines required:

As PROGRAM LINP, and:
IFDATA
INTCON
PURGE

PROGRAM OP (see Chapter 3) solves problems of the form max $px + \frac{1}{2}xDx$, in non-negative variables, subject to linear equality and inequality constraints.

Subroutines required:

A(I,J)	ISOPT
ADDCON	NEWVEC
CHACC	PRICE
CHBSIS	PURGE
CHSLCK	QCON
COPY	QPDATA
DATA	REDUCE
DOAQP	REVERT
FIRSTB	SEEKX
IEXIT	SEEKY
IPRINT	SPRINT

Program PLP (see Chapter 6) is a parametric algorithm to perform parametric variations on the right hand side and objective function elements of an LP.

Subroutines required:

As PROGRAM LINP, and:

CHAGY	PARAB
CHXSL	PARAC
MIDBI	PDATA
MIDCJ	PPRINT

Note: If parametric variations are to be done only on the elements of b_i, then it is only necessary to provide a dummy PARAC (which has only a SUBROUTINE PARAC statement and an END statement): MIDCJ and CHAGY are not needed. Similarly, if only c_j elements are to be varied, only a dummy PARAB is required and MIDBI and CHXSL are not needed.

2. SUBROUTINES

All subroutines are listed alphabetically, followed by the chapter in which each is introduced, and a list of programs in which it is required.

A(I,J)—Chapter 2—BB, LINP, MIF, PLP, QP
ADDCON—Chapter 2—BB, LINP, MIF, PLP, QP
BACKUP—Chapter 5—BB
BBDATA—Chapter 5—BB
BRANCH—Chapter 5—BB
CHACC—Chapter 2—BB, LINP, MIF, PLP, QP

CHAGY—Chapter 6—PLP
CHBSIS—Chapter 2—BB, LINP, MIF, PLP, QP
CHSLCK—Chapter 2—BB, LINP, MIF, PLP, QP
CHXSL—Chapter 6—PLP
COPY—Chapter 2—BB, LINP, MIF, PLP, QP
DATA—Chapter 2—BB, LINP, MIF, PLP, QP
DOANLP—Chapter 2—BB, LINP, MIF, PLP
DOAQP—Chapter 3—QP
DUAL—Chapter 5—BB
FIRSTB—Chapter 2—BB, LINP, MIF, PLP, QP
IEXIT(JK)—Chapter 2—BB, LINP, MIF, PLP, QP
IFDATA—Chapter 4 —MIF
INTCON—Chapter 4—MIF
IPRINT—Chapter 2—BB, LINP, MIF, PLP, QP
ISOPT—Chapter 2—BB, LINP, MIF, PLP, QP
ISTAIL—Chapter 5—BB
LP—Chapter 2—BB, LINP, MIF, PLP
MIDBI—Chapter 6—PLP
MIDCJ—Chapter 6—PLP
NEWVEC—Chapter 2—BB, LINP, MIF, PLP, QP
PARAB—Chapter 6—PLP
PARAC—Chapter 6—PLP
PDATA—Chapter 6—PLP
PNODE—Chapter 5—BB
PPRINT—Chapter 6—PLP
PRICE—Chapter 3—QP
PURGE—Chapter 3—MIF, QP
QCON—Chapter 3—QP
QPDATA—Chapter 3—QP
REDUCE—Chapter 2—BB, LINP, MIF, PLP, QP
RESTRT—Chapter 5—BB
REVERT—Chapter 2—BB, LINP, MIF, PLP, QP
SEEKX—Chapter 2—BB, LINP, MIF, PLP, QP
SEEKY—Chapter 2—BB, LINP, MIF, PLP, QP
SPRINT—Chapter 2—BB, LINP, MIF, PLP, QP

APPENDIX 2

Index of COMMON Variables

All the variables which appear in any COMMON block in these programs are listed alphabetically in Section 1 below. Those which occur in the unlabelled COMMON are signified by 'COMMON'; the labelled COMMONs are signified by their labels only.

Following this alphabetical list, each COMMON block is listed separately in Section 2.

1. ALPHABETICAL LIST OF COMMON VARIABLES

AA(LOOK) COMMON
B(I) COMMON
BIG COMMON
BEFORE BBB
BEST BBB
BMID PARA
BOTOM(JJ) PARA
BOUND(J) COMMON
C(J) COMMON
CMID PARA
D(ID,JD) Q
DRIVER COMMON
DUMBIG PARA
FIXOBJ BBB
FUNC BBB
FUNCL(JJ) BBB
FUNCR(JJ) BBB
G(I)COMMON
GR(K) COMMON
HLDBND(J) BBB
HOLDC(J) Q
IBEST BBB
IJPARA(JJ) PARA
INBASE(J) COMMON
INREV COMMON
INTOBJ BBB
INTX(JJ) BBB
INV(K,L) COMMON
IP PARA
IPARAB PARA
IPARAC PARA
IPRBB BBB
IPRPLP PARA
IR COMMON
IRBB BBB
IRBBM BBB
IRIGHT(JJ) BBB
IRMAX COMMON
IRANGB PARA
IRANGC PARA
IROW(I) AREF
ISBIG COMMON

ISBND COMMON
ISENSB PARA
ISENSC PARA
ISDONE COMMON
ISINT IF
ISEFF(I) COMMON
ISQ(J) Q
ISTATE COMMON
ITAIL BBB
ITR COMMON
ITRBB BBB
ITRBBM BBB
ITRMAX COMMON
JCOL(LOOK) AREF
JDISC(J) BBB
JP PARA
KEEP(I) RETAIN
KEYTOD(ID) Q
KHERE BBB
LEFORT BBB
LEFT(JJ) BBB
LEVEL BBB
M COMMON
MARKI COMMON
MARKK COMMON
MAXA AREF
MAXD BBB
MAXM COMMON
MAXN COMMON
MAXP PARA
MAXQ Q
MNOW COMMON
MORE COMMON
MOREPR COMMON
MXSIZE COMMON
N COMMON
NEGINV COMMON
NEGROW COMMON
NEWD BBB
NEWUP BB
NEWX COMMON
NEWY COMMON
NEXNUM BBB
NUMBES BBB
NUMD BBB
NUMP PARA
NUMQ Q
NUMSLK COMMON
OBJ COMMON
PIV(J) COMMON
PREOBJ BBB
R COMMON
RATEL(JJ) BBB
RATER(JJ) BBB
RATIOD BBB
RATIOU BBB
S(I) COMMON
SBI PARA
SBIN PARA
SCJ PARA
SCJN PARA
SIZE COMMON
SIZE1 COMMON
SLACK(I) COMMON
SMALL COMMON
TOL(JK) COMMON
TOLBB1 BBB
TOLBB2 BBB
TOP(JJ) PARA
UBI PARA
UBIN PARA
UCJ PARA
UCJN PARA
VALUE(JJ) BBB
X(J) COMMON
XBASIS(K) COMMON
XKPOS COMMON
XR(K) COMMON
Y(I) COMMON
YAC(J) COMMON
YACD BBB
YACUP BBB
YAMINC COMMON
YBASIS(L) COMMON
YR(L) COMMON

2. COMMON VARIABLES CLASSIFIED BY THE COMMON BLOCK IN WHICH THEY OCCUR

The variables in each COMMON block are described together, in each case listing first the dimensioned variables and then the undimensioned variables, alphabetically within each of these sets. After a brief description (and, where appropriate, an indication of the intended pronunciation and/or the 'etymology' of the name), there follows a list of all the programs and subroutines in which the value of the variable may be altered, and a list of all the programs and subroutines in which the value of the variable may be used but not altered.

2.1. COMMON

2.1.1. Dimensioned variables

B(I) The array of right hand sides of the linear equality or inequality constraints.

Dimension of B(I) must be equal to MAXM, the maximum number of constraints that the program can store. In the case of MIF (Chapter 4) and QP (Chapter 3), the dimension of B(I) must be sufficiently great to take also the greatest number of added constraints which will be encountered during the calculation. If the calculable maximum is too great, a chance can be taken on a smaller value, and the risk taken that the run will fail because this dimension was not sufficient. All other dimensioned variables in this COMMON and in labelled COMMONs where the index I is used for the dimensions should have the same dimension as B(I).

B(I) is read in DATA; INTCON and QCON create new constraints and PURGE removes constraints.

Value changed in BACKUP, BRANCH, DATA, INTCON, MIDBI, PARAB, PURGE, QCON, RESTRT.

Used in CHACC, CHSLCK, FIRSTB, IFDATA, IPRINT, PLP, PNODE, PPRINT, REVERT, SPRINT.

BOUND(J) The array of upper bounds for each variable.

Dimension of BOUND(J) must be equal to MAXN, the maximum number of variables (not including slack variables) that the program can store.

If a variable is not subject to an upper bound, BOUND(J) = −1·0, except in QP, where BOUND(J) is set at a very large number. In DATA if ISBND = 0, all BOUND(J) will be −1·0; if ISBND = −1, all BOUND(J) will be set equal to 1·0, and if ISBND > 1 the values of specified BOUND(J) are read.

A value of 0·0 for an element of BOUND(J) will prevent the corresponding variable being considered as a candidate for entering the basis. It is so used in BB, whilst the true values are stored in HLDBND(J).

Value changed in BACKUP, BRANCH, DATA, QPDATA, RESTR

Used in BBDATA, CHBSIS, CHSLCK, CHXSL, DUAL, IFDATA, INTCON, IPRINT, ISOPT, MIDBI, MIDCJ, PARAC, PNODE, REVERT, SEEKX, SEEKY, SPRINT.

C(J) The elements of the linear function to be maximized.

In QP the function is $px + \frac{1}{2}xDx$. The vector p of this function is stored in HOLDC(J), and the linear function $c = p + xD$ is computed and stored in C(J) at each iteration.

Dimension, as BOUND(J).

Value changed in DATA, PRICE, MIDCJ, PARAC.

Used in BACKUP, BRANCH, CHACC, CHSLCK, CHXSL, IPRINT, PLP, PPRINT, QPDATA, REVERT, SPRINT.

G(I) The array of changes to SLACK(I) to be made at each basis change.

Dimension, as B(I).

Value changed in SEEKY.

Used in CHSLCK, CHXSL, IEXIT.

GR(K) The array of changes to the current basic variables, XR(K), to be made at each iteration—the 'updated' vector of the entering variable. (Or, rather, those elements corresponding to the explicit basic variables. Those corresponding to implicit basic slack variables are in G(I).)

In BACKUP the array GR(K) is used as a temporary location for a different vector, though its use is similar to the usual one.

Dimension of GR(K) must be equal to MXSIZE, the greatest size of the inverse matrix that is expected to be encountered.

Value changed in BACKUP, NEWVEC, SEEKY.

Used in CHBSIS, CHXSL, IEXIT, QCON, REVERT.

INBASE(J) (in basis) An array of elements indicating whether or not the jth variable is basic. If it is basic, INBASE(J) contains the element K showing which row of the inverse matrix and element of XR(K) is associated with the jth variable. If it is non-basic at its lower bound of zero, INBASE(J) is 0; if it is non-basic at its upper bound, INBASE(J) is −1.

INBASE(J) is set up initially in FIRSTB, and is altered in CHBSIS. It may alter in REDUCE because the position of the rows of the inverse may change. A re-inversion causes it to be again set up.

Dimension, as BOUND(J).

Value changed in BACKUP, CHBSIS, FIRSTB, REDUCE, REVERT.

Used in ADDCON, BRANCH, CHACC, CHAGY, CHSLCK, DOAQP, DUAL, INTCON, IPRINT, ISOPT, MIDCJ, NEWVEC, PARAC, PRICE, SEEKX, SEEKY.

INV(K,L) A matrix of *real* elements and therefore requiring a type statement. INV(K,L) contains the elements of the inverse of the matrix R (see Chapter 1). Both rows and columns may be permuted in order and are identified by XBASIS(K) and YBASIS(L) respectively.

Dimension of both K and L, as discussed under GR(K), above.

Value changed in ADDCON, CHBSIS, FIRSTB, REDUCE, REVERT.

Use in BACKUP, CHAGY, DUAL, INTCON, IPRINT, NEWVEC, PRICE, SEEKX.

ISEFF(I) (is effective) An array of elements indicating whether or not the ith constraint is effective and explicitly represented in the inverse. ISEFF(I) is zero if the constraint is not in the reduced basis R, and shows the associated column, L, of the inverse if the constraint is effective.

ISEFF(I) is set up initially in FIRSTB; is incremented in INTCON, and QCON; is decremented in PURGE as constraints are deleted; is altered in REDUCE as the positions of columns of the inverse are altered.

Dimension, as B(I).

Value changed in ADDCON, FIRSTB, INTCON, PURGE, QCON, REDUCE.

Used in BACKUP, CHACC, CHSLCK, CHXSL, IPRINT, MIDBI, MIDCJ, NEWVEC, PARAB, REVERT, SEEKY.

PIV(J) (pivotal row) This array is used for three purposes:

1. as a row of the A matrix prior to copying it (in COPY) into the AA array (in DATA, INTCON, and QCON);
2. As the 'updated' (pivotal) row of the A matrix required when a pivot is to be sought in a specified row (in CHAGY, IEXIT, DUAL and SEEKX);
3. PIV(J) is used in ISTAIL and SPRINT as a temporary location for printing purposes.

Dimension, as BOUND(J).

Value altered in DATA, DUAL, INTCON, ISTAIL, QCON, SEEKX, SPRINT.

Used in CHAGY, COPY, IEXIT.

S(I) (sign of I) The array of signs of the constraints, 1·0 for a ⩽ constraint; −1·0 for ⩾; 0·0 for =. (These are also the values of the significant elements of the corresponding slack variables.) Note that the ⩾ is *punched* as 2 rather than −1 to enable it to be put into one column of the data card rather than two. S(I) is set up in DATA, incremented in INTCON, and QCON, decremented in PURGE and may be altered in PRICE to change less-than-or-equal to greater-than-or-equal, or vice versa.

Dimension, as B(I).

Value altered in DATA, INTCON, PRICE, PURGE, QCON.

Used in BACKUP, CHBSIS, CHSLCK, CHXSL, DOAQP, DUAL, FIRSTB, IPRINT, ISOPT, MIDBI, MIDCJ, NEWVEC, REDUCE, REVERT, SEEKX, SEEKY, SPRINT.

SLACK(I) The array of slack variables, zero on effective constraints, non-negative for feasibility on ⩽ constraints, non-positive for feasibility on ⩾ constraints, and zero for feasibility on equality constraints (they need not be present in the inverse).

SLACK(I) is set up in CHSLCK if INREV = 1, which it is when CHSLCK follows FIRSTB, or in REVERT, or if LP is entered with ISTATE = 10. SLACK(I) is incremented in INTCON, and QCON, and decremented in PURGE. REDUCE removes a slack vector from explicit representation in the inverse into the implicit representation in the array SLACK(I). In PLP its value is altered in CHXSL on moving from a corner point to the next corner point.

Dimension, as B(I).

Value altered in CHACC, CHSLCK, CHXSL, INTCON, MIDBI, PURGE, QCON, REDUCE.

Used in ADDCON, DOANLP, DOAQP, IPRINT, ISTAIL, PARAB, PPRINT, PRICE, SEEKY, SPRINT.

TOL(JK) (tolerance) An array of tolerances that are used in the LP subroutines. Each tolerance has a specific use. It is explained in greater detail in Chapter 7, Section 2.

Dimension, TOL(8).

Value altered in DATA.

Used in BACKUP, CHACC, CHAGY, CHBSIS, CHSLCK, CHXSL, DUAL, IPRINT, ISOPT, REVERT, SEEKX, SEEKY.

X(J) The values of the variables. This is really a redundant array since the information it contains could be deduced from XR(K) and INBASE(J), and in fact it is merely recomputed at every iteration in CHSLCK. In BB, the newly fixed values of variables are subtracted from the present values in BRANCH. In PLP X(J) is changed in CHXSL on moving from a corner point to the next corner point.

Dimension, as BOUND(J).

Value altered in BRANCH, CHSLCK, CHXSL.

Used in BB, CHACC, INTCON, IPRINT, ISTAIL, PPRINT, PRICE, REVERT, SPRINT.

XBASIS(K) An array of *integer* elements, therefore requiring a type statement. This array is effectively the row labels of the inverse matrix, containing the numbers of the current basic variables. An explicitly basic slack variable on the ith row is represented by N + I in XBASIS(K).

Dimension, as GR(K).

Value altered in ADDCON, CHBSIS, FIRSTB, REDUCE, REVERT.

Used in BACKUP, BRANCH, CHACC, CHXSL, DOAQP, INTCON, IPRINT, ISTAIL, MIDBI, PARAB, PRICE, QCON, SEEKY.

XR(K) (x^R, see Chapter 1.) The values of the variables listed in XBASIS(K). Apart from the alterations during the LP calculations, BB alters the values as variables are fixed and freed in BRANCH and BACKUP. Like X(J), it is altered in CHXSL in PLP.

Dimension, as GR(K).

Value altered in ADDCON, BACKUP, BRANCH, CHBSIS, CHXSL, FIRSTB, REDUCE, REVERT.

Used in CHACC, CHAGY, CHSLCK, INTCON, IPRINT, ISTAIL, MIDBI, SEEKY.

Y(I) Like X(J), a redundant array whose elements could all be deduced from YR(K) and ISEFF(I). Recomputed at each iteration in CHSLCK. It could be combined with SLACK(I) since Y(I) is necessarily zero if SLACK(I) is not zero. Like SLACK(I) it is incremented in INTCON, and QCON, and decremented in PURGE. In QP it is also recomputed at each iteration in PRICE as C(J) changes. In PLP the values are changed on moving from one corner point to the next in CHAGY.

Dimension, as B(I).

Value altered in CHAGY, CHSLCK, INTCON, PRICE, PURGE, QCON.

Used in CHACC, DOAQP, IPRINT, PPRINT, SPRINT.

YAC(J) ($yA - c$) The 'updated' function row of the LP calculation. It is recomputed at each iteration in CHSLCK. Like C(J), it is altered in PRICE in QP. In PLP it is changed in CHAGY at the corner points as C(J) changes.

Dimension, as BOUND(J).

Value altered in CHACC, CHAGY, CHSLCK, ISOPT, MIDCJ, PRICE.

Used in DOAQP, DUAL, IPRINT, PARAC, PPRINT, SEEKX, SPRINT.

YBASIS(L) An array of *integer* elements, therefore requiring a type statement. This array is the column labels of the inverse matrix, containing the numbers of the currently effective constraints. A new constraint is added to the basis in ADDCON and one is removed from the basis in REDUCE. PURGE may alter the numbering of the constraints: it cannot delete an effective constraint. The addition of constraints is always at the end of the list, so it does not affect the numbering of existing constraints.

Dimension, as GR(K).

Value altered in ADDCON, FIRSTB, PURGE, REDUCE.

Used in CHAGY, DUAL, INTCON, IPRINT, ISOPT, NEWVEC, PRICE, REVERT, SEEKX.

YR(L) (y^R, see Chapter 1.) The values of the dual variables of the constraints listed in YBASIS(L). In QP it is recomputed in PRICE at each iteration as C(J) changes. Like Y(I), it is altered in CHAGY in PLP.

Dimension, as GR(K).

Value altered in ADDCON, CHAGY, CHBSIS, FIRSTB, PRICE, REDUCE, REVERT.

Used in CHSLCK, DUAL, INTCON, IPRINT, ISOPT, MIDCJ, SEEKX.

2.1.2. Undimensioned variables

BIG A large number that is treated as infinity; see also Chapter 7, Section 2.

Value altered in DATA.

Used in BACKUP, BBDATA, BRANCH, DOAQP, DUAL, IPRINT, ISTAIL, PNODE, QPDATA, RESTRT, SEEKX, SEEKY

DRIVER This is used when a new variable is sought to reduce the infeasibility in the NEGINV row, and it indicates whether the value of the variable in that row is to be driven up (DRIVER = 1·0) or down (DRIVER = −1·0). In PARAC and MIDCJ, DRIVER is equivalenced to CUPDN which indicates whether the value of C(JP) is increasing (CUPDN = 1·0) or decreasing (CUPDN = −1·0).

Value altered in BACKUP, BRANCH, CHBSIS, CHSXL, DOANLP, DOAQP, FIRSTB, MIDCJ, PARAB, PARAC, REVERT.

Used in CHAGY, IPRINT, MIDCJ, SEEKX.

INREV (in revert) This is an indicator to subroutine CHSLCK whether it is to set up the slack variables from $b - Ax$ (INREV = 1), or to alter the slack variables by subtracting a multiple of the G(I) array (INREV = 0). It is always re-set to zero at the end of CHSLCK. It is also an indicator to the subroutine CHBSIS that only the inverse, and not the associated vectors, is to be updated. It is equal to 1 in subroutine REVERT when the inverse of the basis is recomputed.

Value altered in CHSLCK, DATA, FIRSTB, LP, MIDBI, REVERT.

Used in CHBSIS, IPRINT.

IR The count of the number of re-inversions of the inverse that have been performed while solving an LP problem. It is zeroed in DATA and LP and incremented in REVERT. Subroutine LP zeroes IR before each separate LP calculation. Thus it is possible to control, with IRMAX, the number of re-inversions used in solving each separate LP while accumulating the total in the routine that calls subroutine LP; this is done in BB.

Value altered in DATA, LP, MIF, REVERT.

Used in BB, IEXIT, IPRINT, QP.

IRMAX The maximum of re-inversions that are permitted in solving an LP problem. It is read in DATA and tested upon in subroutine LP.

Value altered in BBDATA, DATA.

Used in IPRINT, LP, MIF, QP.

ISBIG The largest requirement for storage space in these programs is for the inverse matrix. Many apparently large problems in fact never have a reduced form of inverse which approaches either M or N in size. In order to assist the user in developing a judgment about the necessary storage requirement for subsequent runs of his program, ISBIG records the maximum size of the inverse encountered during the calculation.

Value altered in DATA, ADDCON.

Used in BACKUP, IPRINT, ISTAIL, PNODE.

ISBND (is bound) The number of variables subject to upper bounds. Read in on the first LP data card. The effect of the value of ISBND on the value of BOUND(J) is explained in the description of BOUND(J). It is used as a marker to indicate the presence of upper bounded variables.

Value altered in BBDATA, DATA, QPDATA.

Used in IFDATA, IPRINT, REVERT, SEEKY, SPRINT.

ISDONE This variable has the value 0 until the algorithm is complete or an error condition has occurred when it is set to 1. It is used to avoid a STOP statement anywhere other than in the main program. The call to any routine in which the algorithm may effectively terminate must be followed by a test on the value of ISDONE. This means also checking that any routines which themselves call one of the following routines must also be followed by a test of ISDONE (e.g. COPY, which calls IEXIT).

Value altered in BACKUP, BBDATA, DATA, IEXIT, IFDATA, ISTAIL, PDATA, QPDATA.

Used in BB, COPY, DOAQP, INTCON, IPRINT, LINP, MIF, PLP, QP.

ISTATE This variable contains the information about the entering and leaving conditions of an LP, a QP or an ILP. It takes the following values:

ISTATE = 0	an LP or a QP is to be initiated from scratch; there is no basis available.
ISTATE = 1	LP feasible and optimal.
ISTATE = 2	LP or QP infeasible.
ISTATE = 3	LP unbounded.
ISTATE = 4	LP or QP problem insoluble because of insufficient space in the inverse matrix to solve it.
ISTATE = 5	maximum number of iterations reached or exceeded
ISTATE = 6	the *A* matrix is too big for the space allocated.
ISTATE = 7	the program has been unable to achieve an acceptable degree of accuracy after the allowed number of re-inversions.
ISTATE = 8	MIF optimal.
ISTATE = 9	QP optimal.

ISTATE = 10 there is a basis available, complete with x^R and y^R vectors and the LP routine is to start at CHSLCK. It is important that INREV = 1, so that the slack vector is set up in CHSLCK (see subroutine LP).

ISTATE = 11 there is a complete basis including a correct slack vector available which is either feasible or is infeasible with the row of the first infeasibility to be dealt with already identified (in NEGROW or NEGINV). The LP algorithm is to start with SEEKX if infeasible, or with ISOPT to check for optimality if feasible. This is the entry to an LP used after a re-inversion.

ISTATE = 12 as for ISTATE = 11, but the next variable to enter the basis is already identified in NEWX. This is the situation after BRANCH in BB.

Value altered in ADDCON, BB, CHACC, CHAGY, CHXSL, DOANLP, DOAQP, LINP, LP, MIF, MIDBI, MIDCJ, PARAB, PLP, QP.

Used in IPRINT, ISTAIL, PARAC.

ITR The count of the number of iterations that have taken place while solving an LP problem. It is zeroed in DATA and incremented by 1 in FIRSTB and CHBSIS. Subroutine REVERT returns ITR to its count before the re-inversion. Subroutine LP zeroes ITR before each separate LP calculation. Thus it is possible to control, with ITRMAX, the number of iterations used in solving each separate LP while accumulating the total in the routine that calls subroutine LP; this is done in BB.

Value altered in CHBSIS, DATA, FIRSTB, MIF, LP, REVERT.
USED in BB, DOANLP, DOAQP, IPRINT.

ITRMAX (iteration maximum) The maximum number of iterations permitted for solving an LP problem. It is read or set in DATA and tested upon in subroutine LP.

Value altered in DATA, IFDATA.

Used in BBDATA, DOANLP, DOAQP, IPRINT, MIF.

M The number of original constraints in the problem, read in on the first LP data card. In order to read in the additional data required for QP and BB, M (with N) has also to be read in before the additional data for QP and BB.

Value altered in BBDATA, DATA, QPDATA.

Used in DOAQP, IEXIT, IFDATA, IPRINT, PLP, PRICE, PURGE.

MARKI (mark row I) identifies the constraint which is represented by a slack variable explicitly in the basis.
It will normally be eliminated eventually in REDUCE.
Value altered in FIRSTB, REDUCE.
Used in CHSLCK, IPRINT.

MARKK (mark row K) identifies the row of the inverse containing the slack variable indicated by MARKI.
Value altered in FIRSTB, REDUCE.
Used in CHSLCK, IPRINT.

MAXM (maximum M) The maximum number of constraints that the program can store. Its value is the dimension of the arrays B, G, ISEFF, S, SLACK, Y in COMMON, and of the array KEEP in COMMON/RETAIN. The dimension of IROW in COMMON/AREF is MAXM + 1.
Value altered in DATA.
Used in COPY, IEXIT, IPRINT.

MAXN (maximum N) The maximum number of *X* variables, excluding slack variables, that the program can store. Its value is the dimension of the arrays BOUND, C, INBASE, PIV, X and YAC, in COMMON and of the arrays HLDBND and JDISC in COMMON/BBB, and of the arrays HOLDC and ISQ in COMMON/Q.
Value altered in DATA.
Used in IPRINT.

MNOW (M now) The total number of constraints in the system and hence also the identifier of the last one (which is copied into AA, for instance). It is set up in DATA, incremented in INTCON and QCON, and decremented in PURGE.
Value altered in DATA, INTCON, PURGE, QCON.
Used in BACKUP, BB, BRANCH, CHACC, CHSLCK, CHXSL, COPY, DOAQP, FIRSTB, IEXIT, IPRINT, ISTAIL, MIF, PNODE, PPRINT, PRICE, RESTRT, SEEKY, SPRINT.

MORE The indicator of whether there are any more problems to follow the current problem. It is read in on the last data card, and can be used to number a succession of problems, since any non-zero number will indicate a further problem to follow. The last problem must have MORE = 0.
Value altered in DATA.
Used in BB, IPRINT, LINP, MIF, PLP, QP.

MOREPR (more print) This is a printing control variable.

MOREPR = 0 the input cards are printed and the inverse is not printed in subroutine IPRINT.

MOREPR = 1 the input cards are printed, the inverse is printed.

MOREPR = 2 the input cards are not printed, the inverse is printed.

MOREPR = 3 neither the input cards nor the inverse are printed.

Value altered in DATA, IEXIT.

Used in IPRINT.

MXSIZE (maximum SIZE) The maximum size of the inverse matrix, or, equivalently, the maximum number of constraints that will be effective at any basis in the course of solving a problem. The absolute maximum is the maximum of MNOW or N, whichever is the lesser, but for many problems it is safe to assume a lower value. The value of MXSIZE is the dimensions of the arrays GR, INV, XBASIS, XR, YBASIS and YR.

Value altered in DATA.

Used in ADDCON.

N The number of variables in the problem (excluding slacks).

Read in on the first LP data card. Like M, it is read in twice in QP and BB.

Value altered in BBDATA, DATA, QPDATA.

Used in ADDCON, BB, BACKUP, BRANCH, CHACC, CHAGY, CHBSIS, CHSLCK, CHXSL, COPY, DOAQP, DUAL, FIRSTB, IEXIT, IFDATA, INTCON, IPRINT, ISOPT, ISTAIL, MIDBI, MIDCJ, NEWVEC, PARAB, PLP, PNODE, PPRINT, PRICE, QCON, REDUCE, RESTRT, REVERT, SEEKX, SEEKY, SPRINT.

NEGINV (negative row of the inverse) The row of the inverse associated with an infeasible variable (usually, but not necessarily, a negative variable). It is discovered in CHBSIS, although it is not altered there if the previous NEGINV row is still infeasible, even though it is no longer the most infeasible. The position of the most infeasible row may be altered by REDUCE. It is recomputed in REVERT. If (and only if) all the explicit basic variables are feasible the next infeasibility from the implicit constraints (NEGROW) will be made explicit and added to the inverse in ADDCON, whereupon NEGINV will be equal to SIZE, the last row of the inverse. In BB, NEGINV is set when fixing or freeing variables causes an infeasibility in a basic variable. In PLP NEGINV is set when returning to the initial value of B(IP) causes infeasibility. Also it is used in PARAC and MIDCJ to indicate the row of the inverse that is to be used in evaluating the change in C(JP) which is possible without causing the basis to become non-optimal.

Value altered in BACKUP, BRANCH, CHBSIS, CHXSL, DATA, DOANLP, DOAQP, FIRSTB, MIDBI, MIDCJ, PARAB, PARAC, REDUCE, REVERT.

Used in CHSLCK, DUAL, IPRINT, SEEKX, SEEKY.

NEGROW (negative row) The most infeasible row of the A matrix. This is recomputed at each iteration in CHSLCK. Only when NEGINV is zero is NEGROW considered as the next constraint to be satisfied (if possible).

Value altered in CHSLCK, DATA, MIDBI, INTCON.

Used in DOANLP, DOAQP, IPRINT.

NEWX (new x) The next variable to be introduced to the basis. In LINP it is found in ISOPT (if feasible) or SEEKX (if infeasible). It is used in REVERT to determine the next variable to re-introduce. In DOAQP NEWX will be set equal to the variable which has just left the basis if the value of the function has fallen from the last basis. In BRANCH, NEWX is determined in the course of determining the variable on which to branch. In PARAB in order to evaluate the change in B(IP), NEWX is the slack on the IP constraint. In PARAC, NEWX is the variable that has to be introduced to the basis to preserve optimality.

Value altered in BRANCH, DATA, DOAQP, FIRSTB, ISOPT, MIDBI, MIDCJ, PARAB, PARAC, REVERT, SEEKX.

Used in BB, CHAGY, CHBSIS, CHXSL, DOANLP, IPRINT, NEWVEC, QCON, SEEKY.

NEWY (new y) The row of the inverse *or* the row of the A matrix which limits the extent of the current basis change. Determined at each iteration in SEEKY. NEWY = -1 indicates that the limit is set by the entering variable reaching its own upper bound (or zero, if it is entering negatively from its upper bound). If the limit is encountered in one of the variables in the explicit basis going to its upper or lower bound, NEWY = K, indicating the row of this variable. If the limit is in one of the slack variables not represented in the inverse, NEWY = SIZE + I, indicating the ith slack variable.

In ADDCON this constraint is added to the inverse, so that NEWY is now set equal to SIZE, the new last row of the inverse. NEWY is also used (in DOANLP and DOAQP) to signal which row ADDCON is to add to the inverse when a new infeasibility in NEGROW is to be dealt with by making it explicit. In PARAB, NEWY is the variable that has to be made non-basic in order to preserve feasibility.

Value altered in ADDCON, CHXSL, DATA, DOANLP, DOAQP, MIDBI, PARAB, REVERT, SEEKY.

Used in CHBSIS, IPRINT.

NUMSLK (number of slacks) The number of slack variables that are explicitly present in the basis.

Value altered in ADDCON, CHBSIS, FIRSTB, REDUCE, REVERT.

Used in IPRINT.

OBJ (objective) The current value of $cx = yb$. In QP it is altered with C(J) in PRICE, and in BB it is altered as X(J) and B(I) alter. (In that algorithm the actual maximand is FUNC = OBJ + FIXOBJ.)

Value altered in BACKUP, BRANCH, CHAGY, CHBSIS, CHXSL, FIRSTB, MIDCJ, PARAC, PRICE, REVERT.

Used in BB, DOAQP, IPRINT, PPRINT, SPRINT.

R The limit of the value of the entering variable, determined in SEEKY. R is also used effectively as a local variable in SEEKX. In PLP, R and −R are the changes in the values of B(IP) and C(JP) respectively.

Value changed in DATA, CHAGY, CHXSL, MIDBI, MIDCJ, PARAB, PARAC, SEEKX, SEEKY.

Used in CHBSIS, CHSLCK, DOAQP, IPRINT.

SIZE An *integer* variable, requiring a type declaration. The present size of the inverse, incremented in ADDCON and FIRSTB, and decremented in REDUCE.

Value changed in ADDCON, DATA, FIRSTB, REDUCE.

Used in BACKUP, BRANCH, CHACC, CHAGY, CHBSIS, CHXSL, DOANLP, DOAQP, DUAL, IEXIT, INTCON, IPRINT, ISOPT, ISTAIL, MIDBI, NEWVEC, PARAB, PRICE, QCON, REVERT, SEEKX, SEEKY.

SIZE1 (size + 1) An *integer* variable, requiring a type declaration. Its value is the value of SIZE + 1.

Value changed in ADDCON, FIRSTB, REDUCE.

USED in DOANLP, DOAQP, SEEKY.

SMALL A very small value, set in DATA and used as a tolerance, see also Chapter 7, Section 2. It is temporarily set at 0·0 in REVERT, and then returned to its original value.
Value changed in DATA, REVERT.
Used in CHBSIS, IPRINT, PRICE, QCON, SEEKY.

XKPOS (x_k positive) indicates whether the entering variable (NEWX) is entering positively (XKPOS = 1·0) or negatively (XKPOS = −1·0). The latter would be the case if the new variable were previously at its upper bound and was coming down from that level, or if the entering variable were a slack variable on a greater-than-or-equal constraint (which is constrained to take non-positive values). In PARAB and MIDBI, XKPOS is equivalenced to BUPDN which indicates whether the value of B(IP) is increasing (BUPDN = −1·0) or decreasing (BUPDN = 1·0).
Value changed in MIDBI, NEWVEC, PARAB.
Used in CHBSIS, CHSLCK, CHXSL, IPRINT, QCON, SEEKY.

YAMINC (yA minus c i.e., $ya^k - c_k$) The element in the updated function row of the entering variable, YAC(NEWX). It is required in CHBSIS to update the dual (y) values whenever NEWX is determined (except in REVERT where only the inverse, not x and y, is altered).
Value altered in BRANCH, CHAGY, DATA, DOAQP, ISOPT, MIDCJ, SEEKX.
Used in CHBSIS, IPRINT, QCON.

2.2. COMMON/AREF

2.2.1. Dimensioned variables

AA(LOOK) The array of non-zero elements of the coefficient matrix, A, stored row by row. It is built up initially in DATA by the COPY routine, and is incremented as new constraints are created. Elements are deleted and the gaps closed up in PURGE.
Dimension. The dimension of AA must be sufficiently great to hold all the non-zero elements of the original coefficient matrix, and all those generated by the algorithm being used. MAXA should be set equal to this dimension to prevent overrunning this array.
Value altered in COPY, PURGE.
Used in A, ADDCON, CHSLCK, DUAL, IFDATA,

INTCON, IPRINT, PRICE, REVERT, SEEKX, SEEKY, SPRINT.

IROW(I) The array of elements which signify the starting points of rows of A in AA.
Dimension MAXM + 1, i.e., as B(I) plus 1.
Value altered in DATA, COPY, PURGE.
Used in A, ADDCON, CHSLCK, DUAL, IFDATA, INTCON, IPRINT, PRICE, REVERT, SEEKX, SEEKY, SPRINT.

JCOL(LOOK) The array of column labels of the elements of A in array AA.
Dimension as AA(LOOK).
Value altered in COPY, PURGE.
Used in A, ADDCON, CHSLCK, DUAL, INTCON, IPRINT, PRICE, REVERT, SEEKX, SEEKY, SPRINT.

2.2.2. Undimensioned variable

MAXA (maximum A) The maximum number of elements which can be stored in array AA.
Value altered in DATA.
Used in COPY, IEXIT, IPRINT.

2.3. COMMON/BBB

2.3.1. Dimensioned variables

FUNCL(JJ) (function left) The array of upper bounds of the function for values of the variable INTX(JJ) which is fixed at LEVEL JJ at VALUE(JJ), if INTX(JJ) were to be fixed at the next allowable value *below* VALUE(JJ). These upper bounds are initially computed in BRANCH or BACKUP, but may be tightened in ISTAIL. A value of FUNCL(JJ) of −BIG indicates that a value of INTX(JJ) at the next allowable value below VALUE(JJ) is infeasible.
Dimension. The subscript JJ is used throughout to signify the LEVEL, or depth, of the tree of solutions. The dimension of FUNCL(JJ) must be equal to MAXD, the maximum number of discrete variables that the program is able to store.
Value altered in BACKUP, BRANCH, ISTAIL, PNODE, RESTRT.

FUNCR(JJ) (function right) As FUNCL(JJ) but referring to the values of INTX(JJ) to the right hand of the tree, i.e., if INTX(JJ) were to be fixed at the next allowable value *above* VALUE(JJ).

Dimension, as FUNCL(JJ).
Value altered in BACKUP, BRANCH, ISTAIL, PNODE, RESTRT.

HLDBND(J) (hold bound) The original BOUND(J) array of the problem. It is set immediately after DATA and not subsequently altered, though it is used in the calculation.
Dimension, as BOUND(J).
Value altered in BBDATA.
Used in BACKUP, BRANCH.

INTX(JJ) (integer x) The identifying numbers of the variables fixed at each LEVEL, JJ, of the tree. It is fixed in BRANCH, and not altered in BACKUP, since this routine works by reducing LEVEL and hence omitting the later values of INTX(JJ) from further consideration.
Dimension, as FUNCL(JJ).
Value altered in BRANCH, RESTRT.
Used in BACKUP, ISTAIL, PNODE, RESTRT.

IRIGHT(JJ) (I right) The allowable discrete value to the right (above) the current fixed value, VALUE(JJ), of variable INTX(JJ).
Dimension, as FUNCL(JJ).
Value altered in BACKUP, BRANCH.
Used in ISTAIL, PNODE, RESTRT.

JDISC(J) (J discrete) The array of discrete step sizes for each x_j. If x_j is simply constrained to be integer, JDISC(J) is 1. Only one step size is allowed for each variable. If JDISC(J) is 0, x_j is not constrained to take discrete values.
It is read in BB, and set equal to 1 throughout if NUMD = —
Dimension, as BOUND(J).
Value altered in BBDATA.
Used in BACKUP, BRANCH, ISTAIL.

LEFT(JJ) As IRIGHT(JJ), but the allowable value to the left (below) of VALUE(JJ).
Dimension, as FUNCL(JJ).
Value altered in BACKUP, BRANCH.
Used in ISTAIL, PNODE, RESTRT.

RATEL(JJ) (rate to the left) The rate of fall of the function per step to the left of the variable INTX(JJ). It is originally computed in BRANCH, but may be increased in ISTAIL.
Dimension, as FUNCL(JJ).
Value altered in BRANCH, ISTAIL, PNODE, RESTRT.
Used in BACKUP.

RATER(JJ) (rate to the right) As RATEL(JJ) but the rate to the right of the variable INTX(JJ).

Dimension, as FUNCL(JJ).
Value altered in BRANCH, ISTAIL, PNODE, RESTRT.
Used in BACKUP.

VALUE(JJ) The fixed discrete value of the variable INTX(JJ).

Dimension, as FUNCL(JJ).
Value altered in BACKUP, BRANCH.
Used in ISTAIL, PNODE, RESTRT.

2.3.2. Undimensioned variables

BEFORE A previous value of INTX(JJ) that is used to calculate the improvement of the function values, FUNCL(JJ) and FUNCR(JJ), and of the rates, RATEL(JJ) and RATER(JJ) in ISTAIL; see also Chapter 5.

Value altered in BACKUP, BRANCH.
Used in ISTAIL.

BEST The function value of the best discrete solution discovered so far.

Value altered in BBDATA, ISTAIL.
Used in BACKUP, PNODE, RESTRT.

FIXOBJ (fixed objective) The part of the objective function attributable to the current fixed variables.

Value altered in BACKUP, BBDATA, BRANCH.
Used in BB, ISTAIL, PNODE, RESTRT.

FUNC (function) The total objective function, FUNC = OBJ + FIXOBJ. It is altered in BB after each LP calculation.

Value altered in BB.
Used in BRANCH, ISTAIL.

IBEST (integer BEST) The function value of the best discrete solution discovered so far when the optimum function value is known to be integer. (See also Chapter 7 section 1.)

Value altered in BBDATA, ISTAIL.
Used in BACKUP, PNODE, RESTRT.

INTOBJ (integer objective) The character of the optimum function value. It is read in BBDATA.

INTOBJ = 0 the optimum function value may be non-integer.

INTOBJ = 1 the optimum function value will be an integer.

Value altered in BBDATA.
Used in BACKUP, ISTAIL.

IPRBB (I print in BB) This variable controls the amount of print at each tail.

IPRBB $\geqslant$ 1 subroutine IPRINT is called at the initial LP optimum. At a discrete tail (ITAIL = 1) the fixed variables and their values are printed irrespective of the value of IPRBB.

IPRBB $\geqslant$ 1 at a tail, the fixed variables and their values are printed.

IPRBB $\geqslant$ 2 at a tail, function estimates to the right and left of the tree are also printed.

IPRBB = 3 at a tail, the rate of fall of the function estimates to the right and left of the tree are also printed.

If the BB algorithm terminates without completing its search of the tree, IPRBB is set to 3 to ensure a full print out of the node that has been reached.

IPRBB is initially read in BBDATA.
Value altered in BBDATA, ISTAIL.
Used in BB.

IRBB (IR in BB) A count of the number of re-inversions in the BB algorithm.
Value altered in BB, BBDATA.
Used in ISTAIL.

IRBBM (IR in BB, maximum) The maximum number of re-inversions permitted in the BB algorithm. It is read in BBDATA.
Value altered in BBDATA.
Used in ISTAIL.

ITAIL The character of the current solution, discovered in ISTAIL.

ITAIL = 0 the current solution is not a tail, i.e., it is not discrete, and has a function greater than BEST (INTOBJ = 0) or IBEST (INTOBJ = 1).

ITAIL = 1 a new discrete solution with function better than previous BEST, or IBEST.

ITAIL = 2 the function at the current solution is at least as low as BEST, or IBEST.

ITAIL = 3 the current set of discrete constraints is infeasible.

Value altered in BB, ISTAIL.

ITRBB (ITR in BB) A count of the number of iterations in the BB algorithm.
Value altered in BB, BBDATA.
Used in BACKUP, ISTAIL, PNODE.

ITRBBM (ITR in BB, maximum) The maximum number of iterations permitted in the BB algorithm. It is read or set in BBDATA.
Value altered in BBDATA.
Used in BB, ISTAIL.

KHERE (K here) After ISTAIL, the basic variables from 1 to KHERE −1 are known to satisfy the discrete constraints, thus the search for the next variable on which to branch can start from KHERE.
Value altered in ISTAIL.
Used in BRANCH.

LEFORT (left or right) An indicator of whether a move to the left (LEFORT = −1) or to the right (LEFORT = 1) is being made.
Value altered in BACKUP, BBDATA, BRANCH.
Used in ISTAIL, PNODE, RESTRT.

LEVEL The current level of the tree, i.e., the number of variables currently fixed at discrete values.
Value altered in BACKUP, BBDATA, BRANCH.
Used in BB, ISTAIL, PNODE, RESTRT.

MAXD (maximum discrete) The maximum number of discrete variables that the program can store. Its value is the dimension of the arrays FUNCL, FUNCR, INTX, IRIGHT, LEFT, RATEL, RATER and VALUE in COMMON/BBB.
Value altered in BBDATA.

NEWD (new (x) down) The variable which would have to enter the basis to preserve optimality and *reduce* the variable currently being considered for branching.
Value altered in DUAL.
Used in BRANCH.

NEWUP (new (x) up) The variable which would have to enter the basis to preserve optimality and *increase* the variable currently being considered for branching.
Value altered in DUAL.
Used in BRANCH.

NEXNUM (next number) A count of the discrete solutions. It is not really necessary in the algorithm as included here: it would be of interest to help identify the best solution if the program were altered to produce also non-optimal discrete solutions.
Value altered in BBDATA, ISTAIL.
Used in PNODE, RESTRT.

NUMBES (number of the best solution) The value of the count (NEXNUM) assigned to the best discrete solution so far.

Value changed in BBDATA, ISTAIL.
Used in BACKUP, PNODE, RESTRT.

NUMD (number discrete) The number of discrete variables, read on the first BB data card. If NUMD = –1 all the variables may take any integer values. It must not be greater than MAXD.
Value changed in BBDATA.
Used in ISTAIL.

PREOBJ (previous objective) A previous value of the function that is used to calculate the improvement in the function values, FUNCL(JJ) and FUNCR(JJ), and of the rates, RATEL(JJ) and RATER(JJ) in ISTAIL; see also Chapter 5. (N.B. A local variable with the same name is used in DOAQP.)
Value altered in BACKUP, BBDATA, BRANCH.
Used in ISTAIL.

RATIOD (ratio down) YAC(NEWD) divided by the element in the row of the tableau corresponding to the variable at present being considered for branching on, (PIV(NEWD)).
Value altered in DUAL.
Used in BRANCH.

RATIOU (ratio up) As RATIOD, for variable NEWUP.
Value altered in DUAL.
Used in BRANCH.

TOLBB1 (tolerance in BB, 1) This tolerance is used to test whether or not the basic variables have integer values.
Value altered in BBDATA.
Used in BRANCH, ISTAIL.

TOLBB2 (tolerance in BB, 2) When the optimum function value is known to be integer this tolerance is used to test whether or not the function or function estimate has an integer value.
Value altered in BBDATA.
Used in BACKUP, ISTAIL.

YACD [$yA - c$ (down)] YAC(NEWD).
Value altered in DUAL.
Used in BRANCH.

YACUP [$yA - c$ (up)] YAC(NEWUP).
Value altered in DUAL.
Used in BRANCH.

2.4. COMMON/IF

2.4.1. Dimensioned variables

No dimensioned variables.

2.4.2. *Undimensioned variable*

ISINT (is it integer) This variable is used to indicate whether or not an integer solution has been found.
ISINT = 0 the solution is non-integer.
ISINT = 1 the solution is integer
Value altered in INTCON.
Used in MIF.

2.5. COMMON/PARA

2.5.1. *Dimensioned variables*

BOTOM(JJ) The array of the lower bounds of the parametric variations for each parametric request.
Dimension of BOTOM(JJ) must be equal to MAXP.
Value altered in PDATA.
Used in PLP.

IJPARA(JJ) The array of the variables to be parametrized. If IJPARA(JJ) is positive then B(IJPARA(JJ)) is to be varied, while if it is negative then C(–IJPARA(JJ)) is to be varied.
Dimension, as BOTOM(JJ).
Value altered in PDATA.
Used in PLP.

TOP(JJ) The array of upper bounds of the parametric variations for each parametric request.
Dimension, as BOTOM(JJ).
Value altered in PDATA.
Used in PLP.

2.5.2. *Undimensioned variables*

BMID (*b* middle) The value of B(IP) at the initial basis. The routine MIDBI returns to the basis associated with BMID.
Value altered in PARAB.
Used in MIDBI.

CMID (*c* middle) The value of C(JP) at the initial basis. The routine MIDCJ returns to the basis associated with CMID.
Value altered in PARAC.
Used in MIDCJ.

DUMBIG (dummy BIG) This variable has a large value and it is used to represent infinity for printing purposes.
Value altered in PDATA.
Used in PARAB, PARAC.

IP The constraint whose right hand side, B(IP), is being varied.
Value altered in PLP.
Used in CHXSL, MIDBI, PARAB, PPRINT.

IPARAB This variable contains the information about the state of the parametrization of B(IP). It takes the following values:

IPARAB = 0 parametrization of an element of B is not taking place.

IPARAB = 1 parametrization of B(IP) has started.

IPARAB = 2 the initial basis is feasible within a range of values of B(IP).

IPARAB = 3 the current basis is feasible within a range of values of B(IP).

IPARAB = 4 the current basis is feasible within a range of values of B(IP) but the constraint IP is ineffective so that only the value of SLACK(IP) will alter as B(IP) changes.

IPARAB = 5 the current basis is feasible and the constraint IP is effective. However, the value of B(IP) may change to either plus or minus infinity, depending upon the direction of movement, without causing infeasibility.

IPARAB = 6 the current basis is infeasible within a range of values of B(IP)

IPARAB = 7 the current basis is feasible within a range of values of B(IP) but only the range and not the solution values are to be printed.

IPARAB = 8 end of the parametric variation of B(IP).

IPARAB = 9 the current basis is feasible within a range of values of B(IP) but only the solution values and not the range are to be printed.

IPARAB = 10 an equality constraint cannot be made effective so that a parametric analysis of any type cannot be performed on the right hand side of this constraint.

The value of IPARAB affects the printing in PPRIN
Value altered in PARAB, PDATA, PLP.
Used in PPRINT.

IPARAC This variable contains the information about the state of the parametrization of C(JP). It takes the following values:

IPARAC = 0 parametrization of an element of C is not taking place.

IPARAC = 1 parametrization of C(JP) has started.

IPARAC = 2 the initial basis is optimal within a range of values of C(JP).

IPARAC = 3 the current basis is optimal within a range of values of C(JP).

IPARAC = 4 the current basis is optimal within a range of values of C(JP) but the variable JP is non-basic so that only the value of YAC(JP) will alter as C(JP) alters.

IPARAC = 5 the current basis is optimal and the variable JP is basic. However, the value of C(JP) may change to either plus or minus infinity, depending upon the direction of movement, without causing non-optimality.

IPARAC = 6 the current basis is non-optimal within a range of values of C(JP).

IPARAC = 7 the current basis is optimal with a range of values of C(JP) but only the range and not the solution values are to be printed.

IPARAC = 8 end of the parametric variation of C(JP).

IPARAC = 9 the current basis is optimal within a range of values of C(JP) but only the solution values and not the range are to be printed.

The value of IPARAC affects the printing in PPRINT.
Value altered in PARAC, PDATA, PLP.
Used in PPRINT.

IPRPLP (I print in PLP) A printing control variable.

Parametrizing an element of B:

IPRPLP = 0 the *x* and slack variables are printed at each corner point.

IPRPLP = 1 the dual and function row variables are also printed at each corner point.

Parametrizing an element of C:

IPRPLP = 0 the dual and function row variables are printed at each corner point.

IPRPLP = 1 the *x* and slack variables are also printed at each corner point.

Value altered in PDATA.
Used in PPRINT.

IRANGB (I range *b*) This marker indicates whether a range analysis of an element of *b* is being performed.

IRANGB = 1 a range analysis is being performed.
IRANGB = 0 otherwise.

Value altered in PDATA, PLP.
Used in PARAB, PPRINT.

IRANGC (I range c) This marker indicates whether a range analysis of an element of c is being performed.
IRANGC = 1 a range analysis is being performed.
IRANGC = 0 otherwise.
Value altered in PDATA, PLP.
Used in PARAC, PPRINT.

ISENSB (I sensitivity b) This marker indicates whether a sensitivity analysis of an element of b is being performed.
ISENSB = 1 a sensitivity analysis is being performed.
ISENSB = 0 otherwise.
Value altered in PLP.
Used in PARAB, PPRINT.

ISENSC (I sensitivity c) This marker indicates whether a sensitivity analysis of an element of c is being performed.
ISENSC = 1 a sensitivity analysis is being performed.
ISENSC = 0 otherwise.
Value altered in PLP.
Used in PARAC, PPRINT.

JP The variable whose element in the objective function, C(JP), is being varied.
Value altered in PLP.
Used in CHAGY, MIDCJ, PARAC, PPRINT.

MAXP (maximum parametric) The maximum number of parametric requests that the program can store. Its value is the dimension of the arrays BOTOM, IJPARA and TOP.
Value altered in PDATA.

NUMP The number of parametric requests which is read on the first PLP data card. It must not be greater than MAXP.
Value altered in PLP.
Used in PDATA.

SBI (small b_i) The lower end of the range within which B(IP) is to be parametrized. In a sensitivity analysis SBI is initially equal to the value of B(IP), and at the end of the computation SBI is equal to the lower end of the range of values within which the initial basis is feasible. Throughout a range analysis SBI is equal to the value of B(IP).
Value altered in PARAB, PLP.

SBIN (small b_i now) The lower end of the range of B(IP) within which the current basis is feasible.

Value altered in PARAB.
Used in PPRINT.

SCJ (small c_j) The lower end of the range within which C(JP) is to be parametrized. In a sensitivity analysis SCJ is initially equal to the value of C(JP), and at the end of the computation SCJ is equal to the lower end of the range of values within which the initial basis is optimal. Throughout a range analysis SCJ is equal to the value of C(JP).
Value altered in PARAC, PLP.

SCJN (small c_j now) The lower end of the range of C(JP) within which the current basis is optimal.
Value altered in PARAC.
Used in PPRINT.

UBI (upper b_i) The upper end of the range within which B(IP) is to be parametrized. In a sensitivity analysis UBI is initially equal to the value of B(IP), and at the end of the computation UBI is equal to the upper end of the range of values within which the initial basis is feasible. Throughout a range analysis UBI is equal to the value of B(IP).
Value altered in PARAB, PLP.

UBIN (upper b_i now) The upper end of the range of B(IP) within which the current basis is feasible.
Value altered in PARAB.
Used in PPRINT.

UCJ (upper c_j) The upper end of the range within which C(JP) is to be parametrized. In a sensitivity analysis UCJ is initially equal to the value of C(JP), and at the end of the computation UCJ is equal to the upper end of the range of values within which the initial basis is optimal. Throughout a range analysis UCJ is equal to the value of C(JP).
Value altered in PARAC, PLP.

UCJN (upper c_j now) The upper end of the range of C(JP) within which the current basis is optimal.
Value altered in PARAC.
Used in PPRINT.

2.5.3. Equivalenced variables

BUPDN (b up down) equivalenced to XKPOS. BUPDN = −1·0 indicates that B(IP) is increasing and BUPDN = 1·0 that B(IP) is decreasing.

Value altered in PARAB.
Used in CHXSL, MIDBI.

CUPDN (*c* up down) equivalenced to DRIVER. CUPDN = 1·0 indicates that C(JP) is increasing and CUPDN = −1·0 that C(JP) is decreasing.
Value altered in PARAC.
Used in CHAGY, MIDCJ.

2.6. COMMON/Q

2.6.1. Dimensioned variables

D(ID, JD) The matrix D of the function $px + \frac{1}{2}xDx$. It can always be made symmetrical, but advantage has not been taken of this feature in storing D in QP. Only rows and columns which have at least one non-zero entry need be stored. Read in QPDATA, before the call to DATA.
Dimensions, equal to MAXQ, the maximum number of variables entering the function non-linearly that the program can store.
Value altered in QPDATA.
Used in PRICE, QCON.

ISQ(J) (is quadratic) An array indicating whether each variable, x_j, enters the function non-linearly. If not, ISQ(J) = 0. If it does, ISQ(J) gives the cross reference (ID or JD) to the row and column of D(ID, JD) in which the quadratic coefficient occurs.
Dimension, as BOUND(J).
Value altered in QPDATA.
Used in QCON.

HOLDC(J) (hold *c*) The elements of p in the function $px + \frac{1}{2}xDx$. (The vector C(J) changes at each iteration and holds $c = p + \bar{x}D$.)
Dimension, as BOUND(J).
Value altered in QPDATA.
Used in PRICE, QCON.

KEYTOD(ID) (key to D) A row and column key to the x_j variables associated with the matrix D.
Dimension, as D(ID,JD).
Value altered in QPDATA.
Used in PRICE, QCON.

2.6.2. Undimensioned variables

MAXQ (maximum quadratic) The maximum number of quadratic variables the program can store. Its value is the dimensions of the arrays D and KEYTOD.

Value altered in QPDATA.

NUMQ (number quadratic) The number of variables entering the function non-linearly (the quadratic variables). Read on the first QP data card for the problem, and it must not be greater than MAXQ.

Value altered in QPDATA.
Used in PRICE, QCON.

2.7. COMMON/RETAIN

2.7.1. Dimensioned variables

KEEP(I) An array which indicates whether or not a constraint may be deleted in PURGE. IF KEEP(I) $\neq 0$, the row will not be deleted. The elements of KEEP(I) that refer to the original constraints are not used in these routines as PURGE only deletes constraints whose row number is greater than M. Thus KEEP(I) is used to indicate whether or not the constraints generated in INTCON and QCON are to be retained.

Dimension, as B(I).

Value altered in IFDATA, INTCON, PURGE, PRICE, QPDATA, QCON.

2.7.2. Undimensioned variables

No undimensioned variables.

APPENDIX 3

Data Input Format

This is a description of the input cards. It should be compared with the data punching sheets in Section 2 of Appendix 4.

All the data should be right adjusted within the field and should be integer except for C(J), BOUND(J), B(I), A(I,J) which may take real values and TYPE, card 2 of PLP, which is a character.

1. INPUT TO LINP

Card 1	Col	1–10	M	number of constraints
		11–20	N	number of variables
		21–30	ISBND	number of bounded variables = –1, all the variables have an upper bound of 1
		31–40	MOREPR	= 0 print the input cards, do not print the inverse in IPRINT = 1 print the input cards, print the inverse = 2 do not print the input cards, print the inverse = 3 do not print the input cards, do not print the inverse
		41–50	ITRMAX	maximum number of iterations = 0, will be set to 3 * (M + N + number of bounded variables)
		51–60	IRMAX	maximum number of re-inversions
Card 2	Col	1–3	J	number of a non-zero element of the objective function, *c*
		5–10	C(J)	j^{th} element of the objective function
		11–13	J	

		15-20	C(J)	
		.		
		.		
		.		
		71-73	J	
		75-80	C(J)	

Card 2 is repeated until all the non-zero elements of the objective function have been specified, up to eight per card.

Card 3	Col	1-10	9999999999	indicates the end of the c elements

If ISBND is greater than 0 the next card is Card 4, otherwise the next card is Card 6.

Card 4	Col	1-3	J	number of an upper bounded variable
		5-10	BOUND(J)	value of the upper bound on the jth variable
		11-13	J	
		15-20	BOUND(J)	
		.		
		.		
		.		
		71-73	J	
		75-80	BOUND(J)	

Card 4 is repeated until all the upper bounds have been specified, up to eight per card. (Any that are not specified are assumed to have no upper bound.)

Card 5	Col	1-10	9999999999	indicates the end of the upper bounds
Card 6	Col	1-3	I	number of an element of the b vector
		4	S(I)	= 0, an equality constraint = 1, a less-than-or-equal constraint = 2, a greater-than-or-equal constraint
		5-10	B(I)	the ith element of the b vector
		11-13	I	
		14	S(I)	
		15-20	B(I)	
		.		
		.		
		71-73	I	
		74	S(I)	
		75-80	B(I)	

Card 6 is repeated until all the elements of the right-hand side vector have been specified, up to eight per card. (Any not specified are assumed by the program to be $\leqslant$ a very large number.)

Card	Col	Variable	Description
Card 7	Col 1–10	9999999999	indicates the end of the b elements

Card	Col	Variable	Description
Card 8	Col 5–10	I	number of a row of the A matrix
	11–13	J	number of a column of the A matrix
	15–20	A(I,J)	a non-zero element of the A matrix
	21–23	J	
	25–30	A(I,J)	
	.		
	.		
	.		
	71–73	J	
	75–80	A(I,J)	

All the elements on a card must belong to the same row but need not be in correct column order. The rows must be entered in correct row order. Card 8 is repeated until all the non-zero elements of the A matrix have been specified, up to seven per card.

Card	Col	Variable	Description
Card 9	Col 1–10	9999999999	indicates the end of the A matrix elements
Card 10	Col 1–10	MORE	$= 0$, if no further problems $\neq 0$, if there are further problems

2. INPUT TO QP

Card	Col	Variable	Description
Card 1	Col 1–10	M	number of constraints
	11–20	N	number of variables
	21–30	NUMQ	number of quadratic variables
Card 2	Col 1–5	ID	the variable associated with the row of the D matrix
	6–10	JD	the variable associated with the column of the D matrix
	11–20	D(ID,JD)	a non-zero element (ID,JD) of D. By symmetry D(ID,JD) and D(JD,ID) have the same value and hence it is unnecessary to specify both coefficients
	21–25	ID	
	26–30	JD	

31-40 D(ID,JD)

.

.

.

71-80 D(ID,JD)

The elements of D do not have to be in any order. Card 2 is repeated until all the non-zero elements of D have been specified, up to four per card.

Card 3 Col 1-10 9999999999 indicates the end of the elements of D

Card 4 to Card 13 are as for LINP Card 1 to Card 10, the vector p of the quadratic function taking the place of c of the LP input.

3. INPUT TO MIF

As for LINP except that if ITRMAX is read in as 0 it will be set to 3 * N * (M + N + number of bounded variables). All the elements of A, B, C and BOUND must be integers.

4. INPUT TO BB

Card	Col	Variable	Description
Card 1	Col 1-10	M	number of constraints
	11-20	N	total number of variables
	21-30	NUMD	number of discrete variables = −1, all the variables have a step size, JDISC(J), of 1.
	31-40	INTOBJ	= 1, if the value of the objective function at the optimal integer solution will be integer. = 0, otherwise.
	41-50	IPRBB	at an integer solution the values of the original and the slack variables are printed irrespective of the value of IPRBB. ⩾ 1 subroutine IPRINT is called at the initial LP optimum. At a tail a message with the total number of iterations is printed and the fixed variables and their values are also printed. ⩾ 2 at a tail the values of the fixed variables and the function estimates to the

		right and to the left of the tree are also printed.
		= 3 at a tail the rate of fall of the function estimates to the right and left of the tree are also printed.
51–60	ITRBBM	maximum number of iterations for BB = 0, is set to N * ITRMAX
61–70	IRBBM	maximum number of re-inversions for BB
71–80	IREST	= 0, the current run is not a restart = 1, the calculation is to be restarted

If NUMD = 0 or −1 Cards 2 and 3 are not needed.

Card 2	Col	1–3	J	number of a discrete variable
		5–10	JDISC(J)	step size of the jth discrete variable
		11–13	J	
		15–20	JDISC(J)	
		.		
		.		
		.		
		71–73	J	
		75–80	JDISC(J)	

Card 2 is repeated until the step sizes for the NUMD discrete variables have been specified, up to eight per card.

Card 3 Col 1–10 9999999999 indicates the end of the step sizes.

Card 4 to Card 13 are as for LINP Card 1 to Card 10.

If IREST = 1 card 13 is followed by the card deck punched out by the previous run.

Notes

1. ITRBBM is the maximum number of iterations for BB while ITRMAX is the maximum number of iterations for solving an LP in subroutine LP. On entry to LP the number of iterations for solving an LP, ITR, is set to zero, and is not permitted to exceed ITRMAX. In BB the number of iterations is accumulated in ITRBB and is not permitted to exceed ITRBBM.
2. IRBBM is the maximum number of re-inversions for BB while IRMAX is the maximum number of re-inversions for solving an LP in subroutine LP. On entry to LP the number of re-inversions for solving an LP, IR, is set to zero, and is not permitted to exceed IRMAX. In BB the number of re-inversions is accumulated in IRBB and is not permitted to exceed IRBBM.
3. IRMAX is set to 3 if it is read in as 0 and IRBBM is greater than 3, but IRMAX is set equal to IRBBM if IRMAX is 0 and $0 < \text{IRBBM} \leqslant 3$.

5. INPUT TO PLP

Card 1	Col 1–10	NUMP	number of parametric, sensitivity or range requests, i.e. the number of cards of type 2 to follow. = 0 if no parametric variation is to be performed; the program simply solves the LP.
	11–20	IPRPLP	= 0, the dual and function row variables are printed when parametrizing c_j; the original and slack variables are printed when parametrizing b_i. = 1, the dual, the function row, the original and the slack variables are printed when parametrizing either b_i or c_j.

Card 2 can be of three types:

1. To parametrize an element of b or c between specified limits.

Card 2	Col 1	TYPE	character B, if an element of b is to be varied or C, if an element of c is to be varied.
	8–10	I or J	number of row, I, whose b element is to be varied, or column, J, whose c element is to be varied.
	11–20	TLOW	lower bound of the parametric variation.
	21–30	THIGH	upper bound of the parametric variation. TLOW and THIGH must be such that TLOW $\leqslant b_i \leqslant$ THIGH or TLOW $\leqslant c_j \leqslant$ THIGH according as b_i or c_j is to be varied.

2. To perform a sensitivity analysis on an element of b or c.

Card 2	Col 1	TYPE	B or C
	8–10	I or J	
	11–20	B(I) or C(J)	the value of the element in the LP
	21–30	B(I) or C(J)	(i.e. the same value repeated).

3. To perform a range analysis on all elements of b or c.

Card 2	Col 1	TYPE	B or C
	2–10	–1	all the elements of b or c are to be analysed.

Card 2 is repeated NUMP times. The three types of Card 2 can be in any order. In the output, the range analyses, if requested, will be printed first. The remaining analyses will be printed in the requested order.

Card 3 to Card 12 are as for LINP Card 1 to Card 10.

APPENDIX 4

Test Problems

This appendix is composed of three sections; 1, descriptions of and solutions to a series of small numerical test problems; 2, the data-punching sheets for the cards that are needed to input the problems; and 3, the computer output for the LP problem.

1. TEST PROBLEMS FOR SOLUTION

These very small numerical problems are to test the running of the programs.

1.1. An LP problem

$$\begin{aligned} \text{Max} \quad & x_1 + 3x_2 + 10x_3 \\ \text{s.t.} \quad & 12x_1 + 5x_2 + 30x_3 \leqslant 120 \\ & 2x_1 + 10x_2 + 30x_3 \leqslant 95 \\ & x_1 \geqslant 0, \quad x_2 \geqslant 0, \quad 0 \leqslant x_3 \leqslant 2. \end{aligned}$$

LP solution in four iterations:

$x_1 = 3{\cdot}8636, \quad x_2 = 2{\cdot}7273, \quad x_3 = 2,$
$y_1 = 0{\cdot}0364, \quad y_2 = 0{\cdot}2818,$
$yA - c = [0,\ 0,\ -0{\cdot}45]$ (third element is negative because x_3 is non-basic at its upper bound).

1.2. Beale's QP problem [2]

$$\text{Max } z = px + \tfrac{1}{2}xDx$$

$$\text{where } p = [\ 8 \quad 6 \quad 4\ ]$$

$$D = \begin{bmatrix} -4 & -2 & -2 \\ -2 & -4 & 0 \\ -2 & 0 & -2 \end{bmatrix}$$

$$\text{s.t. } x_1 + x_2 + 2x_3 \leqslant 3.$$

Solution in six iterations, following the original Beale Algorithm:

$$x_1 = \tfrac{12}{9},\quad x_2 = \tfrac{7}{9},\quad x_3 = \tfrac{4}{9}$$
$$y_1 = \tfrac{2}{9}\qquad z = 8\tfrac{8}{9}$$

Two added constraints:

$$-x_1 \quad -0{\cdot}5x_2 \quad -0{\cdot}4x_3 \leqslant -1{\cdot}9$$
$$0{\cdot}03774x_1 - 0{\cdot}98113x_2 + 0{\cdot}41509x_3 \leqslant -0{\cdot}52830$$

with dual values $y_2 = y_3 = 0$.

Same solution in five iterations following the algorithm as listed in Chapter 2; with two added constraints:

$$3x_1 + \quad 2x_2 + \quad x_3 \leqslant \ 6$$
$$-0{\cdot}8x_1 + 2{\cdot}8x_2 - 1{\cdot}6x_3 \leqslant 0{\cdot}4$$

$\bar{c} = p + D\bar{x}$: $\bar{c}_1 = \tfrac{2}{9}$, $\bar{c}_2 = \tfrac{2}{9}$, $\bar{c}_3 = \tfrac{4}{9}$.

Note that the constraints which determine the optimum point are quite different for the two different versions of the algorithm. They might even differ from either of these if run on a different computer. *Any* added constraints are valid, so long as they have zero dual values at the optimum.

1.3. An all-integer problem

Problem 1.1 can be treated as an ILP problem and solved by MIF, or by BB.

Integer solution by MIF (Chapter 4) in 18 iterations (basis changes):

$$x_1 = 2,\quad x_2 = 3,\quad x_3 = 2;\quad cx = 31.$$

Two (remaining) added constraints:

$$x_1 + 8x_2 + 25x_3 \leqslant 78$$
$$x_1 + 3x_2 + 10x_3 \leqslant 31$$

Note that the constraints that are generated are machine dependent. The value of the coefficients will vary depending upon the machine word length and the values of the tolerances. However, the solution (the values of the x's) is machine independent.

The same solution was obtained by BB (Chapter 5) in ten iterations (basis changes).

1.4. An all-integer problem with an equality constraint

Almost identical with 1.1, but the second constraint replaced by:

$$2x_1 + 10x_2 + 30x_3 = 94 \quad \text{(changing} \leqslant \text{to =, and 95 to 94).}$$

Same solution as 1.3.

MIF, 11 iterations, one added constraint:

$$x_1 + x_2 + 5x_3 \leqslant 15$$

Solution by BB in eight iterations.

1.5. A problem in discrete variables

By suitable scaling, problem 1.3 is converted to:

$$\begin{aligned} \text{Max} \quad & 2x_1 + \ \ 3x_2 + 10x_3 \\ \text{s.t.} \quad & 24x_1 + \ \ 5x_2 + 30x_3 \leqslant 1200 \\ & 4x_1 + 10x_2 + 30x_3 \leqslant \ \ 950 \\ & x_1 \geqslant 0,\ x_2 \geqslant 0,\ 0 \leqslant x_3 \leqslant 20 \end{aligned}$$

x_1 step size, 5; x_2 and x_3 step size, 10.

Solution by BB in 10 iterations:

$$x_1 = 10, \quad x_2 = 30, \quad x_3 = 20; \quad cx = 310.$$

1.6. Data to test PLP on problem 1.1

Parametric range of b_1: $50 \leqslant b_1 \leqslant 300$; 'central' value, 120
Parametric range of b_2: $95 \leqslant b_2 \leqslant 150$; 'central' value, 95
Parametric range of c_1: $-1 \leqslant c_1 \leqslant 1$; 'central' value, 1
Parametric range of c_2: $1 \leqslant c_2 \leqslant 5$; 'central' value, 3
Parametric range of c_3: $10 \leqslant c_3 \leqslant 20$; 'central' value, 10

2. PUNCHING FORMS FOR THE SAMPLE PROBLEMS

2.1. An LP problem

The input to LINP:

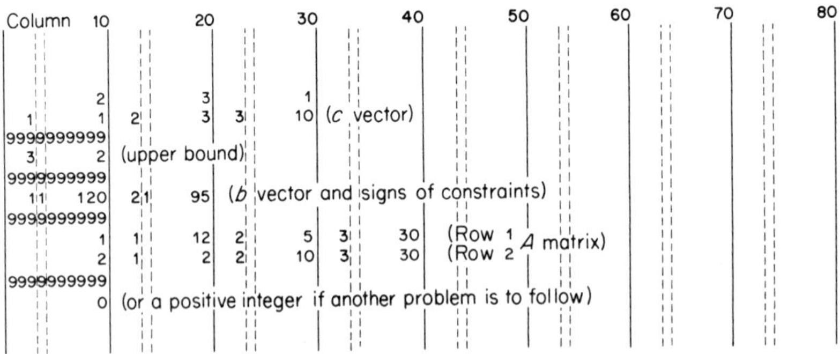

```
Column    10        20        30        40        50        60        70        80
           2         3         1
 1         1   2     3   3    10 (c vector)
9999999999
 3         2 (upper bound)
9999999999
 11      120  21     95 (b vector and signs of constraints)
9999999999
           1   1    12   2     5   3    30  (Row 1  A matrix)
           2   1     2   2    10   3    30  (Row 2
9999999999
           0 (or a positive integer if another problem is to follow)
```

Note that on the first card the first three coefficients in columns 1–30 are problem parameters, and that the last three coefficients in columns 31–60 have been left blank and hence will be read as zeros. Thus MOREPR will have a value of zero which will generate for this problem the computer output in Section 3. ITRMAX, having been read as zero, will be assigned a value of 3 * (M + N + number of bounded variables). IRMAX will have a value of zero; it should not be necessary to recompute the inverse for a small problem such as the one above. This form of the input where only the number of constraints, M, variables N, and bounded variables, ISBND, need be specified is useful for small problems or when the program is used by students. For larger problems, however, the user may wish to specify alternative values for MOREPR, ITRMAX and IRMAX.

2.2. Beale's QP problem

The input to QP:

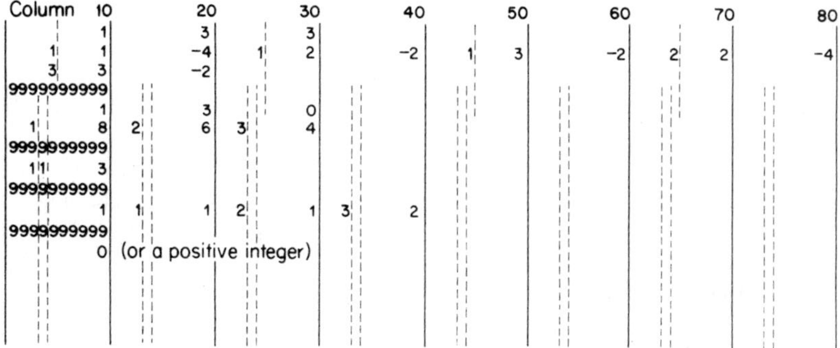

Note that because the D matrix is symmetric only half the non-zero off-diagonal elements need be specified. Thus D(1,2) is specified to have the value −2, and the program will also assign the value −2 to D(2,1).

As in 2.1, the user may leave the last three coefficients of the first LP card blank and they will be read as zeros. Again this feature is useful for small problems and for student use.

2.3. An all-integer problem

The input to MIF is the same as the input to LINP except that the A matrix and b vector coefficients must have integer values. The cards of Section 2.1 can be used as input to MIF.

The input to BB:

```
Column  10        20        30        40        50        60        70        80
         2         3        -1         1
```

This card precedes the cards in section 2.1. Note that on this card the first four coefficients in columns 1–40 are problem parameters.

The coefficients in columns 41–80 have been left blank and will be read as zeros. Thus IPRBB will be zero so that only the successively better integer solutions will be printed. ITRBBM will be set to N * ITRMAX, IRBBM will be zero and IREST will be zero indicating the current run is not a restart. For small problems and student use these values of the parameters will be satisfactory though for larger problems these parameters may have to be specified by the user.

2.4. An all-integer problem with an equality constraint

As Section 2.3 except that the card for the right hand sides and signs is replaced by:

```
Column  10        20        30        40        50        60        70        80
   11  120   20   94
```

2.5. A problem in discrete variables

The input to BB:

```
Column  10        20        30        40        50        60        70        80
         2         3         3         1
   1     5   2    10   3    10
9999999999
         2         3         1
   1     2   2     3   3    10
9999999999
   3    20
9999999999
   11 1200   21  950
9999999999
         1   1    24   2     5   3    30
         2   1     4   2    10   3    30
9999999999
         0 (or a positive integer)
```

As before only the problem parameters have been specified, the other parameters are permitted to take their default values.

2.6. Data to test PLP on problem 1.1

Column	10	20	30	
	11	1		
B	1	50	300	To perform a parametric analysis of b_1, b_2, c_1, c_2 and c_3 within a specified range
B	2	95	150	
C	1	−1	1	
C	2	1	5	
C	3	10	20	
C	−1			To perform a range analysis of the elements of b and c
B	−1			
B	2	95	95	To perform a sensitivity analysis on b_2, b_1, c_1 and c_3.
B	1	120	120	
C	1	1	1	
C	3	10	10	

These cards precede the cards in Section 2.1. Note that IPRPLP, in this example, has been set equal to 1 so that all the solution variables are printed at each corner point.

3. DESCRIPTION OF THE OUTPUT

The output for problem 1.1 in Figure A4.1 is generated from the input in Section 2 and from the program as given in the text. The first two lines summarize the information on the first data card. Then the data cards are listed; each card is numbered and printed on two lines. Within a card a unit of data, e.g. J and C(J), are enclosed in brackets, ( ), and within the brackets the fields are separated with solidi, /.

In the second half of the output the problem and its optimal solution are printed. This is headed by a statement, OPTIMUM, about the state of the following solution. The value of the objective function at the optimal solution is followed by the vector of upper bounds and then the x vector which is the values of the original variables at the optimum. The A matrix is enclosed in dotted lines (- - -) and brackets. On the left hand side of the A matrix is the y vector which is the values of the dual variables at the optimum, and on the right hand side is the b vector and the vector of slack variables. In this problem, as both of the problem constraints are effective, the two slack variables have a value of zero. Beneath the A matrix is the c vector and the values of the function row variables labelled Y'A C. In this problem x_1 and x_2 are basic variables and the values of the associated function row variables are zero while x_3 is non-basic at its upper bound and the value of the function row variable is negative.

The line in the output labelled ISEFF shows that the two constraints are effective; the first constraint is in the second column of the inverse basis

```
M (NO. OF CONSTRAINTS) =      2. N (NO. OF VARIABLES--REAL, NOT SLACK) =      3.
NUMBER OF UPPER BOUNDED VARIABLES =      1.

INPUT CARDS FOR THE C ELEMENTS . . . .
CARD    2
( 1/0/        1.00000)( 2/0/        3.00000)( 3/0/       10.00000)( 0/0/        0.00000)
( 0/0/        0.00000)( 0/0/        0.00000)( 0/0/        0.00000)( 0/0/        0.00000)
CARD    3
(999/9/999999.00000)( 0/0/        0.00000)( 0/0/        0.00000)( 0/0/        0.00000)
( 0/0/        0.00000)( 0/0/        0.00000)( 0/0/        0.00000)( 0/0/        0.00000)

INPUT CARDS FOR THE UPPER BOUNDS ON SINGLE VARIABLES . . . .
CARD    4
( 3/0/        2.00000)( 0/0/        0.00000)( 0/0/        0.00000)( 0/0/        0.00000)
( 0/0/        0.00000)( 0/0/        0.00000)( 0/0/        0.00000)( 0/0/        0.00000)
CARD    5
(999/9/999999.00000)( 0/0/        0.00000)( 0/0/        0.00000)( 0/0/        0.00000)
( 0/0/        0.00000)( 0/0/        0.00000)( 0/0/        0.00000)( 0/0/        0.00000)

INPUT CARDS FOR THE B VECTOR, THE RIGHT-HAND SIDES OF THE CONSTRAINTS . . . .
CARD    6
( 1/1/      120.00000)( 2/1/       95.00000)( 0/0/        0.00000)( 0/0/        0.00000)
( 0/0/        0.00000)( 0/0/        0.00000)( 0/0/        0.00000)( 0/0/        0.00000)
CARD    7
(999/9/999999.00000)( 0/0/        0.00000)( 0/0/        0.00000)( 0/0/        0.00000)
( 0/0/        0.00000)( 0/0/        0.00000)( 0/0/        0.00000)( 0/0/        0.00000)

INPUT CARDS FOR THE ROWS OF THE A MATRIX . . . .
CARD    8
( 0/0/        1.00000)( 1/0/       12.00000)( 2/0/        5.00000)( 3/0/       30.00000)
( 0/0/        0.00000)( 0/0/        0.00000)( 0/0/        0.00000)( 0/0/        0.00000)
CARD    9
( 0/0/        2.00000)( 1/0/        2.00000)( 2/0/       10.00000)( 3/0/       30.00000)
( 0/0/        0.00000)( 0/0/        0.00000)( 0/0/        0.00000)( 0/0/        0.00000)
CARD   10
(999/9/999999.00000)( 0/0/        0.00000)( 0/0/        0.00000)( 0/0/        0.00000)
( 0/0/        0.00000)( 0/0/        0.00000)( 0/0/        0.00000)( 0/0/        0.00000)




OPTIMUM

OBJECTIVE                 32.04545455

                  J. . .  1          2          3

            BOUND VECTOR. . . .
                       -1.0000    -1.0000     2.0000

              X VECTOR. . . .
                        3.8636     2.7273     2.0000
 I    Y VECTOR                                              B          B-AX
                 ---------------------------------                    (SLACK)
                 (                               )
 1      0.0364 (   12.0000     5.0000    30.0000 ) LE    120.00      0.0000
                 (                               )
 2      0.2818 (    2.0000    10.0000    30.0000 ) LE     95.00      0.0000
                 (                               )
                 ---------------------------------

              C VECTOR. . . .
                        1.0000     3.0000    10.0000

                 Y'A-C. . . .
                        0.0000     0.0000    -0.4545

ISEFF
  2  1

INBASE
  2  1 -1

    4 SIMPLEX ITERATIONS.

(N.B., THE MAXIMUM SIZE OF THE INVERSE DURING THE CALCULATION WAS     2)
```

Figure A4.1

and the second constraint in the first column. The line labelled INBASE shows that x_1 and x_2 are basic in the second and first rows of the inverse basis respectively and that x_3 is non-basic at its upper bound.

Finally the number of Simplex iterations and the maximum size of the inverse basis during the calculations are printed.

The output in Figure A4.1 is generated by subroutine SPRINT. In the text this subroutine is called when the number of variables is less than eight. For the purpose of illustrating the form of the output when the number of variables is eight or more the following statements were removed from subroutine IPRINT

```
IF(N.GE.8) GO TO 90
CALL SPRINT
GO TO 400
```

and problem 1.1 was run on the modified program with MOREPR set at 2 instead of left blank. The output that was generated is shown in Figure A4.2.

The output starts by printing the value of MOREPR. The input cards are not listed with MOREPR = 2 but the inverse basis at the optimum is printed. Only the non-zero elements of the A matrix are printed; each element is numbered and below the element is its column number. The matrix is represented row-wise and after the A matrix elements the number of the initial non-zero element in each row is printed (see the description of the arrangement of the A matrix in Chapter 2). In this example the first element is the first element of row 1 and the fourth element is the first of row 2.

After the state of the basis, OPTIMUM, the value of the objective function at the optimal solution, the elements of the objective function, the values of the variables at the optimal solution, $\bar{x}$, and the function row variables, labelled Y'A-C, are printed. These are followed by the b vector, the sign of the constraints, the vector of dual variables, $\bar{y}$, and the slack variables, labelled B–AX. The value of these variables should be compared with those in Figure A4.1.

The columns 1 and 2 of the inverse matrix refer to the rows 2 and 1 (the line of output labelled YBASIS) of the A matrix respectively. The reverse cross-referencing is contained in the array ISEFF. Thus YR(1) = ·2818 = Y(2). The rows 1 and 2 of the inverse matrix refer to the columns 2 and 1 (the column of output labelled XBASIS) of the A matrix respectively. The reverse cross-referencing is contained in the array INBASE. Thus XR(1) = 2·7273 = X(2). The inverse matrix in Figure A4.2 is the inverse of

$$\begin{array}{l} \\ \text{constraint 2} \\ \text{constraint 1} \end{array} \begin{array}{c} \begin{array}{cc} x_2 & x_1 \end{array} \\ \begin{bmatrix} 10 & 2 \\ 5 & 12 \end{bmatrix} \end{array}$$

```
MOREPR =      2

M (NO. OF CONSTRAINTS) =      2, N (NO. OF VARIABLES--REAL, NOT SLACK) =      3,
NUMBER OF UPPER BOUNDED VARIABIES =      1.



OPTIMUM


NON-ZERO ELEMENTS OF THE A MATRIX, FOLLOWED BY THEIR COLUMN LABELS....

        1         2         3          4         5         6
   12.000     5.000    30.000      2.000    10.000    30.000
        1         2         3          1         2         3

THE FOLLOWING VECTORS SHOW THE STARTING POINTS OF THE SUCCESSIVE ROWS OF A IN THE ABOVE LIST OF THE NON-ZERO ELEMENTS.'.


   1    2
   1    4

OBJECTIVE            32,04545455

                                  J        1          2          3

                           C VECTOR      1.0        3.0       10.0

                       BOUND VECTOR  -1.0000    -1.0000     2.0000

                           X VECTOR   3.8636     2.7273     2.0000

                              Y'A-C     0.00       0.00      -0.45



 THE SIGN(I) VECTOR INDICATES THE SIGN OF THE I-TH CONSTRAINT, 0 FOR EQ, 1 FOR LE, -1 FOR GE.

                                  I        1          2

                           B VECTOR    120.0       95.0

                               SIGN       1.         1.

                           Y VECTOR   0.0364     0.2818

                               B-AX   0.0000     0.0000
```

```
               COLUMN        1              2

               YBASIS        2              1

                  YR         0,2818         0,0364

ROW  XBS       XR       INVERSE MATRIX

 1    2        2.7273        0.1091        -0.0182
 2    1        3.8636       -0.0455         0.0909



   BIG  0.1000E 12, DRIVER          0.0,  INREV             0,       IR             0,   IRMAX             0,  ISBND           1
ISDONE           1, ISTATE            1,    ITR             4,  ITRMAX           18,       M             2,  MARKI           0
 MAXKK           0,   MAXA         1000,   MAXM            70,    MAXN          150,    MORE             0, MXSIZE          50
     N           3, NEGINV            0, NEGROW             0,    NEWX            0,    NEWY             2, NUMSLK           0
     R    3.86364,    SIZE            2,  SMALL   0.1000E-08,  TOL(1)   0.1000E-05,  TOL(2)   0.1000E-04,  TOL(3)  0.1000E-05
TOL(4)  0.1000E-04, TOL(5)   0.1000E-04, TOL(6)   0.1000E-04,  TOL(7)   0.1000E-04,  TOL(8)   0.1000E-03,  XKPOS         1,0
YAMINC    -0.00000

ISEFF
  2  1

INBASE
  2  1 -1

   [illegible] SIMPLEX ITERATIONS,

(N.B , THE MAXIMUM SIZE OF THE INVERSE DURING THE CALCULATION WAS     2)
```

Figure A4.2

After the inverse matrix, are printed the values of many of the variables in COMMON. NEGINV = 0 and NEGROW = 0 show that the basis is feasible and NEWX = 0 and YAMINC = 0·0 show that the basis is also optimal.

Finally, as in Figure A4.1, the arrays ISEFF, INBASE, the number of Simplex iterations and the maximum size of the inverse are printed.

References

1. L. E. Briskin, 'A note on Trauth and Woolsey's integer programming algorithm', *Management Science,* **16,** 651 (1970).
2. E. M. L. Beale, 'Numerical Methods', in *Nonlinear Programming* (Ed. J. Abadie), North Holland Publishing Company, 1967, pp. 143–163.
3. G. B. Dantzig, *Linear Programming and Extensions,* Princeton University Press, 1963.
4. A. Dutt Roy, 'Application of ILP to Timetabling', *M.Sc. Thesis,* Institute of Computer Science, London University, 1972.
5. R. Gomory, 'An Algorithm for Integer Solutions to Linear Programs', in *Recent Advances in Mathematical Programming* (Eds. R. Graves and P. Wolfe), McGraw-Hill, 1963, pp. 269–302.
6. J. Haldi, '25 Integer Programming Test Problems', *Working Paper No. 43,* Graduate School of Business Studies, Stanford University.
7. H. W. Kuhn, 'Foundations of Mathematical Programming', London University, Audio-Visual Centre (Forthcoming).
8. A. H. Land and A. G. Doig, 'An Automatic Method of Solving Discrete Programming Problems', *Econometrica,* **28,** No. 3, 497–520 (July 1960).
9. A. H. Land and G. Morton, 'An Inverse-basis method for Beales' Quadratic Programming Algorithm', *Management Science,* **19,** No. 5, 510–516 (Jan. 1973).
10. J. D. C. Little, K. G. Murty, D. W. Sweeney and Caroline Karel, 'An Algorithm for the Travelling Salesman Problem', *Operations Research,* **11,** 972–989 (1963).
11. C. A. Trauth and R. E. Woolsey 'Integer Linear Programming: A Study in Computational Efficiency', *Management Science,* **15,** 481–493 (1969).